A NEWMAN SYNTHESIS

A

Newman Synthesis

ARRANGED BY

Erich Przywara, S.J.

NEW YORK · 1945

Sheed and Ward

PUBLISHERS' NOTE

The original German edition of this work appeared in six volumes, each prefaced by an "argument" setting out generally the plan of the whole work and more fully the plan of the particular volume concerned. Naturally there was a certain amount of repetition, and in this one-volume edition it has been thought better to combine and compress the "arguments" into this one brief explanation, given as far as possible in Fr. Przywara's own words.

His task is to reconstitute Newman's thought, systematically and in its completeness, as it was present in Newman's own mind. The arrangement he follows is of the very simplest.

The growth of man to full spiritual maturity is seen in three stages: *first*—fallen man's path to Christianity—the apprehension by his conscience of God as giver of the moral law, the perception of his own situation as one of sin, misery and profound need of God's help; *secondly,* his conviction of Christianity and of Christ as his divinely willed and commissioned Messiah and Saviour—through the fact of Christ in His historical life on earth, fulfilling the Old Testament, radiating miracle, living on in the Church—"head and body one Christ"; *finally* redeemed man's path *in* Christianity, the way of faith which leads to the beatific vision of the one God in three Persons, the way of complete surrender to God's guidance and of brotherly love as a member of Christ's one body, a life lived from and in God. These three stages are divided into a score of sections and each section is further subdivided into some hundred steps, which mark out the whole upward journey of the soul. Thus the spiritual life, dynamically and in its totality, lies in analysis before the reader: upon the points of that analysis, Fr. Przywara threads passages from Newman—choosing those which careful research shows to be representative of the final state of his mind. The book is thus all Newman: the passages fall into sequence without the aid of any connecting links externally supplied: Newman surveys the whole of the conflict and co-operation of nature and grace.

* * * * *

The preparation of this book for the press has had the active help and guidance of Fr. Francis Bacchus of the Birmingham Oratory at every stage, and we should like to acknowledge our debt to him in respect of a labour that could not have been accomplished without such a great knowledge of Newman as he was able to place at our disposal.

CONTENTS

ix

LIST OF ABBREVIATIONS

IN REFERENCE TO WORKS QUOTED

Apo., *Apologia, pro Vita Sua.*
Ari., *The Arians of the Fourth Century.*
Call., *Callista.*
D.A., *Discussions and Arguments.*
Diff., *Certain Difficulties felt by Anglicans in Catholic teaching considered.*
Dev., *Essay on the Development of Doctrine.*
Ess., *Essays Critical and Historical.*
G.A., *Essay in Aid of a Grammar of Assent.*
H.S., *Historical Sketches.*
Idea, *Idea of a University, defined and illustrated.*
Jfc., *Lectures on Justification.*
L.G., *Loss and Gain.*
M.D., *Meditations and Devotions.*
Mir., *Two Essays on Miracles.*
Mix., *Discourses to Mixed Congregations.*
O.S., *Sermons Preached on Various Occasions.*
P.S., *Parochial and Plain Sermons.*
Prepos., *Lectures on the Present Position of Catholics in England.*
S.D., *Sermons bearing on Subjects of the Day.*
S.N., *Sermon Notes.*
T.T., *Tracts Theological and Ecclesiastical.*
U.S., *Oxford University Sermons.*
V.M., *Via Media.*
V.V., *Verses on Various Occasions.*

I: GOD

ANALYTICAL SUMMARY

God's existence is immediately and irrefutably disclosed as soon as we open our eyes to life as it really is;

against the background of life's beginning and ending, God appears without beginning and without end;

against the background of its helpless dependence, God appears, whose Being is alone self-grounded;

against the background of its limitation and division, God appears— infinite perfection;

God—the Divine Majesty.

(Nos. 1-4.)

But it is in the experience of a tender and reverent conscience that we hear, as it were, His voice addressing us personally;

that He in our experience of guilt, remorse and penance increasingly reveals Himself as the transcendent ground of all morality, the supreme Lawgiver, commanding good and forbidding evil, the strict inflexible Judge, the Mighty, Pure, Infinite Holiness which strikes our hearts with awe.

But in spite of all this, there is a voice of infinite mercy: "Come to Me! ..."

(Nos. 5-9.)

Thus His Image grows with the actual development of our interior life ever mightier, without limit:

and the more we apprehend Him, the more does He elude our grasp, so that it is precisely in the realisation that our quest can never reach its goal that we attain our profoundest knowledge of Him as the Infinite and Incomprehensible.

(Nos. 10-12.)

And nevertheless, precisely as the infinite and incomprehensible, He is our God, and "our heart is restless until it rests in Him."

(Nos. 13-16.)

I. THE NOTION OF GOD

I

Is not the being of a God reported to us by testimony, handed down by history, inferred by an inductive process, brought home to us by metaphysical necessity, urged on us by the suggestions of our conscience? It is a truth in the natural order, as well as in the supernatural. So much for its origin; and when obtained, what is its worth? Is it a great truth or a small one? Is it a comprehensive truth? Say that no other religious idea whatever were given but it, and you have enough to fill the mind; you have at once a whole dogmatic system. The word "God" is a Theology in itself, indivisibly one, inexhaustibly various from the vastness and simplicity of its meaning. Admit a God, and you introduce among the subjects of your knowledge, a fact encompassing, closing in upon, absorbing, every other fact conceivable. How can we investigate any part of any order of Knowledge, and stop short of that which enters into every order? All true principles run over with it, all phenomena converge to it; it is truly the First and the Last . . .

According to the teaching of Monotheism, God is an Individual, Self-dependent, All-perfect, Unchangeable Being; intelligent, living, personal and present; almighty, all-seeing, all-remembering; between whom and His creatures there is an infinite gulf; who has no origin, who is all-sufficient for Himself; who created and upholds the universe; who will judge every one of us, sooner or later, according to that Law of right and wrong which He has written on our hearts. He is One who is sovereign over, operative amidst, independent of, the appointments which He has made; One in whose hands are all things, who has a purpose in every event, and a standard for every deed, and thus has relations of His own towards the subject-matter of each particular science which the book of knowledge unfolds; who has with an

I

adorable, never-ceasing energy implicated Himself in all the history of creation, the constitution of nature, the course of the world, the origin of society, the fortunes of nations, the action of the human mind; and who thereby necessarily becomes the subject-matter of a science, far wider and more noble than any of those which are included in the circle of secular education.

Idea, 25, 26; and 36.

2

Reason teaches you there must be a God; else how was this all-wonderful universe made? It could not make itself; man could not make it, he is but a part of it; each man has a beginning, there must have been a first man, and who made him? To the thought of God then we are forced from the nature of the case; we must admit the idea of an Almighty Creator, and that Creator must have been from everlasting. He must have had no beginning, else how came He to be? Else, we should be in our original difficulty, and must begin our argument over again. The Creator, I say, had no beginning; for, if He was brought into being by another before Him, then how came that other to be? And so we shall proceed in an unprofitable series or catalogue of creators, which is as difficult to conceive as an endless line of men. Besides, if it was not the Creator Himself who was from everlasting, then there would be one being who was from everlasting, and another who was Creator; which is all one with saying there are two Gods. It is least trial then to our reason, it is simplest and most natural, to pronounce, that the Creator of the world had no beginning;—and if so, He is self-existing; and if so, He can undergo no change. What is self-existing and everlasting has no growth or decay; It is what It ever was, and ever shall be the same. As It originated in nothing else, nothing else can interfere with It or affect It. Besides, everything that is has originated in It; everything therefore is dependent on It, and It is independently of everything.

Mix., 285-6.

2

3

Every one spontaneously embraces the doctrine of the existence of God, as a first principle, and a necessary assumption. It is not so much proved to him, as borne in upon his mind irresistibly, as a truth which it does not occur to him, nor is possible for him, to doubt; so various and so abundant is the witness for it contained in the experience and the conscience of every one. He cannot unravel the process, or put his finger on the independent arguments, which conspire together to create in him the certainty which he feels; but certain of it he is, and he has neither the temptation nor the wish to doubt it, and he could, should need arise, at least point to the books or the persons from whence he could obtain the various formal proofs on which the being of a God rests, and the irrefragable demonstration thence resulting against the freethinker and the sceptic. At the same time he certainly would find, if he was in a condition to pursue the subject himself, that unbelievers had the advantage of him so far as this,—that there were a number of objections to the doctrine which he could not satisfy, questions which he could not solve, mysteries which he could neither conceive nor explain; he would perceive that the body of proof itself might be more perfect and complete than it is; he would not find indeed anything to invalidate that proof, but many things which might embarrass him in discussion, or afford a plausible, though not a real, excuse for doubting about it.

Mix., 261-2.

4

As in the human frame there is a living principle, acting upon it and through it by means of volition, so, behind the veil of the visible universe, there is an invisible, intelligent Being, acting on and through it, as and when He will. . .

This invisible Agent is in no sense a soul of the world, after the analogy of human nature, but, on the contrary, is absolutely distinct from the world, as being its Creator, Upholder, Governor, and Sovereign Lord. . .

I mean then by the Supreme Being, one who is simply self-dependent, and the only Being who is such; moreover, that He is without beginning or Eternal, and the only Eternal; that in consequence He has lived a whole eternity by Himself; and hence that He is all-sufficient, sufficient for His own blessedness, and all-blessed, and ever-blessed.

Further I mean a Being who having these prerogatives, has the Supreme Good, or rather is the Supreme Good, or has all the attributes of Good in infinite intenseness; all wisdom, all truth, all justice, all love, all holiness, all beautifulness; who is omnipotent, omniscient, omnipresent; ineffably one, absolutely perfect; and such, that what we do not know, and cannot even imagine of Him, is far more wonderful than what we do and can.

I mean One who is sovereign over His own will and actions, though always according to the eternal Rule of right and wrong, which is Himself.

I mean, moreover, that He created all things out of nothing, and preserves them every moment, and could destroy them as easily as He made them; and that, in consequence, He is separated from them by an abyss, and is incommunicable in all His attributes.

And further, He has stamped upon all things, in the hour of their creation, their respective natures, and has given them their work and mission, and their length of days, greater or less in their appointed place.

I mean, too, that He is ever present with His works, one by one, and confronts every thing He has made by His particular and most loving Providence, and manifests Himself to each according to its needs; and has on rational beings imprinted the moral law, and given them power to obey it, imposing on them the duty of searching service and worship, and scanning them through and through with His omniscient eye, and putting before them a present trial and a judgment to come.

Idea, 61-3.

4

5

As we have our initial knowledge of the universe through sense, so do we in the first instance begin to learn about its Lord and God from conscience; and, as from particular acts of that instinct, which makes experiences, mere images (as they ultimately are) upon the retina, the means of our perceiving something real beyond them, we go on to draw the general conclusion that there is a vast external world, so from the recurring instances in which conscience acts, forcing upon us importunately the mandate of a Superior, we have fresh and fresh evidence of the existence of a Sovereign Ruler, from whom those particular dictates which we experience proceed; so that, with limitations which cannot here be made without digressing from my main subject, we may, by means of that induction from particular experiences of conscience, have as good a warrant for concluding the Ubiquitous Presence of One Supreme Master, as we have from parallel experience of sense, for assenting to the fact of a multiform and vast world, material and mental.

G.A., 63.

6

Conscience does not repose on itself, but vaguely reaches forward to something beyond self, and dimly discerns a sanction higher than self for its decisions, as is evidenced in that keen sense of obligation and responsibility which informs them. And hence it is that we are accustomed to speak of conscience as a voice,... and moreover a voice, ... or the echo of a voice, imperative and constraining, like no other dictate in the whole of our experience...

If a man has been betrayed into any kind of immorality, he has a lively sense of responsibility and guilt, though the act be no offence against society,—of distress and apprehension, even though it may be of present service to him,—of compunction and regret, though in itself it be most pleasurable,—of confusion of face, though it may have no witnesses ...

If, as is the case, we feel responsibility, are ashamed, are frightened, at transgressing the voice of conscience, this implies that there is One to whom we are responsible, before whom we are ashamed, whose claims upon us we fear. If, on doing wrong, we feel the same tearful, broken-hearted sorrow which overwhelms us on hurting a mother; if, on doing right, we enjoy the same sunny serenity of mind, the same soothing, satisfactory delight which follows on our receiving praise from a father, we certainly have within us the image of some person, to whom our love and veneration look, in whose smile we find our happiness, for whom we yearn, towards whom we direct our pleadings, in whose anger we are troubled and waste away. These feelings in us are such as require for their exciting cause an intelligent being: we are not affectionate towards a stone, nor do we feel shame before a horse or a dog; we have no remorse or compunction on breaking mere human law: yet, so it is, conscience excites all these painful emotions, confusion, foreboding, self-condemnation; and on the other hand it sheds upon us a deep peace, a sense of security, a resignation, and a hope, which there is no sensible, no earthly object to elicit. "The wicked flees, when no one pursueth;" then why does he flee? whence his terror? Who is it that he sees in solitude, in darkness, in the hidden chambers of his heart? If the cause of these emotions does not belong to this visible world, the Object to which his perception is directed must be Supernatural and Divine; and thus the phenomena of Conscience, as a dictate, avail to impress the imagination with the picture of a Supreme Governor, a Judge, holy, just, powerful, all-seeing, retributive, and is the creative principle of religion. . .

G.A., 107-110.

7

Take an ordinary child, but still one who is safe from influences destructive of his religious instincts. Supposing he has offended his parents, he will all alone and without effort, as if it were the most natural of acts, place himself in the presence of God, and beg of Him to set him right with them. Let us consider how much is contained in this simple act. First, it involves the impression on his mind of an unseen Being with whom he is in immediate relation, and that relation so familiar that he can address Him whenever he himself chooses; next, of One whose goodwill towards him he is assured of, and can take for granted—nay, who loves him better, and is nearer to him, than his parents; further, of One who can hear him, wherever he happens to be, and who can read his thoughts, for his prayer need not be vocal; lastly, of One who can effect a critical change in the state of feeling of others towards him. That is, we shall not be wrong in holding that this child has in his mind the image of an Invisible Being, who exercises a particular providence among us, who is present every where, who is heart-reading, heart-changing, ever-accessible, open to impetration. What a strong and intimate vision of God must he have already attained, if, as I have supposed, an ordinary trouble of mind has the spontaneous effect of leading him for consolation and aid to an Invisible Personal Power!

Moreover, this image brought before his mental vision is the image of One who by implicit threat and promise commands certain things which he, the same child coincidently, by the same act of his mind, approves; which receive the adhesion of his moral sense and judgment, as right and good. It is the image of One who is good, inasmuch as enjoining and enforcing what is right and good, and who, in consequence, not only excites in the child hope and fear,—nay (it may be added), gratitude towards Him, as giving a law and maintaining it by reward and punishment,—but kindles in him love towards Him, as giving him a good law, and therefore as being good Himself, for it is the property of goodness to kindle love, or rather the very object of love is goodness; and all those distinct elements of the moral law, which the typical child, whom I am supposing, more or less consciously loves and approves,—truth, purity, justice, kindness, and the like,—are but shapes and aspects of goodness. And having in his degree a sensibility towards them all, for the sake of them all he is moved to love the Lawgiver, who enjoins them upon him. And, as he can contemplate these qualities and their manifestations under the common name of goodness, he is prepared to think of them as indivisible, correlative, supplementary of each other in one and

7

the same Personality, so that there is no aspect of goodness which God is not; and that the more, because the notion of a perfection embracing all possible excellences, both moral and intellectual, is especially congenial to the mind, and there are in fact intellectual attributes, as well as moral, included in the child's image of God, as above represented.

G.A., 112-114.

8

The image of God, if duly cherished, may expand, deepen, and be completed, with the growth of their powers and in the course of life, under the varied lessons, within and without them, which are brought home to them concerning that same God, One and Personal, by means of education, social intercourse, experience, and literature.

To a mind thus carefully formed upon the basis of its natural conscience, the world, both of nature and of man, does but give back a reflection of those truths about the One Living God, which have been familiar to it from childhood. Good and evil meet us daily as we pass through life, and there are those who think it philosophical to act towards the manifestations of each with some sort of impartiality, as if evil had as much right to be there as good, or even a better, as having more striking triumphs and a broader jurisdiction. And because the course of things is determined by fixed laws, they consider that those laws preclude the present agency of the Creator in the carrying out of particular issues. It is otherwise with the theology of a religious imagination. It has a living hold on truths which are really to be found in the world, though they are not upon the surface. It is able to pronounce by anticipation, what it takes a long argument to prove—that good is the rule, and evil the exception. It is able to assume that, uniform as are the laws of nature, they are consistent with a particular Providence. It interprets what it sees around it by this previous inward teaching, as the true key of that maze of vast complicated disorder; and thus it gains a more and more consistent and luminous vision of God from the most unpromising materials. Thus conscience is a connecting principle between the creature and his Creator; and the firmest hold of theological truths is gained by habits of personal religion. When men begin all their works with the thought of God, acting for His sake, and to fulfil His will, when they ask His blessing on themselves and their life, pray to Him for the objects they desire, and see Him in the event, whether it be according to their prayers or not, they will find everything that happens tend to confirm them in the truths about Him which live in their imagination, varied and unearthly as those truths may be. Then they are brought into His presence as that of a Living Person, and are able to hold converse with Him, and that with a directness and simplicity, with a confidence and intimacy, *mutatis mutandis*, which we use towards an earthly superior; so that it is doubtful whether we realize the company of our fellow-men with greater keenness than these favoured minds are able to contemplate and adore the Unseen, Incomprehensible Creator.

G.A., 116-118.

9

"His eyes were as a flame of fire," and "His countenance shone as the sun shineth in his strength."

(1) O my God, the day will come when I shall see that countenance and those eyes, when my soul returns to Him to be judged.

(2) Those eyes are so *piercing;* they see through me; nothing is hid from them. Thou countest every hair of my head; Thou knowest every breath I breathe; Thou sees every morsel of food I take.

(3) Those eyes are so *pure.* They are so clear that I can look into their depths, as into some transparent well of water, though I cannot see the bottom; for Thou art infinite.

(4) Those eyes are so *loving;* so gentle, so sweet; they seem to say, "Come to Me."

M.D., 299-300.

THIS is only one instance* of a general principle which holds good in all such real apprehension as is possible to us, of God and His Attributes. Not only do we see Him at best only in shadows, but we cannot bring even those shadows together, for they flit to and fro, and are never present to us at once. We can indeed combine the various matters which we know of Him by an act of the intellect, and treat them theologically, but such theological combinations are no objects for the imagination to gaze upon. Our image of Him never is one, but broken into numberless partial aspects, independent each of each. As we cannot see the whole starry firmament at once, but have to turn ourselves from east to west, and then round to east again, sighting first one constellation and then another, and losing these in order to gain those, so it is, and much more, with such real apprehensions as we can secure of the Divine Nature. We know one truth about Him and another truth,—but we cannot image both of them together; we cannot bring them before us by one act of the mind; we drop the one while we turn to take up the other. None of them are fully dwelt on and enjoyed, when they are viewed in combination. . . Break a ray of light into its constituent colours, each is beautiful, each may be enjoyed; attempt to unite them, and perhaps you produce only a dirty white. The pure and indivisible Light is seen only by the blessed inhabitants of heaven; here we have but such faint reflections of it as its diffraction supplies; but they are sufficient for faith and devotion. Attempt to combine them into one, and you gain nothing but a mystery, which you can describe as a notion, but cannot depict as an imagination. . . We must contemplate the God of our conscience as a Living Being, as one Object and Reality, *under* the aspect of this or that attribute. We must patiently rest in the thought of the Eternal, Omnipresent, and All-knowing, rather than of Eternity, Omnipresence, and Omniscience; and we must not hurry on and force a series of deductions, which, if they are to be realized, must distil like dew into our minds, and form them-

* The writer had just been treating of the mystery of the Trinity.

selves spontaneously there, by a calm contemplation and gradual
understanding of their premisses.

G.A., 131-2, 314.

11

We all confess that He is infinite; He has an infinite number of
perfections, and He is infinite in each of them. . .

The outward exhibition of infinitude is mystery; and the
mysteries of nature and of grace are nothing else than the mode in
which His infinitude encounters us and is brought home to our
minds. Men confess that He is infinite, yet they start and object,
as soon as His infinitude comes in contact with their imagination
and acts upon their reason. They cannot bear the fulness, the
superabundance, the inexhaustible flowing forth, and "vehement rushing," and encompassing flood of the Divine attributes.
They restrain and limit them to their own comprehension, they
measure them by their own standard, they fashion them by their
own model; and when they discern aught of the unfathomable
depth, the immensity, of any single excellence or perfection of
the Divine Nature, His love, or His justice, or His power, they
are at once offended, and turn away, and refuse to believe. . .

The invisible air, how gentle is it, and intimately ours! We
breathe it momentarily, nor could we live without it; it fans
our cheek, and flows around us, and we move through it without
effort, while it obediently recedes at every step we take, and ob-
sequiously pursues us as we go forward. Yet let it come in its
power, and that same silent fluid, which was just now the servant of our necessity or caprice, takes us up on its wings with the
invisible power of an Angel, and carries us forth into the regions
of space, and flings us down headlong upon the earth. Or go to
the spring, and draw thence at your pleasure, for your cup or your
pitcher, in supply of your wants; you have a ready servant, a
domestic ever at hand, in large quantity or in small, to satisfy
your thirst, or to purify you from the dust and mire of the world.
But go from home, reach the coast; and you will see that same
humble element transformed before your eyes. You were equal
to it in its condescension, but who shall gaze without astonish-

ment at its vast expanse in the bosom of the ocean? who shall hear without awe the dashing of its mighty billows along the beach? who shall without terror feel it heaving under him, and swelling and mounting up, and yawning wide, till he, its very sport and mockery, is thrown to and fro, hither and thither, at the mere mercy of a power which was just now his companion and almost his slave? Or, again, approach the flame: it warms you, and it enlightens you; yet approach not too near, presume not, or it will change its nature. That very element which is so beautiful to look at, so brilliant in its character, so graceful in its figure, so soft and lambent in its motion, will be found in its essence to be of a keen resistless nature; it tortures, it consumes, it reduces to ashes that of which it was just before the illumination and the life. So is it with the attributes of God; our knowledge of them serves us for our daily welfare; they give us light and warmth and food and guidance and succour; but go forth with Moses upon the mount and let the Lord pass by, or with Elias stand in the desert amid the wind, the earthquake, and the fire, and all is mystery and darkness; all is but a whirling of the reason, and a dazzling of the imagination, and an overwhelming of the feelings, reminding us that we are but mortal men and He is God, and that the outlines which Nature draws for us are not his perfect image, nor to be pronounced inconsistent with those further lights and depths with which it is invested by revelation.

Mix., 309-310; 319-320.

12

O my Lord God . . . I adore Thee, because Thou art so mysterious, so incomprehensible. Unless thou wert incomprehensible, Thou wouldst not be God. For how can the Infinite be other than incomprehensible to me.

M.D., 308.

IV. GOD AND THE SELF

13

ALMIGHTY God, Thou art the One Infinite Fulness. From eternity Thou art the One and only absolute and most all-sufficient seat and proper abode of all conceivable best attributes, and of all, which are many more, and cannot be conceived. I hold this as a matter of reason, though my imagination starts from it. I hold it firmly and absolutely, though it is the most difficult of all mysteries. I hold it from the actual experience of Thy blessings and mercies towards me, the evidences of Thy awful Being and attributes, brought home continually to my reason, beyond the power of doubting or disputing. I hold it from that long and intimate familiarity with it, so that it is part of my rational nature to hold it; because I am so constituted and made up upon the idea of it, as a keystone, that not to hold it would be to break my mind to pieces. I hold it from that intimate perception of it in my conscience, as a fact present to me, that I feel it as easy to deny my own personality as the personality of God, and have lost my grounds for believing that I exist myself, if I deny existence to Him. I hold it because I could not bear to be without Thee, O my Lord and Life, because I look for blessings beyond thought by being with Thee. I hold it from the terror of being left in this wild world without stay or protection. I hold it from humble love to Thee, from delight in Thy glory and exaltation, from my desire that thou shouldst be great and the only great one. I hold it for Thy sake and because I love to think of Thee as so glorious, perfect, and beautiful. There is one God and none other but He.

M.D., 591, 592.

14

Since, O eternal God, Thou art so incommunicably great, so one, so perfect in that oneness, surely one would say, Thou ever must be most distant from Thy creatures, didst Thou create any;—separated from them by Thy eternal ancientness on their beginning to be, and separated by Thy transcendency of excellence, and Thy absolute contrariety to them. . . For what is every creature in Thy sight, O Lord, but a vanity and a breath, a smoke that stays not, but flits and passes away, a poor thing which only vanishes so much the sooner, because Thou lookest on it, and it is set in the illumination of Thy countenance? . . . There is an infinite gulf between Thee and me, O my God.

M.D., 592-594.

15

By Thee we cross the gulf that lies between Thee and us. The Living God is lifegiving. Thou art the Fount and Centre, as well as the Seat of all good. . . Remaining one and sole and infinitely removed from all things, still Thou art the fulness of all things, in Thee they consist, of Thee they partake, and into Thee, retaining their own individuality, they are absorbed. And thus, while we droop and decay in our own nature, we live by Thy breath; and Thy grace enables us to endure Thy presence.

M.D., 595-596.

16

Charles' characteristic, perhaps above anything else, was an habitual sense of the Divine Presence; a sense which, of course, did not ensure uninterrupted conformity of thought and deed to itself, but still, there it was—the pillar of the cloud before him and guiding him. He felt himself to be God's creature, and responsible to Him—God's possession, not his own. He had a great wish to succeed in the schools; a thrill came over him when he thought of it; but ambition was not his life; he could have reconciled himself in a few minutes to failure.

L.G., 220-231.

II: PREPARATION FOR CHRISTIANITY

ANALYTICAL SUMMARY

The man, however, who is not yet a Christian is a "fallen" man, and has no need of the Christian revelation to tell him so. Deep in the consciousness of all races, since they are all descended from one "fallen" pair, lives a more or less obscure feeling that they "were conceived in sin" and a longing for a "Redeemer" who, in accordance with the promise spoken during man's last hour in the earthly Paradise, will "crush the serpent's head."

Christianity meets this fallen man with the message of salvation, but of a salvation which depends on unconditional and unqualified faith, the entire surrender of the intellect to the authority of God, whose word is truth, a salvation which proclaims the atoning death of a God-Man for the sin of the world, and demands from whosoever will receive it that he be "crucified with Christ to the world" and the world to him.

But everything depends in the first instance on this, that fallen man should see himself as fallen, and not imagine that he is pure complete and perfect, his own Master, Redeemer and Sanctifier.

Christianity demands the obedience of faith.

How shall a man be prepared for this "sacrifice of his intellect" who approaches truth in a spirit of pride and wilfulness?

Will not that man rather lend a humble hearing to its voice, who has learnt in the simplicity of innocence to follow the voice of his conscience and by obedience to conscience has made himself ready for the obedience of faith?

(Nos. 1-8.)

15

Christianity tells of a death of atonement for the death of sin.

Must not that message be "Folly" rather than "Wisdom" to one who knows nothing of sin either in his own life or in the world at large, who accepts everything "as an inevitable stage in an upward process," and rejects with disgust all mention of sin, sorrow for sin, penance, and atonement as relics of an outworn savagery?

Or will not he rather bow the knee before the Crucified and "take up his cross daily" to whom a tender and scrupulous conscience has revealed all the most subtle and profound ramifications of sin in human flesh, and from whom the duel experienced in his personal life between the law of the spirit and the law of the flesh has extorted the cry: "Who shall deliver me from the body of this death?"

(Nos. 9-18.)

No doubt, to whatever height his longing may rise, it can never give him a claim to its satisfaction nor even a certainty that it will be satisfied. On the contrary, it is precisely the voice of his conscience which tells him that he is completely unworthy of such a satisfaction, and must await the good pleasure of God, if perchance in His free mercy He may graciously incline to him.

(See esp. nos. 14-18).

If, however, he has reasonable grounds for accepting this merciful intervention as a fact (the fact, that is to say, of a revelation), he will then commit himself unreservedly to the wise guidance of the God who has thus bowed to his need. It may be that God's providence permits him at first to seek his salvation in corrupt and false forms of religion. If, however, he follows the best lights of an upright conscience, his road will for a certainty lead him sooner or later into the one fold of the good Shepherd, who knows His sheep and from whose hand no man can tear them.

(Nos. 19-26.)

16

I. READINESS TO BELIEVE

I

Is not this the error, the common and fatal error, of the world, to think itself a judge of Religious Truth without preparation of heart? "I am the good Shepherd, and know My sheep, and am known of Mine." "He goeth before them, and the sheep follow Him, for they know His voice." "The pure in heart shall see God"; "to the meek mysteries are revealed"; "he that is spiritual judgeth all things." "The darkness comprehendeth it not." Gross eyes see not; heavy ears hear not. But in the schools of the world the ways towards Truth are considered high roads open to all men, however disposed, at all times. Truth is to be approached without homage. Everyone is considered on a level with his neighbour; or rather the powers of the intellect, acuteness, sagacity, subtleness, and depth, are thought the guides into Truth. Men consider that they have as full a right to discuss religious subjects, as if they were themselves religious. They will enter upon the most sacred points of Faith at the moment, at their pleasure,—if it so happen, in a careless frame of mind, in their hours of recreation, over the wine cup. Is it wonderful that they so frequently end in becoming indifferentists, and conclude that Religious Truth is but a name, that all men are right and all wrong, from witnessing externally the multitude of sects and parties, and from the clear consciousness they possess within, that their own inquiries end in darkness?

U.S., 198, 199.

2

The Apostles appealed to men's hearts, and according to their hearts, so they answered them. They appealed to their secret belief in a superintending providence, to their hopes and fears thence resulting; and they professed to reveal to them, the nature,

17

personality, attributes, will, and works of Him "whom their hearers ignorantly worshipped." They came as commissioned from Him, and declared that mankind was a guilty and outcast race,—that sin was a misery,—that the world was a snare,—that life was a shadow,—that God was everlasting,—that His Law was holy and true, and its sanctions certain and terrible;—that He also was all-merciful,—that He had appointed a Mediator between Him and them, who had removed all obstacles, and was desirous to restore them, and that He had sent themselves to explain how. They said that that Mediator had come and gone; but had left behind Him what was to be His representative till the end of all things, His mystical Body, the Church, in joining which lay the salvation of the world. So they preached, and so they prevailed; using indeed persuasives of every kind as they were given them, but resting at bottom on a principle higher than the senses or the reason. They used many arguments, but as outward forms of something beyond argument. Thus they appealed to the miracles they wrought, as sufficient signs of their power, and assuredly divine, in spite of those which other systems could show or pretended. They expostulated with the better sort on the ground of their instinctive longings and dim visions of something greater than the world. They awed and overcame the passionate by means of what remained of heaven in them, and of the involuntary homage which such men pay to the more realized tokens of heaven in others. They asked the more generous-minded whether it was not worth while to risk something on the chance of augmenting and perfecting those precious elements of good which their hearts still held; and they could not hide what they cared not to "glory in," their own disinterested sufferings, their high deeds, and their sanctity of life. They won over the affectionate and gentle by the beauty of holiness, and the embodied mercies of Christ as seen in the ministrations and ordinances of His Church. Thus they spread their nets for disciples, and caught thousands at a cast; thus they roused and inflamed their hearers into enthusiasm, till "the Kingdom of Heaven suffered violence, and the violent took it by force." . . . Those who had the seed of God within them. . .

18

would find day by day, as love increased, increasing experience that what they had ventured boldly amid conflicting evidence of sight against sight, and reason against reason, with many things against it, and more things for it, they had ventured well. The examples of meekness, cheerfulness, contentment, silent endurance, private self-denial, fortitude, brotherly love, persever-ance in well-doing, which would from time to time meet them in their new kingdom,—the sublimity and harmony of the Church's doctrine,—the touching and subduing beauty of her services and appointments,—their consciousness of her virtue, divinely imparted, upon themselves, in subduing, purifying, changing them,—the bountifulness of her alms-giving,—her power, weak as she was and despised, over the statesmen and philosophers of the world,—her consistent and steady aggression upon it, moving forward in spite of it on all sides at once, like the wheels in the Prophet's vision, and this in contrast with the ephemeral and variable outbreaks of sectarianism,—the unanimity and intimacy existing between her widely-separated branches,—the mutual sympathy and correspondence of men of hostile nations and foreign languages,—the simplicity of her ascetics, the gravity of her Bishops, the awful glory shed around her Martyrs, and the mysterious and recurring traces of mira-culous agency here and there, once and again, according as the Spirit willed,—these and the like persuasives acted on them day by day, turning the whisper of their hearts into an habitual conviction.

Jfc., 269-272.

3

Those Jews became Christians in Apostolic times who were already what may be called crypto-Christians; and those Chris-tians in this day remain Christian only in name, and (if it so happen) at length fall away, who are nothing deeper or better than men of the world, *savants*, literary men, or politicians. . .

And so our Lord: "He that hath ears, let him hear." "If any man will do His will, he shall know of the doctrine." And "He that is of God, heareth the words of God." Thus too the Angels

19

at the Nativity announce "Peace to men of good will." And we read in the Acts of the Apostles of "Lydia, whose heart the Lord opened to attend to those things which were said by Paul." And we are told on another occasion, that "as many as were ordained," or disposed by God, "to life everlasting, believed." And St. John tells us, "He that knoweth God, heareth us; he that is not of God, heareth us not; by this we know the spirit of truth, and the spirit of error." . . . The Evidences of Christianity . . . then, presuppose a belief and perception of the Divine Presence, a recognition of His attributes and an admiration of His Person viewed under them; a conviction of the worth of the soul and of the reality and momentousness of the unseen world, an understanding that, in proportion as we partake in our own persons of the attributes which we admire in Him, we are dear to Him; a consciousness on the contrary that we are far from exemplifying them, a consequent insight into our guilt and misery, an eager hope of reconciliation to Him, a desire to know and to love Him, and a sensitive looking-out in all that happens, whether in the course of nature or of human life, for tokens, if such there be, of His bestowing on us what we so greatly need.

G.A., 413-415, 417-8.

4

I come then to this conclusion;—if I must submit my reason to mysteries, it is not much matter whether it is a mystery more or a mystery less, when faith anyhow is the very essence of all religion, when the main difficulty to an inquirer is firmly to hold that there is a Living God, in spite of the darkness which surrounds Him, the Creator, Witness, and Judge of men. When once the mind is broken in, as it must be, to the belief of a Power above it, when once it understands, that it is not itself the measure of all things in heaven and earth, it will have little difficulty in going forward. I do not say it will, or can, go on to other truths, without conviction; I do not say it ought to believe the Catholic faith without grounds and motives; but I say that, when once it believes in God, the great obstacle to faith has been taken away,—a proud, self-sufficient spirit. When once a man really, with the eyes of his soul and by the power of Divine grace recognises his Creator, he has passed a line; that has happened to him which cannot happen twice; he has bent his stiff neck, and triumphed over himself. If he believes that God has no beginning, why not believe that He is Three yet One? if he owns that God created space, why not own also that He can cause a body to subsist without dependence on place? if he is obliged to grant that God created all things out of nothing, why doubt His power to change the substance of bread into the Body of His Son? It is as strange that, after an eternal rest, He should begin to create, as that, when He had once created, He should take on Himself a created nature; it is as strange that man should be allowed to fall so low, as we see before our eyes in so many dreadful instances, as that Angels and Saints should be exalted even to religious honours; it is as strange that such large families in the animal world should be created without souls and subject to vanity, as that one creature, the Blessed Mother of God, should be exalted over all the rest.

Mix., 274-5.

5

Men are too well inclined to sit at home, instead of stirring themselves to inquire whether a revelation has been given; they expect its evidences to come to them without their trouble; they act, not as suppliants, but as judges. . . . Like this is the conduct of those who resolve to treat the Almighty with dispassionateness, a judicial temper, clearheadedness, and candour. It is the way with some men, (surely not a good way,) to say, that without these lawyerlike qualifications conversion is immoral. It is their way, a miserable way, to pronounce that there is no religious love of truth where there is fear of error. On the contrary, I would maintain that the fear of error is simply necessary to the genuine love of truth. No inquiry comes to good which is not conducted under a deep sense of responsibility, and of the issues depending upon its determination. Even the ordinary matters of life are an exercise of conscientiousness; and where conscience is, fear must be. So much is this acknowledged just now, that there is almost an affectation, in popular literature, in the case of criticisms on the fine arts, on poetry, and music, of insisting upon conscientiousness in writing, painting, or singing; and that earnestness and simplicity of mind, which makes men fear to go wrong in these minor matters, has surely a place in the most serious of all undertakings.

G.A., 425-6.

6

A religious mind is ever marvelling, and irreligious men laugh and scoff at it because it marvels. A religious mind is ever looking out of itself, is ever pondering God's words, is ever "looking into" them with the Angels, is ever realizing to itself Him on whom it depends, and who is the centre of all truth and good. Carnal and proud minds are contented with self; they like to remain at home; when they hear of mysteries, they have no devout curiosity to go and see the great sight, though it be ever so little out of their way; and when it actually falls in their path, they stumble at it. As great then as is the difference between hanging upon the thought of God and resting in ourselves, lifting up the heart to God and bringing all things in heaven and earth down to ourselves, exalting God and exalting reason, measuring things by God's power and measuring them by our own ignorance, so great is the difference between him who believes in the Christian mysteries and him who does not. And were there no other reason for the revelation of them but this gracious one, of raising us, refining us, making us reverent, making us expectant and devout, surely this would be more than a sufficient one.

P.S., *iv*, 293.

7

To be detached is to be loosened from every tie which binds the soul to the earth, to be dependent upon nothing sublunary, to lean on nothing temporal; it is to care simply nothing what other men choose to think or say of us, or do to us; to go about our own work, because it is our duty, as soldiers go to battle without a care for the consequences; to account credit, honour, name, easy circumstances, comfort, human affections, just nothing at all, when any religious obligation involves the sacrifice of them. It is to be as reckless of all these goods of life on such occasions, as under ordinary circumstances we are lavish and wanton, if I must take an example, in our use of water,—or as we make a present of our words without grudging to friend or stranger,—or as we get rid of wasps, or flies, or gnats, which trouble us, without any sort of compunction, without hesitation before the act, and without a second thought after it.

H.S., iii, 130.

8

There [in the Gospel] Callista learned . . . that the present must be sacrificed for the future; that what is seen must give way to what is believed. Nay, more, she drank in the teaching which at first sight seems so paradoxical, that even present happiness and present greatness lie in relinquishing what at first sight seems to promise them; that the way to true pleasure is, not through self-indulgence, but through mortification; that the way to power is weakness, the way to success failure, the way to wisdom foolishness, the way to glory dishonour. She saw that there was a higher beauty than that which the order and harmony of the natural world revealed, and a deeper peace and calm than that which the exercise, whether of the intellect or of the purest human affection, can supply. She now begun to understand that strange, unearthly composure, which had struck her in Chione, Agellius, and Caecilius; she understood that they were detached from the world, not because they had not the possession, nor the natural love of its gifts, but because they possessed a higher blessing already, which they loved above everything else.

Call., 327.

II. THE CONSCIOUSNESS OF SIN

9

THESE passages [i.e. passages in which Our Lord implies that hardness of belief is a fault], cannot mean that faith is against reason, or that reason does not ordinarily precede faith, for this is a doctrine quite contrary to Revelation, but I think I shall not be wrong in understanding them thus,—that with good dispositions faith *is* easy; and that without good dispositions faith is *not* easy. . .

Now in order to show what this good will, or good disposition is, and how it bears upon faith, I observe as follows: What is the main guide of the soul, given to the whole race of Adam, outside the true fold of Christ as well as within it, given from the first dawn of reason, given to it in spite of that grievous penalty of ignorance, which is one of the chief miseries of our fallen state? It is the light of conscience, "the true Light," as the same Evangelist says, in the same passage, "which enlighteneth every man that cometh into this world." Whether a man be born in pagan darkness, or in some corruption of revealed religion,—whether he has heard the name of the Saviour of the world or not,—whether he be the slave of some superstition, or is in possession of some portions of Scripture, and treats the inspired word as a sort of philosophical book, which he interprets for himself, and comes to certain conclusions about its teaching,—in any case, he has within his breast a certain commanding dictate, not a mere sentiment, not a mere opinion, or impression, or view of things, but a law, an authoritative voice, bidding him do certain things and avoid others. I do not say that its particular injunctions are always clear, or that they are always consistent with each other; but what I am insisting on here is this, that it *commands*,—that it praises, it blames, it promises, it threatens, it implies a future, and it witnesses the unseen. It is more than a man's own self. The man himself has not power over it, or only with extreme difficulty; he did not make it, he cannot destroy it. He may silence it in particular cases or directions, he may distort its enunciations, but he cannot, or it is quite the exception if he can, he cannot emancipate himself from it. He can disobey it, he may refuse to use it; but it remains.

This is Conscience; and, from the nature of the case, its very existence carries on our minds to a Being exterior to ourselves; for else whence did it come? and to a Being superior to ourselves; else whence its strange, troublesome peremptoriness? I say, with-

24

out going on to the question *what* it says, and whether its particular dictates are always as clear and consistent as they might be, its very existence throws us out of ourselves, and beyond ourselves, to go and seek for Him in the height and depth, whose Voice it is. . . And in proportion as we listen to that Word, and use it, not only do we learn more from it, not only do its dictates become clearer, and its lessons broader, and its principles more consistent, but its very tone is louder and more authoritative and constraining. And thus it is, that to those who use what they have, more is given; for, beginning with obedience, they go on to the intimate perception and belief of one God. His voice within them witnesses to Him, and they believe His own witness about Himself. They believe in His existence, not because others say it, not in the word of man merely, but with a personal apprehension of its truth. This, then, is the first step in those good dispositions which lead to faith in the Gospel.

And my second remark is this: that, in spite of all that this Voice does for them, it does not do enough, as they most keenly and sorrowfully feel. They find it most difficult to separate what it really says, taken by itself, from what their own passion or pride, self-love or self-will, mingles with it. Many is the time when they cannot tell how much that true inward Guide commands, and how much comes from a mere earthly source. So that the gift of conscience raises a desire for what it does not itself fully supply. It inspires in them the idea of authoritative guidance, of a divine law; and the desire of possessing it in its fulness, not in mere fragmentary portions or indirect suggestion. It creates in them a thirst, an impatience, for the knowledge of that Unseen Lord, and Governor, and Judge, who as yet speaks to them only secretly, who whispers in their hearts, who tells them something, but not nearly so much as they wish and as they need. Thus you see, my Brethren, a religious man, who has not the blessing of the infallible teaching of revelation, is led to *look out* for it, for the very reason that he *is* religious. He has something, but not all; and if he did not desire more, it would be a proof that he had not used, that he had not profited by, what he had. Hence he will be on the look-out. Such is the definition, I may say, of every

25

religious man, who has not the knowledge of Christ; he is on the look-out. As the Jewish believers were on the look-out for a Messias who they knew was to come, so at all times, and under all dispensations, and in all sects, there are those who know there is a truth, who know they do not possess it except in a very low measure, who desire to know more, who know that He alone who has taught them what they know, can teach them more, who hope that He *will* teach them more, and so are on the look-out for His teaching.

There is another reason why they will be thus waiting and watching for some further knowledge of God's will than they at present possess. It is because the more a person tries to obey his conscience, the more he gets alarmed at himself, for obeying it so imperfectly. His sense of duty will become more keen, and his perception of transgression more delicate, and he will understand more and more how many things he has to be forgiven. But next, while he thus grows in self-knowledge, he also understands more and more clearly that the voice of conscience has nothing gentle, nothing of mercy in its tone. It is severe, and even stern. It does not speak of forgiveness, but of punishment. It suggests to him a future judgment; it does not tell him how he can avoid it. Moreover it does not tell him how he is to get better; he feels himself very sinful at the best; he feels himself in bondage to a tyranny which, alas! he loves too well, even while he hates it. And thus he is in great anguish, and cries out in the Apostle's words, "Unhappy man that I am, who shall deliver me from the body of this death!"

O.S., 63-67.

10

The special attribute under which it [conscience] brings Him before us, to which it subordinates all other Attributes, is that of justice—retributive justice. We learn from its informations to conceive of the Almighty, primarily, not as a God of Wisdom, of Knowledge, of Power, of Benevolence, but as a God of Judgment and Justice; as One, who, not simply for the good of the offender, but as an end good in itself, and as a principle of

26

government, ordains that the offender should suffer for his offence. If it tells us anything at all of the characteristics of the Divine Mind, it certainly tells us this; and, considering that our shortcomings are far more frequent and important than our fulfilment of the duties enjoined upon us, and that of this point we are fully aware ourselves, it follows that the aspect under which Almighty God is presented to us by Nature, is (to use a figure) of One who is angry with us, and threatens evil. Hence its effect is to burden and sadden the religious mind, and is in contrast with the enjoyment derivable from the exercise of the affections, and from the perception of beauty, whether in the material universe or in the creations of the intellect. . .

It is scarcely necessary to insist, that wherever Religion exists in a popular shape, it has almost invariably worn its dark side outwards. It is founded in one way or other on the sense of sin; and without that vivid sense it would hardly have any precepts or any observances. Its many varieties all proclaim or imply that man is in a degraded, servile condition, and requires expiation, reconciliation, and some great change of nature.

G.A., 390-392.

II

I have implied that the laws on which this world is governed do not go so far as to prove that evil will never die out of the creation ; nevertheless, they look in that direction. No experience indeed of life can assure us about the future, but it can and does give us means of conjecturing what is likely to be; and those conjectures coincide with our natural forebodings. Experience enables us to ascertain the moral constitution of man, and thereby to presage his future from his present. It teaches us, first, that he is not sufficient for his own happiness, but is dependent upon the sensible objects which surround him, and that these he cannot take with him when he leaves the world; secondly, that disobedience to his sense of right is even by itself misery, and that he carries that misery about him, wherever he is, though no divine retribution followed upon it; and thirdly, that he cannot change his nature and his habits by wishing, but is simply

himself, and will ever be himself and what he now is, wherever
he is, as long as he continues to be,—or at least that pain has no
natural tendency to make him other than he is, and that the
longer he lives, the more difficult he is to change. How can we
meet these not irrational anticipations, except by shutting our
eyes, turning away from them, and saying that we have no call,
no right, to think of them at present, or to make ourselves miserable about what is not certain, and may be not true ?

G.A., 399-400.

12

Now we come to the third natural informant on the subject of
Religion; I mean the system and the course of the world. This
established order of things, in which we find ourselves, if it has a
Creator, must surely speak of His will in its broad outlines and
its main issues. This principle being laid down as certain, when
we come to apply it to things as they are, our first feeling is one
of surprise and (I may say) of dismay, that His control of this
living world is so indirect, and His action so obscure. This is the
first lesson that we gain from the course of human affairs. What
strikes the mind so forcibly and so painfully is, His absence (if I
may so speak) from His own world. It is a silence that speaks.
It is as if others had got possession of His work. Why does not
He, our Maker and Ruler, give us some immediate knowledge
of Himself? Why does He not write His Moral Nature in large
letters upon the face of history, and bring the blind, tumultuous
rush of its events into a celestial, hierarchical order? Why does
He not grant us in the structure of society at least so much of a
revelation of Himself as the religions of the heathen attempt to
supply? Why from the beginning of time has no one uniform
steady light guided all families of the earth, and all individual
men, how to please Him? Why is it possible without absurdity
to deny His will, His attributes, His existence? Why does He not
walk with us one by one, as He is said to have walked with His
chosen men of old time? We both see and know each other; why,
if we cannot have the sight of Him, have we not at least the
knowledge? On the contrary, He is specially "a Hidden God";

28

and with our best efforts we can only glean from the surface of the world some faint and fragmentary views of Him. I see only a choice of alternatives in explanation of so critical a fact:—either there is no Creator, or He has disowned His creatures. Are then the dim shadows of His Presence in the affairs of men but a fancy of our own, or, on the other hand, has He hid His face and the light of His countenance, because we have in some special way dishonoured Him? My true informant, my burdened conscience, gives me at once the true answer to each of these antagonist questions:—it pronounces without any misgiving that God exists:—and it pronounces quite as surely that I am alienated from Him; that "His hand is not shortened, but that our iniquities have divided between us and our God." Thus it solves the world's mystery, and sees in that mystery only a confirmation of its own original teaching.

G.A., 396-8.

13

If I looked into a mirror, and did not see my face, I should have the sort of feeling which actually comes upon me, when I look into this living busy world, and see no reflexion of its Creator. . . . Were it not for this voice, speaking so clearly in my conscience and my heart, I should be an atheist, or a pantheist, or a polytheist when I looked into the world. . . The sight of the world is nothing else than the prophet's scroll, full of "lamentations, and mourning, and woe."

To consider the world in its length and breadth, its various history, the many races of man, their starts, their fortunes, their mutual alienation, their conflicts; and then their ways, habits, governments, forms of worship; their enterprises, their aimless courses, their random achievements and acquirements, the impotent conclusion of long-standing facts, the tokens so faint and broken of a superintending design, the blind evolution of what turn out to be great powers or truths, the progress of things, as if from unreasoning elements, not towards final causes, the greatness and littleness of man, his far-reaching aims, his short duration, the curtain hung over his futurity, the disappointments of life, the defeat of good, the success of evil, physical pain, mental anguish, the prevalence and intensity of sin, the pervading idolatries, the corruptions, the dreary hopeless irreligion, that condition of the whole race, so fearfully yet exactly described in the Apostle's words, "having no hope and without God in the world." . . .

What shall be said to this heart-piercing, reason-bewildering fact? I can only answer, that either there is no Creator, or this living society of men is in a true sense discarded from His presence. . . *If* there be a God, *since* there is a God, the human race is implicated in some terrible aboriginal calamity. It is out of joint with the purposes of its Creator. This is a fact, a fact as true as the fact of its existence; and thus the doctrine of what is theologically called original sin becomes to me almost as certain as that the world exists, and as the existence of God.

Apo., 241-43.

14

Nothing, however, is told us in nature of the limits of the two rules, of love and of justice, or how they are to be reconciled; nothing to show that the rule of mercy, as acting on moral agents, is more than the supplement, not the substitute of the fundamental law of justice and holiness. And, let it be added, taking us even as we are, much as each of us has to be forgiven, yet a religious man would hardly wish the rule of justice obliterated. It is a something which he can depend on and recur to; it gives a character and a certainty to the course of Divine Governance; and, tempered by the hope of mercy, it suggests animating and consolatory thoughts to him; so that, far from acquiescing in the theory of God's unmixed benevolence, he will rather protest against it as the invention of those who, in their eagerness to conciliate the enemies of the Truth, care little about distressing and sacrificing its friends.

Different, indeed, is his view of God and of man, of the claims of God, of man's resources, of the guilt of disobedience, and of the prospect of forgiveness, from those flimsy self-invented notions, which satisfy the reason of the mere man of letters, or the prosperous and self-indulgent philosopher! .... To see truly the cost and misery of sinning, we must quit the public haunts of business and pleasure, and be able, like the Angels, to see the tears shed in secret,—to witness the anguish of pride and impatience, where there is no sorrow,—the stings of remorse, where yet there is no repentance,—the wearing, never-ceasing struggle between conscience and sin,—the misery of indecision,—the harassing, haunting fears of death, and a judgment to come,— and the superstitions which these engender. Who can name the overwhelming total of the world's guilt and suffering,—suffering crying for vengeance on the authors of it, and guilt foreboding it!

U.S., 114-15.

15

Not only in their possessions and their offspring, but in their own persons, have men mortified themselves, with the hope of expiating deeds of evil. Burnt-offerings, calves of a year old, thousands of rams, and ten thousands of rivers of oil, their first-born for their transgression, the fruit of their body for the sin of their soul, even these are insufficient to lull the sharp throbbings of a heavy-laden conscience. Think of the bodily tortures to which multitudes have gloomily subjected themselves, and that for years, under almost every religious system, with a view of ridding themselves of their sins, and judge what man conceives of the guilt of disobedience. . .

Doubtless these desperate and dark struggles are to be called superstition, when viewed by the side of true religion; and it is easy enough to speak of them as superstition, when we have been informed of the gracious and joyful result in which the scheme of Divine Governance issues. But it is man's truest and best religion, *before* the Gospel shines on him. If our race *be* in a fallen and depraved state, what ought our religion to be but anxiety and remorse, till God comforts us? Surely, to be in gloom,—to view ourselves with horror,—to look about to the right hand and to the left for means of safety,—to catch at everything, yet trust in nothing,—to do all we can, and try to do more than all,—and,

31

after all, to wait in miserable suspense, naked and shivering, among the trees of the garden, for the hour of His coming, and meanwhile to fancy sounds of woe in every wind stirring the leaves about us,—in a word, to be superstitious,—is nature's best offering, her most acceptable service, her most mature and enlarged wisdom, in the presence of a holy and offended God. They who are not superstitious without the Gospel, will not be religious with it.

U.S., 116-18.

16

The very difficulties of nature make it likely that a revelation should be made; the very mysteries of creation call for some act on the part of the Creator, by which those mysteries shall be alleviated to you or compensated. One of the greatest of the perplexities of nature is this very one, that the Creator should have left you to yourselves. You know there is a God, yet you know your own ignorance of Him, of His will, of your duties, of your prospects. A revelation would be the greatest of possible boons which could be vouchsafed to you. After all, you do not know, you only conclude that there is a God; you see Him not, you but hear of Him. He acts under a veil; He is on the point of manifesting himself to you at every turn, yet He does not. He has impressed on your hearts anticipations of His majesty; in every part of creation has He left traces of His presence and given glimpses of His glory; you come up to the spot, He has been there, but He is gone. He has taught you His law, unequivocally indeed, but by deduction and by suggestion, not by direct command. He has always addressed you circuitously, by your inward sense, by the received opinion, by the events of life, by vague traditions, by dim histories; but as if of set purpose, and by an evident law, He never actually appears to your longing eyes or your weary heart, He never confronts you with Himself. What can be meant by all this? a spiritual being abandoned by its Creator! there must doubtless be some awful and all-wise reason for it; still a sore trial it is; so sore, surely, that you must gladly hail the news of His interference to remove or diminish it.

The news then of a revelation, far from suspicious, is borne in upon our hearts by the strongest presumptions of reason in its behalf. It is hard to believe that it has not been given, as indeed the conduct of mankind has ever shown. You cannot help expecting it from the hands of the All-merciful, unworthy as you feel yourselves of it. It is not that you can claim it, but that He inspires hope of it; it is not you that are worthy of the gift, but it is the gift which is worthy of your Creator. It is so urgently probable, that little evidence is required for it, even though but little were given. . . The very fact, I say, that there is a Creator, and a hidden one, powerfully bears you on and sets you down at the very threshold of revelation, and leaves you there looking up earnestly for Divine tokens that a revelation has been made.

Mix., 276-78.

17

Now take a man from each of these two classes, and suppose the news actually reaches them both, that a message has been received from the unseen world: how will they respectively act? It is plain: on him who has been looking out, or hoping, or at least longing, for such a mercy, its operation will be wonderful. It will affect him profoundly; it will thrill through him; so much so, that, provided only the message, on examination, be of a nature to answer his needs, he will be under a strong temptation to believe it, if he can, on very little evidence, or on none at all. At all events he will set about inquiring what its evidence is, and will do his best to find it all out, whether it be more or less. On the other hand, the man who is without the due religious dispositions I have been describing, simply is not moved at all. He takes no interest in the report, and will not go to the pains to inquire about it. He will sit at home; and it will not even occur to him that he ought to rise, and look about him. He is as little stirred, as if he heard that a great man had arisen in the antipodes, or that there was a revolution in Japan. Here then we have come to the critical difference between the two descriptions of men. The one is active, and the other passive, when Christ is preached as the Saviour of the world. The one goes to meet

33

the truth; the other thinks that the Truth ought to come to *him*. The one examines into the proof that God has spoken; the other waits till this is proved to him. He feels no personal interest in it; he thinks it not his own concern, but (if I may so say) God Almighty's concern. He does not care to make the most of his knowledge; he does not put things together; he does not add up his facts and cumulate his arguments; he leaves all this to be done for him by Him who speaks to him; and if he is to have any trouble in the matter, then he is willing to dismiss it altogether. And next, supposing proof is actually offered him, he feels no sort of gratitude or delicacy towards Him who offers it: he says without compunction, "I do not see this"; and "that does not follow"; for he is a critic and a judge, not an inquirer, and he negotiates and bargains, when he ought to be praying for light. And thus he learns nothing rightly, and goes the way to reject a divine message, because he will not throw himself upon and into the evidence; while his neighbour, who has a real concern for his own salvation, finds it and believes.

Returning, then, to what I said when I began, we see now how it was that our Lord praised easiness of belief, and condemned hardness of belief. To be easy in believing is nothing more or less than to have been ready to inquire; to be hard of belief is nothing else but to have been loth and reluctant to inquire. Those whose faith He praised had no stronger evidence than those whose unbelief He condemned; but they had used their eyes, used their reason, exerted their minds, and persevered in inquiry till they found; while the others, whose unbelief He condemned, had heard indeed, but had let the divine seed lie by the roadside, or in the rocky soil, or among the thorns which choked it.

O.S., 69-71.

18

"If, on the other hand," continued Caecilius . . . "if all your thoughts go one way; if you have needs, desires, aims, aspirations, all of which demand an Object, and imply, by their very existence, that such an Object does exist also; and if nothing here does satisfy them, and if there be a message which professes to come from that Object, of whom you already have the presentiment, and to teach you about Him, and to bring the remedy you crave; and if those who try that remedy say with one voice that the remedy answers; are you not bound, Callista, at least to look that way, to inquire into what you hear about it, and to ask for His help, if He be, to enable you to believe in Him?"

"This is what a slave of mine used to say," cried Callista abruptly " . . . and another, Agellius, hinted the same thing . . . What is your remedy, what your Object, what your love, O Christian teacher? Why are you all, so mysterious, so reserved in your communications?"

Caecilius was silent for a moment, and seemed at a loss for an answer. At length he said, "Every man is in that state which you confess of yourself. We have no love for Him who alone lasts. We love those things which do not last, but come to an end. Things being thus, He whom we ought to love has determined to win us back to Him. With this object He has come into His own world, in the form of one of us men. And in that human form He opens His arms and woos us to return to Him, our Maker. This is our Worship, this is our Love, Callista."

"You talk as Chione," Callista answered, "only that she felt and you teach. She could not speak of her Master without blushing for joy—And Agellius, when he said one word about his Master, he too began to blush——"

It was plain that the priest could hardly command his feelings, and they sat for a short while in silence. Then Callista began, as if musing on what she had heard.

"A loved One," she said, "yet ideal; a passion so potent, so fresh, so innocent, so absorbing, so expulsive of other loves, so enduring; yet of One never beheld:—Mysterious! It is our own notion of the First and only Fair, yet embodied in a substance, yet dissolving again into a sort of imagination. It is beyond me."

"There is but one Lover of souls," cried Caecilius, "and He loves each one of us, as though there were no one else to love. He died for each one of us, as if there were no one else to die for. He died on the shameful cross. 'Amor meus crucifixus est.' The love which he inspires lasts, for it is the love of the Unchangeable.

It satisfies, for He is inexhaustible. The nearer we draw to Him, the more triumphantly does He enter into us; the longer He dwells in us, the more intimately have we possession of Him. It is an espousal for eternity. This is why it is so easy for us to die for our faith, at which the world marvels."

Call., 220-22.

III. SURRENDER

19

OF the two, I would rather have to maintain that we ought to begin with believing everything that is offered to our acceptance, than that it is our duty to doubt of everything. The former, indeed, seems the true way of learning. In that case, we soon discover and discard what is contradictory to itself; and error having always some portion of truth in it, and the truth having a reality which error has not, we may expect, that when there is an honest purpose and fair talents, we shall somehow make our way forward, the error falling off from the mind, and the truth developing and occupying it. Thus it is that the Catholic religion is reached, as we see, by inquirers from all points of the compass, as if it mattered not where a man began, so that he had an eye and a heart for the truth.

G.A., 377.

20

Certainly, I have always contended that obedience even to an erring conscience was the way to gain light, and that it mattered not where a man began, so that he began on what came to hand, and in faith; and that any thing might become a divine method of Truth; that to the pure all things are pure, and have a self-correcting virtue and a power of germinating.

Apo., 206.

21

There are few religions which have no points in common; and these, whether true or false, when embraced with an absolute conviction, are the pivots on which changes take place in that

36

collection of credences, opinions, prejudices, and other assents, which make up what is called a man's selection and adoption of a form of religion, a denomination, or a Church. . .

And if this intercommunion of religions holds good, even when the common points between them are but errors held in common, much more natural will be the transition from one religion to another, without injury to existing certitudes, when the common points, the objects of those certitudes, are truths; and still stronger in that case and more constraining will be the sympathy, with which minds that love truth, even when they have surrounded it with error, will yearn towards the Catholic faith, which contains within itself, and claims as its own, all truth that is elsewhere to be found, and more than all, and nothing but truth. This is the secret of the influence, by which the Church draws to herself converts from such various and conflicting religions. They come, not so much to lose what they have, as to gain what they have not; and in order that, by means of what they have, more may be given to them. St. Augustine tells us that there is no false teaching without an intermixture of truth; and it is by the light of those particular truths, contained respectively in the various religions of men, and by our certitudes about them, which are possible wherever those truths are found, that we pick our way, slowly perhaps, but surely, into the One Religion which God has given, taking our certitudes with us, not to lose, but to keep them more securely. . .

And thus it is conceivable that a man might travel in his religious profession all the way from heathenism to Catholicity, through Mahometanism, Judaism, Unitarianism, Protestantism, and Anglicanism, without any one certitude lost, but with a continual accumulation of truths, which claimed from him and elicited in his intellect fresh and fresh certitudes.

G.A., 248-51.

22

All religions, the various heathen religions as well as the Mosaic religion, have many things in them which are very much the same. They seem to come from one common origin, and so far

37

have the traces of truth upon them. They are all branches, though they are corruptions and perversions, of that patriarchal religion which came from God. And of course the Jewish religion came entirely and immediately from God. Now God's works are like each other, not different; if, then, the Gospel is from God, and the Jewish religion was from God, and the various heathen religions in their first origin were from God, it is not wonderful, rather it is natural, that they should have in many ways a resemblance one with another. And, accordingly, that the Gospel is in certain points like the religions which preceded it, is but an argument that "God is One, and that there is none other but He"; the difference between them being that the heathen religions are a true religion corrupted; the Jewish, a true religion dead; and Christianity the true religion living and perfect.

P.S., v, 170-71.

23

True religion is the summit and perfection of false religions: it combines in one whatever there is of good and true, severally remaining in each. And in like manner the Catholic Creed is for the most part the combination of separate truths, which heretics have divided among themselves, and err in dividing. So, that, in matter of fact, if a religious mind were educated in and sincerely attached to some form of heathenism or heresy, and then were brought under the light of truth, it would be drawn off from error into the truth, not by losing what it had, but by gaining what it had not—not by being unclothed, but by being "clothed upon," "that mortality may be swallowed up of life." That same principle of faith which attaches it to its original human teaching, would attach it to the truth; and that portion of its original teaching which was to be cast off as absolutely false, would not be directly rejected, but indirectly rejected *in* the reception of the truth which is its opposite. True conversion is of a positive, not a negative character.

D.A., 200.

For a time perhaps the mind remains contented in the home of its youth, where originally it found itself, till in due season the special idea, however it came by it, which is ultimately to form and rule it, begins to stir; and gradually energising more and more, and growing and expanding, it suddenly bursts the bonds of that external profession, which, though its first, was never really its proper habitation. During this interval it uses the language which it has inherited, and thinks it certainly true; yet all the while its own genuine thoughts and modes of thinking are germinating and ramifying and penetrating into the old teaching which only in name belongs to it; till its external manifestations are plainly inconsistent with each other, though sooner in the apprehension of others than in its own, nay perhaps for a season it maintains what it has received by education the more vehemently, by way of keeping in check or guarding the new views, which are opening upon it, and startle it by their strangeness.

What happens in Science, Philosophy, Politics, or the Arts, may happen, I say, in Religion too; there is such a thing as an inchoate faith or incomplete creed, which is not yet fully Catholic, yet is Catholic as far as it goes, tends to Catholicism, and is in the way to reach it, whether in the event it actually is happy enough to reach it or not. And from the beginning such a creed, such a theology was, I grant, the work of a supernatural principle, which, exercising itself first in the rudiments of truth, finished in its perfection. Man cannot determine in what instances that principle of grace is present and in what not, except by the event; but wherever it is, whether it can be ascertained by man or not, whether it reaches its destination, which is Catholicity, or whether it is ultimately frustrated and fails, still in every case the Church claims that work as her own; because it tends to her, because it is recognized by all men, even enemies, to belong to her, because it comes of that divine power, which is given her in fulness, and because it anticipates portions of that divine creed which is committed to her infallibility as an everlasting deposit. And in this sense it is perfectly true that a Protestant may hold and teach one doctrine of Catholicism without holding or teaching another; but then, as I have said, he is in the way to hold others, in the way to profess all, and he is inconsistent if he does not, and till he does. Nay, he is already reaching forth to the whole truth, from the very circumstance of his really grasping any portion of it.

So strongly do I feel this, that I account it no paradox to say, that, let a man but master the one doctrine with which I began these Discourses, the Being of a God, let him really and truly, and not in words only, or by inherited profession, or in the conclusions of reason, but by a direct apprehension, be a Monotheist, and he is already three-fourths of the way towards Catholicism.

Idea (1852 *edition*), 160-2.*

25

The growth of plants . . . is slow, gradual, continual; yet one day by chance they grow more than another, they make a shoot, or at least we are attracted to their growth on that day by some actual circumstance, and it remains on our memory. So with our souls. . . .

Many men do not at all recollect any one marked and definite time *when* they began to seek God. Others recollect a time, not, properly speaking, when they began, but when they made what may be called a shoot forward, the fact either being so, in consequence of external events, or at least for some reason or other their attention being called to it. Others, again, continue forming a religious character, and religious opinions as the result of it, though holding at the same time some outward profession of faith inconsistent with them; as, for instance, suppose it has been their unhappy condition to be brought up as heathens, Jews, infidels or heretics. They hold the notions they have been taught for a long while, not perceiving that the character forming within them is at variance with these, till at length the inward growth forces itself forward, forces on the opinions accompanying it, and the dead outward surface of error, which has no root in

---

* The Lecture in which this passage occurs was omitted in subsequent editions.

their minds, from some accidental occurrence, suddenly falls off; suddenly—just as a building might suddenly fall, which had been going many years, and which falls at this moment rather than that, in consequence of some chance cause, as it is called, which we cannot detect.

P.S., viii, 225-7.

26
PRAYER FOR THE LIGHT OF TRUTH

O MY GOD, I confess that *Thou canst* enlighten my darkness. I confess that Thou *alone* canst. I *wish* my darkness to be enlightened. I do not know whether Thou wilt: but that Thou canst and that I wish, are sufficient reasons for me to *ask,* that Thou at least has not forbidden my asking. I hereby promise that by Thy grace which I am asking, I will embrace whatever I at last feel certain is the truth, if ever I come to be certain. And by Thy grace I will guard against all self-deceit which may lead me to take what nature would have, rather than what reason approves.

M.D., 386.

III: MIRACLES

ANALYTICAL SUMMARY

Profound insight into his own misery and sinfulness makes man look longingly for atonement, redemption and the help of grace and for these to direct his gaze upward to God. Everything depends on God's personal help.

But can the creature compel the Creator? Has the wrong-doer a right to the pardon of the party he has wronged?

God alone can of his free mercy descend to man and make Himself known to man: "See here am I."

But how can man know that it is God who approaches Him? Everything which surrounds man, everything which constitutes his being, is created, not divine, and obeys the laws of nature. If God should reveal Himself in the course of nature, how is the "previous" situation altered? And it is precisely this "previous" situation from which "fallen man suffers."

If, then, God alone can bring help, and no natural means; if this divine aid cannot be recognised as God's immediate aid, should it appear as simply an instance of the operation of nature's normal laws:

if God is truly God, and therefore distinct from nature with a distinctive mode of operation, so that He is able to intervene in the normal course of nature in such wise that His own footsteps become audible: here necessarily is the miraculous.

If man has needed this and longed "that Thou would'st rend the heavens and come down,"

if Christ and Christianity are God's word and God's grace, and not simply another aspect of the normal course of nature, then the extent of

43

God's *personal interposition and action will determine the extent of the method reserved for Himself alone—namely, the miraculous.*

(Nos. 1-3.)

It is no doubt true that God *intervenes and acts in a visible and therefore a "creaturely" mode of action—but it is a creaturely mode which exceeds the normal operation of creatures.*

It is no doubt also true that this *"creaturely" mode of action which exceeds the normal operation of creatures does not abolish the laws which regulate their activity—but it is a mode of action by which its pre-existing laws are combined to produce an effect nowhere found in the normal operation of created agents and as only the Hand of the Sovereign Master can combine them.*

And finally, it is no doubt true that this *extraordinary combination of laws is no arbitrary patchwork introduced into the marvellous edifice of nature—but manifests the entrance of a new and mighty "Nature" into the sphere of pre-existing nature.*

"Head and Body One Christ."

(Nos. 4-8.)

MIRACLES

I

And the whole tenor of Scripture from beginning to end is to this effect: the matter of revelation is not a mere collection of truths, not a philosophical view, not a religious sentiment or spirit, not a special morality,—poured out upon mankind as a stream might pour itself into the sea, mixing with the world's thought, modifying, purifying, invigorating it;—but an authoritative teaching, which bears witness to itself and keeps itself together as one, in contrast to the assemblage of opinions on all sides of it, and speaks to all men, as being ever and everywhere one and the same, and claiming to be received intelligently, by all whom it addresses, as one doctrine, discipline, and devotion directly given from above. In consequence, the exhibition of credentials, that is, of evidence, that it is what it professes to be, is essential to Christianity, as it comes to us; for we are not left at liberty to pick and choose out of its contents according to our judgment, but must receive it all, as we find it, if we accept it at all.

G.A., 387.

2

Science and Revelation agree in supposing that nature is governed by uniform and settled laws.

Scripture, properly understood, is decisive in removing all those irregular agents which are supposed to interrupt, at their own pleasure, the order of Nature.

Almost every religion but that of the Bible, and those derived from it, has supposed the existence of an indefinite number of beings, to a certain extent independent of each other, able to interfere in the affairs of life, and whose interference (supposing it to exist) being reducible to no law, took away all hope of obtain-

45

ing any real information concerning the actual system of the universe. On the other hand, the inspired writers are express in tracing all miraculous occurrences to the direct interposition, or at least the permission of the Deity; and since they also imply that miracles are displayed, not at random, but with a purpose, their declarations in this respect entirely agree with the deductions which scientific observation has made concerning the general operation of established laws, and the absence of any arbitrary interference with them on the part of beings exterior to the present system of things.

The supposition, then, of a system of established laws, on which all philosophical investigation is conducted, is also the very foundation on which the evidence for Revealed Religion rests.

U.S., 5-6.

3

A Revelation, that is, a direct message from God to man, itself bears in some degree a miraculous character; inasmuch as it supposes the Deity actually to present Himself before His creatures, and to interpose in the affairs of life in a way above the reach of those settled arrangements of nature, to the existence of which universal experience bears witness. And as a Revelation itself, so again the evidences of a Revelation may all more or less be considered miraculous. Prophecy is an evidence only so far as foreseeing future events is above the known powers of the human mind, or miraculous. In like manner, if the rapid extension of Christianity be urged in favour of its divine origin, it is because such extension under such circumstances, is supposed to be inconsistent with the known principles and capacities of human nature. And the pure morality of the Gospel, as taught by illiterate fishermen of Galilee, is an evidence, in proportion as the phenomenon disagrees with the conclusions of general experience, which leads us to believe that a high state of mental cultivation is ordinarily requisite for the production of such moral teachers.

It might even be said that, strictly speaking, no evidence of a

Revelation is conceivable which does not partake of the character of a miracle; since nothing but a display of power over the existing system of things can attest the immediate presence of Him by whom it was originally established; or, again, because no event which results entirely from the ordinary operation of nature can be the criterion of one that is extraordinary. . . .

[Physical miracles] are the most striking and conclusive evidence, because the laws of matter being better understood than those to which mind is conformed, the transgression of them is more easily recognised. They are the most simple and obvious; because, whereas the freedom of the will resists the imposition of undeviating laws, the material creation, on the contrary, being strictly subjected to the regulation of its Maker, looks to Him alone for a change in its constitution.

Yet miracles [of this kind] are but a branch of the evidences, and other branches have their respective advantages. Prophecy, as has often been observed, is a growing evidence, and appeals more forcibly to those who are acquainted with the Miracles only through testimony. A philosophical mind will perhaps be most strongly affected by the fact of the very existence of the Jewish polity, or of the revolution effected by Christianity. While the beautiful moral teaching and evident honesty of the New Testament writers is the most persuasive argument to the unlearned but single-hearted inquirer.

Nor must it be forgotten that the evidences of Revelation are cumulative, that they gain strength from each other; and that, in consequence, the argument from [physical] Miracles is immensely stronger when viewed in conjunction with the rest, than when considered separately, as in an inquiry of the present nature.

Mir. (1825-26), 6-8.

4

While writers expatiate so largely on the laws of nature, they altogether forget the existence of a moral system: a system which, though but partially understood, and but general in its appointments as acting upon free agents, is as intelligible in its laws and provisions as the material world. Connected with this moral government, we find certain instincts of mind; such as conscience, a sense of responsibility, and an approbation of virtue; an innate desire of knowledge, and an almost universal feeling of the necessity of religious observances; while, in fact, Virtue is, on the whole, rewarded, and Vice punished. And though we meet with many and striking anomalies, yet it is evident that they are but anomalies, and possibly but in appearance so, and with reference to our partial information.

These two systems, the Physical and the Moral, sometimes act in union, and sometimes in opposition to each other; and as the order of nature certainly does in many cases interfere with the operation of moral laws (as, for instance, when good men die prematurely, or the gifts of nature are lavished on the bad), there is nothing to shock probability in the idea that a great moral object should be effected by an interruption of physical order.

But, further than this, however physical laws may embarrass the operation of the moral system, still on the whole they are subservient to it; contributing, as is evident, to the welfare and convenience of man, providing for his mental gratification as well as animal enjoyment, sometimes even supplying correctives to his moral disorders.

If, then, the economy of nature has so constant a reference to an ulterior plan, a Miracle is a deviation from the subordinate for the sake of the superior system, and is very far indeed from improbable, when a great moral end cannot be effected except at the expense of physical regularity.

Nor can it fairly be said to argue an imperfection in the Divine plans, that this interference should be necessary. For we must view the system of Providence as a whole; which is not more imperfect because of the mutual action of its parts, than a machine, the separate wheels of which effect each others movement.

Mir., 16-18.

5

Considering, then, our instinctive sense of duty and moral obligation, yet the weak sanction which reason gives to the practice of virtue, and withal the uncertainty of the mind when advancing beyond the first elements of right and wrong; considering, moreover, the feeling which wise men have entertained of the need of some heavenly guide to instruct and confirm them in goodness, and that unextinguishable desire for a Divine message which has led men in all ages to acquiesce even in pretended revelations, rather than forego the consolation thus afforded them; and, again, the possibility (to say the least) of our being destined for a future state of being, the nature and circumstances of which it may concern us much to know, though from nature we know nothing; considering, lastly, an experience of a watchful and merciful Providence, and the impracticability already noticed of a Revelation without a Miracle, it is hardly too much to affirm that the moral system points to an interference with the course of nature, and that Miracles wrought in evidence of a Divine communication, instead of being antecedently improbable, are, when directly attested, entitled to a respectful and impartial consideration.

Mir., 19, 20.

6

Facts are only so far improbable as they fall under no general rule; whereas it is as parts of an existing system that the Miracles of Scripture demand our attention, as resulting from the known attributes of God, and corresponding to the ordinary arrangements of His providence.

Even as detached events they might excite a rational awe towards the mysterious Author of nature. But they are presented to us, not as unconnected and unmeaning occurrences, but as holding a place in an extensive plan of Divine government, completing the moral system, connecting Man and his Maker, and introducing him to the means of securing his happiness in another and eternal state of being. . . .

As parts of a system, the Miracles recommend and attest each other, evidencing not only general wisdom, but a digested and extended plan. And while this appearance of design connects them with the acknowledged works of a Creator, who is in the natural world chiefly known to us by the presence of final causes, so, again, a plan conducted as this was, through a series of ages, evinces not the varying will of successive individuals, but the steady and sustaining purpose of one Sovereign Mind.

And this remark especially applies to the coincidence of views observable between the Old and New Testament.

Mir., 22, 24, 25.

7

As a gradual revelation of Gospel truth accompanied the miracles of the Prophets, so to those who admit the Catholic doctrines as enunciated in the Creed, and commented on by the Fathers, the subsequent expansion and variation of super-natural agency in the Church, instead of suggesting difficulties, will seem to be in correspondence, as they are contemporaneous, with the developments and additions in dogmatic statements which have occurred between the Apostolic and the present age, and which are but a result and an evidence of spiritual life. . . .

We have been accustomed to believe that Christianity is little more than a creed or doctrine, introduced into the world once for all, and then left to itself, after the manner of human institutions, and under the same ordinary governance with them, stored indeed with hopes and fears for the future, and containing certain general promises of aid for this life, but unattended by any special Divine Providence or any immediately supernatural gift. . . . On the other hand, if we believe that Christians are under an extraordinary dispensation, such as Judaism was, and that the Church is a supernatural ordinance, we shall in mere consistency be disposed to treat even the report of miraculous occurrences with seriousness, from our faith in a Present Power adequate to their production.

Mir., 170, 171, 184, 185.

8

To my mind, certainly, it is incomparably more difficult to believe that the Divine Being should do one miracle and no more, than that He should do a thousand; that He should do one great miracle only, than that He should do a multitude of less besides.

This beautiful world of nature, His own work, He broke its harmony; He broke through His own laws which He had imposed on it; He worked out His purposes, not simply through it, but in violation of it.

If He did this only in the lifetime of the Apostles, if He did it but once, eighteen hundred years ago and more, that isolated infringement looks as the mere infringement of a rule:

If Divine Wisdom would not leave an infringement, an anomaly, a solecism on His work, He might be expected to introduce a series of miracles, and turn the apparent exception into an additional law of His providence.

Prepos., 306.

IV: THE OLD AND THE NEW TESTAMENT

ANALYTICAL SUMMARY

Christ is the one supreme miracle; He, the revelation which we believe, is also the proof of its divine origin.

For only if He is what He professes to be, the promised Messiah whom His people did not recognise, does the great and otherwise insoluble enigma find its solution, the riddle which still exists a living reality under our eyes, since Jew and Christian dwell side by side on earth:

the rejection of the chosen people but the fulfilment of all the promises made to it in the one Church:

the enigma of a broken yet fulfilled covenant.

(Nos. 1-2.)

Only if He is the Messiah, Prophet and Lawgiver of a New Covenant, and absolute Master of the Old, is it no scandal, but our salvation that He in the Sermon on the Mount opposes to the words spoken by "those of old time" His own "But I say unto you,"

is it no contradiction but the truth, that He constitutes His "little flock" when "a Kingdom" was expected,

that He founds a Kingdom in which human weakness and sin continue nevertheless to exist, when a "heaven on earth" was expected.

(No. 3.)

If He is not what He solemnly professed Himself to be, what He accepted as Peter's confession of faith, and before the Sanhedrin attested on oath to His own condemnation—

the "Son of the living God"—"the only begotten of the Father full of grace and truth"—

He Himself in His Life as a Whole, in the history of His effect upon succeeding generations—

53

is a contradiction so great that we must despair in our capacity for knowledge.

We must overthrow and violate all the laws of science and consequently renounce entirely the investigation of truth.

But "Christ conquers."

(Nos. 4-8.)

I. FULFILMENT OF THE OLD TESTAMENT

I

CHRISTIANITY is the continuation and conclusion of what professes to be an earlier revelation, which may be traced back into prehistoric times, till it is lost in the darkness that hangs over them. . . When mankind had universally denied the first lesson of their conscience by lapsing into polytheism, is it a thing of slight moment that there was just one exception to the rule, that there was just one people who, first by their rulers and priests, and afterwards by their own unanimous zeal, professed, as their distinguishing doctrine, the Divine Unity and Government of the world, and that, moreover, not only as a natural truth, but as revealed to them by that God Himself of whom they spoke,—who so embodied it in their national polity, that a Theocracy was the only name by which it could be called? It was a people founded and set up in Theism, kept together by Theism, and maintaining Theism for a period from first to last of 2,000 years, till the dissolution of their body politic; and they have maintained it since in their state of exile and wandering for 2,000 years more. They begin with the beginning of history, and the preaching of this august dogma begins with them. They are its witnesses and confessors, even to torture and death; on it and its revelation are moulded their laws and government; on this their politics, philosophy, and literature are founded; of this truth their poetry is the voice, pouring itself out in devotional compositions which Christianity, through all its many countries and ages, has been unable to rival; on this aboriginal truth, as time goes on, prophet after prophet bases his further revelations, with a sustained reference to a time when, according to the secret counsels of its Divine Object and Author, it is to receive completion and perfection,—till at length that time comes.

55

The last age of their history is as strange as their first. When that time of destined blessing came, which they had so accurately marked out, and were so carefully waiting for—a time which found them, in fact, more zealous for their Law, and for the dogma it enshrined, than they ever had been before—then, instead of any final favour coming on them from above, they fell under the power of their enemies, and were overthrown, their holy city razed to the ground, their polity destroyed, and the remnant of their people cast off to wander far and away through every land except their own, as we find them at this day; lasting on, century after century, not absorbed in other populations, not annihilated, as likely to last on, as unlikely to be restored, as far as outward appearances go, now as a thousand years ago. . . They were the favoured servants of God, and yet a peculiar reproach and note of infamy is affixed to their name. It was their belief that His protection was unchangeable, and that their Law would last for ever;—it was their consolation to be taught by an uninterrupted tradition, that it could not die, except by changing into a new self, more wonderful than it was before;—it was their faithful expectation that a promised King was coming, the Messiah, who would extend the sway of Israel over all people;— it was a condition of their covenant, that, as a reward to Abraham, their first father, the day at length should dawn when the gates of their narrow land should open, and they should pour out for the conquest and occupation of the whole earth;—and, I repeat, when the day came, they did go forth, and they did spread into all lands, but as hopeless exiles, as eternal wanderers.

Are we to say that this failure is a proof that, after all, there was nothing providential in their history? . . . It is an historical fact, that, at the very time that the Jews were driven out from their home to wander over the earth, their Christian brethren, born of the same stock, and equally citizens of Jerusalem, did also issue forth from the same home, but in order to subdue that same earth and make it their own; that is, they undertook the very work which, according to the promise, their nation actually was ordained to execute; and, with a method of their own indeed and with a new end, and only slowly and painfully, but still really and thoroughly, they did it. And since that time the two children of the promise have ever been found together—of the promise forfeited and the promise fulfilled; and whereas the Christian has been in high place, so the Jew has been degraded and despised—the one has been "the head," and the other "the tail"; so that, to go no farther, the fact that Christianity actually has done what Judaism was to have done, decides the controversy, by the logic of facts, in favour of Christianity . . . If the Jews, instead of hailing their own Messiah, crucified Him, then the strange scourge which has pursued them after the deed, and the energetic wording of the curse before it, are explained by the very strangeness of their guilt:—or rather their sin is their punishment; for in rejecting their Divine King, they *ipso facto* lost the living principle and tie of their nationality. . .

On the whole, then, I observe, on the one hand, that, Judaism having been the channel of religious traditions which are lost in the depth of their antiquity, of course it is a great point for Christianity to succeed in proving that it is the legitimate heir to that former religion. Nor is it, on the other, of less importance to the significance of those early traditions to be able to determine that they were not lost together with their original storehouse, but were transferred, on the failure of Judaism, to the custody of the Christian Church. And this apparent correspondence between the two is in itself a presumption for such correspondence being real. Next, I observe, that if the history of Judaism is so wonderful as to suggest the presence of some special divine agency in its appointments and fortunes, still more wonderful and divine is the history of Christianity; and again it is more wonderful still, that two such wonderful creations should span almost the whole course of ages, during which nations and states have been in existence, and should constitute a professed system of continued intercourse between earth and heaven from first to last amid all the vicissitudes of human affairs. This phenomenon again carries on its face, to those who believe in a God, the probability that it has that divine origin which it professes to have; and (when viewed in the light of the strong presumption which I have insisted on, that in God's mercy a

57

revelation from Him will be granted to us, and of the contrast presented by other religions, no one of which professes to be a revelation and direct definite, and integral as His is), this phenomenon, I say, of cumulative marvels raises that probability, both for Judaism and Christianity, in religious minds, almost to a certainty.

G.A., 431-9.

2

First, then, as to what Scripture declares. From the book of Genesis we learn that the chosen people was set up in this one idea, viz. to be a blessing to the whole earth, and that, by means of one of their own race, a greater than their father Abraham. This was the meaning and drift of their being chosen. . .

Such was the categorical prophecy, literal and unequivocal in its wording, direct and simple in its scope. One man, born of the chosen tribe, was the destined minister of blessing to the whole world; and the race, as represented by that tribe, was to lose its old self in gaining a new self in Him. Its destiny was sealed upon it in its beginning. An expectation was the measure of its life. It was created for a great end, and in that end it had its ending. . .

It is quite clear that the Jews did thus understand their prophecies, and did expect their great Ruler, in the very age in which our Lord came, and in which they, on the other hand, were destroyed, losing their old self without gaining their new. . .

Now, considering that at that very time our Lord did appear as a teacher, and founded not merely a religion, but (what was then quite a new idea in the world) a system of religious warfare, an aggressive and militant body, a dominant Catholic Church, which aimed at the benefit of all nations by the spiritual conquest of all; and that this warfare, then begun by it, has gone on without cessation down to this day, and now is as living and real as ever it was; that that militant body has from the first filled the world, that it has had wonderful successes, that its successes have on the whole been of extreme benefit to the human race, tha it has imparted an intelligent notion about the Supreme God to millions who would have lived and died in irreligion, that it has raised the tone of morality wherever it has come, has abolished great social anomalies and miseries, has elevated the female sex to its proper dignity, has protected the poorer classes, has destroyed slavery, encouraged literature and philosophy, and had a principal part in that civilization of human kind, which, with some evils, has still on the whole been productive of far greater good,—considering, I say, that all this began at the destined, expected, recognized season when the old prophecy said that in one Man, born of the tribe of Judah, all the tribes of the earth were to be blessed,—I feel I have a right to say (and my line of argument does not lead me to say more), that it is at the very least a remarkable coincidence; that is, one of those coincidences which, when they are accumulated, come close upon the idea of miracle, as being impossible without the Hand of God directly and immediately in them.

G.A., 441-445.

II. THE NEW TESTAMENT

3

Christianity was quite aware from the first of its own prospective future, so unlike the expectations which the prophets would excite concerning it, and it meets the difficulty thence arising, by anticipation, by giving us its own predictions of what it was to be in historical fact, predictions which are at once explanatory comments upon the Jewish Scriptures, and direct evidences of its own prescience.

I think it observable then, that, though our Lord claims to be the Messiah, He shows so little of conscious dependence on the old Scriptures, or of anxiety to fulfil them; as if it became Him, who was the Lord of the Prophets, to take His own course, and to leave their utterances to adjust themselves to Him as they could, and not to be careful to accommodate Himself to them. The evangelists do indeed show some such natural zeal in His behalf, and thereby illustrate what I notice in Him by the contrast. They betray an earnestness to trace in His Person and history the accomplishment of prophecy, as when they discern

59

it in His return from Egypt, in His life at Nazareth, in the gentleness and tenderness of His mode of teaching, and in the various minute occurrences of His passion; but He Himself goes straightforward on His way, of course claiming to be the Messiah of the Prophets,* still not so much recurring to past prophecies, as uttering new ones, with an antithesis not unlike that which is so impressive in the Sermon on the Mount, when He first says, "It has been said by them of old time," and then adds, "But I say unto you." . . .

1. First, then, the fact has been often insisted on as a bold conception, unheard of before, and worthy of divine origin, that He should even project a universal religion, and that to be effected by what may be called a propagandist movement from one centre. Hitherto it had been the received notion in the world, that each nation had its own gods. The Romans legislated upon that basis, and the Jews had held it from the first, holding of course also, that all gods but their own God were idols and demons. . .

While the Jews, relying on their Scriptures with great appearance of reason, looked for a deliverer who should conquer with the sword, we find that Christianity, from the first, not by an afterthought upon trial and experience, but as a fundamental truth, magisterially set right that mistake, transfiguring the old prophecies, and bringing to light, as St. Paul might say, "the mystery which had been hidden from ages and generations, but now was made manifest in His saints, the glory of this mystery among the Gentiles, which is Christ in you," not simply over you, but in you, by faith and love, "the hope of glory."

2. I have partly anticipated my next remark, which relates to the means by which the Christian enterprise was to be carried into effect. That preaching was to have a share in the victories of the Messiah was plain from Prophet and Psalmist; but then Charlemagne preached, and Mahomet preached, with an army to

* He appeals to the prophecies in evidence of His Divine mission, in addressing the people of Nazareth (Luke iv, 18), St. John's disciples (Matt. xi, 5), and the Pharisees (Matt. xxi, 42, and John v, 39) but not in details. The appealt, details He reserves for His disciples. *Vide* Matt. xi, 10; xxvi, 24, 31, 54 Luke xxii, 37; xxiv, 27, 46.

back them. The same Psalm which speaks of those "who preach good tidings," speaks also of their King's "foot being dipped in the blood of His enemies;" but what is so grandly original in Christianity is, that on its broad field of conflict its preachers were to be simply unarmed, and to suffer, but to prevail. . .

3. Now we come to a third point. . . I have granted that they [i.e. the prophecies of the Old Covenant] seemed to say that the coming of Christ would issue in a period of peace . . . [and] seem to predict a reversal of the consequences of the fall, and that reversal has not yet been granted to us, it is true; but let us consider how distinctly Christianity warns us against any such anicipation. While it is so forcibly laid down in the Gospels that the history of the kingdom of heaven begins in suffering and sanctity, it is as plainly said that it results in unfaithfulness and sin; that is to say, that, though there are at all times many holy, many religious men in it, and though sanctity, as at the beginning, is ever the life and the substance and the germinal seed of the Divine Kingdom, yet there will ever be many too, there will be more, who by their lives are a scandal and injury to it, not a defence. This again is an astonishing announcement, and the more so when viewed in contrast with the precepts delivered by our Lord in His Sermon on the Mount, and His description to the Apostles of their weapons and their warfare. . . Yet our Lord's words are express: He tells us that "Many are called, few are chosen;" . . . and "the kingdom is like to a net which gathered together all kind of fishes;" and "at the end of the world the Angels shall go forth, and shall separate the wicked from among the just."

Moreover, He not only speaks of His religion as destined to possess a wide temporal power, such, that, as in the case of the Babylonian, "the birds of the air should dwell in its branches," but He opens on us the prospect of ambition and rivalry in its leading members, when He warns His disciples against desiring the first places in His kingdom; nay, of grosser sins, in His description of the Ruler, who "began to strike his fellow-servants, and to eat and drink and be drunken,"—passages which have an awful significance, considering what kind of men have before

61

now been His chosen representatives, and have sat in the chair of His Apostles.

If then it be objected that Christianity does not, as the old prophets seem to promise, abolish sin and irreligion within its pale, we may answer, not only that it did not engage to do so, but that actually in a prophetical spirit it warned its followers against the expectation of so doing.

G.A., 447-456.

III. CHRIST

4

In the Old Covenant, Almighty God first of all spoke the Ten Commandments from Mount Sinai, and afterwards wrote them. So Our Lord first spoke His own Gospel, both of promise and of precept, on the Mount, and His Evangelists have recorded it. Further, when He delivered it, He spoke by the way of parallel to the Ten Commandments. And His style, moreover, corresponds to the authority which He assumes. It is of that solemn, measured, and severe character, which bears on the face of it tokens of its belonging to One who spake as none other man could speak. The Beatitudes, with which His sermon opens, are an instance of this incommunicable style, which befitted, as far as human words could befit, God Incarnate.

Nor is this style peculiar to the ·Sermon on the Mount. All through the Gospels it is discernible, distinct from any other part of Scripture, showing itself in solemn declarations, canons, sentences, or sayings, such as legislators propound, and scribes and lawyers comment on. Surely everything our Saviour did and said is characterized by mingled simplicity and mystery. His emblematical actions, His typical miracles, His parables, His replies, His censures, all are evidence of a legislature in germ, afterwards to be developed, a code of divine truth which was ever to be before men's eyes, to be the subject of investigation and interpretation, and the guide in controversy. "Verily, verily I say unto you."—"But, I say unto you,"—are the tokens of a supreme Teacher and Prophet."

V.M. I, 292-3.

. . . Our Lord's character, as it is recorded by the evangelists, as carrying with it its own evidence, dispensing with extrinsic proof, and claiming authoritatively by itself the faith and devotion of all to whom it is presented . . . such an argument is as old as Christianity itself. The young man in the Gospel calls our Lord "Good Master," and St. Peter introduces Him to the first Gentile converts as one who "went about doing good; and in these last times we can refer to the testimony even of unbelievers in behalf of an argument which is as simple as it is constraining. *"Si la vie et la mort de Socrate sont d'un sage,"* says Rousseau, *"la vie et la mort de Jésus sont d'un Dieu."* And he clenches the argument by observing that were the picture a mere conception of the sacred writers, *l'inventeur en serait plus étonnant que le héros."* The force of the argument lies in its directness; it comes to the point at once, and concentrates in itself evidence, doctrine, and devotion. In theological language, it is the *motivum credibilitatis,* the *objectum materiale,* and the *formale,* all in one; it unites human reason and supernatural faith in one complex act; and it comes home to all men, educated and ignorant, young and old. And it is the point to which, after all and in fact, all religious minds tend, and in which they ultimately rest, even if they do not start from it. Without an intimate apprehension of the personal character of our Saviour, what professes to be faith is little more than an act of ratiocination. If faith is to live, it must love; it must lovingly live in the Author of faith as a true and living Being, *in Deo vivo et vero;* according to the saying of the Samaritans to their townswoman: "We now believe, not for thy saying, for we ourselves have heard Him." Many doctrines may be held implicitly; but to see Him as if intuitively is the very promise and gift of Him who is the object of the intuition. We are constrained to believe when it is He that speaks to us about Himself.

D.A., 366-7.

6

A Deliverer of the human race through the Jewish nation had been promised from time immemorial. The day came when He was to appear, and He was eagerly expected; moreover, One actually did make His appearance at that date in Palestine, and claimed to be He. He left the earth without apparently doing much for the object of His coming. But when He was gone, His disciples took upon themselves to go forth to preach to all parts of the earth with the object of preaching *Him*, and collecting converts *in His Name*. After a little while they are found wonderfully to have succeeded. Large bodies of men in various places are to be seen, professing to be His disciples, owning Him as their King, and continually swelling in number and penetrating into the populations of the Roman Empire; at length they convert the Empire itself. All this is historical fact. Now, we want to know the farther historical fact, viz., the cause of their conversion; in other words, what were the topics of that preaching which was so effective? If we believe what is told us by the preachers and their converts, the answer is plain. They "preached Christ;" they called on men to believe, hope, and place their affections, in that Deliverer who had come and gone; and the moral instrument by which they persuaded them to do so, was a description of the life, character, mission, and power of that Deliverer, a promise of His invisible Presence and Protection here, and of the Vision and Fruition of Him hereafter. From first to last to Christians, as to Abraham, He Himself is the centre and fulness of the dispensation, They, as Abraham, "see His day, and are glad."

A temporal sovereign makes himself felt by means of his subordinate administrators, who bring his power and will to bear upon every individual of his subjects who personally know him not; the universal Deliverer, long expected, when He came, He too, instead of making and securing subjects by a visible graciousness or majesty, departs;—*but* is found, through His preachers, to have imprinted the Image or idea of Himself in the minds of His subjects individually; and that Image, apprehended and worshipped in individual minds, becomes a principle of association, and a real bond of those subjects one with another, who are thus united to the body by being united to that Image; and moreover that Image, which is their moral life, when they have been already converted, is also the original instrument of their conversion. It is the Image of Him who fulfils the one great need of human nature, the Healer of its wounds, the Physician of the soul, this Image it is which both creates faith, and then rewards it. . . .

How, without the Hand of God, could a new idea, one and the same, enter at once into myriads of men, women, and children of all ranks, especially the lower, and have power to wean them from their indulgences and sins, and to nerve them against the most cruel tortures, and to last in vigour as a sustaining influence for seven or eight generations, till it founded an extended polity, broke the obstinacy of the strongest and wisest government which the world has ever seen, and forced its way from its first caves and catacombs to the fulness of imperial power?

G.A., 463·5.

7

The life of Christ brings together and concentrates truths concerning the chief good and the laws of our being, which wander idle and forlorn over the surface of the moral world, and often appear to diverge from each other. It collects the scattered rays of light, which, in the first days of creation, were poured over the whole face of nature, into certain intelligible centres, in the firmament of the heaven, to rule over the day and over the night, and to divide the light from the darkness. Our Saviour has in Scripture all those abstract titles of moral excellence bestowed upon Him which philosophers have invented. He is the Word, the Light, the Life, the Truth, Wisdom, the Divine Glory. St. John announces in the text, "The Life was manifested, and we *have seen* It."

U.S., 27-8.

8

When, then, they have logical grounds presented to them for holding that the recorded picture of our Lord is its own evidence, that it carries with it its own reality and authority, that

65

His "revelatio" is "revelata" in the very act of being a "revelatio," it is as if He Himself said to them, as He once said to His
disciples, "It is I, be not afraid"; and the clouds at once clear off,
and the waters subside, and the land is gained for which they
are looking out.

D.A., 372.

V: THE CHURCH

ANALYTICAL SUMMARY

Christ lives on in His Church, as the one supreme miracle.   For—how else can we explain the fact that in the Church alone from the seed of Holy Scriptures has sprung the rich harvest of one holy doctrine;

whereas outside her borders the same Holy Scriptures have proved the bone of a never-ending contention until their authority has been completely destroyed?

that the infallible doctrinal magisterium which is the sole ground of the Church's internal unity of doctrine, despite the uncompromising challenge to the independence of human reason which it obviously involves, nevertheless in the teeth of this same reason has maintained itself for centuries and still maintains itself;

that it is actually under the discipline it provides that its adversary has been able for the first time to develop fully its real capacity and powers, so that this infallible magisterium has proved the saviour of reason from itself;

which, because it disciplines reason, redeems reason.

(Nos. 1-12.)

Further , how else can we explain the fact that in the doctrinal development of this Church conflicting systems and doctrines of human wisdom of every kind have played their chaotic part—and nevertheless one single doctrinal system, self-grounded, developing only itself and self-contained, has existed from the first, exists to-day and will continue to exist?

that in the process the variability of human nature and thought has run up and down its entire gamut—and nevertheless that which has achieved such a splendid development is but the One divinely Immutable Revelation?

(Nos. 13-20.)

Finally—how are we to explain the fact that this one Church as Catholic *has found room for men of all races, cultures and classes—and nevertheless in the nineteenth century is the same as she was in the first century?*

that her foes have put forth against her their utmost strength and have failed?

that just when she appeared completely crushed, corrupt and dead, it proved but the cloud before a new and more brilliant burst of sunlight?

How can "strength" come "from weakness, life from death," if not because "God is in the Flesh"?

"Head and Body One Christ"?

(Nos. 21-25.)

I. THE INFALLIBLE CHURCH

I

IF Christianity is a fact, and impresses an idea of itself on our minds and is a subject-matter of exercises of the reason, that idea will in course of time expand into a multitude of ideas, and aspects of ideas, connected and harmonious with one another, and in themselves determinate and immutable, as is the objective fact itself which is thus represented. It is a characteristic of our minds, that they cannot take an object in, which is submitted to them simply and integrally. We conceive by means of definition or description; whole objects do not create in the intellect whole ideas, but are, to use a mathematical phrase, thrown into series, into a number of statements, strengthening, interpreting, correcting each other, and with more or less exactness approximating, as they accumulate, to a perfect image. . .

And the more claim an idea has to be considered living, the more various will be its aspects; and the more social and political is its nature, the more complicated and subtle will be its issues, and the longer and more eventful will be its course. And in the number of these special ideas, which from their very depth and richness cannot be fully understood at once, but are more and more clearly expressed and taught the longer they last,—having aspects many and bearings many, mutually connected and growing one out of another, and all parts of a whole, with a sympathy and correspondence keeping pace with the ever-changing necessities of the world, multiform, prolific, and ever resourceful,—among these great doctrines surely we Christians shall not refuse a foremost place to Christianity. . .

Certainly it is a sort of degradation of a divine work to consider it under an earthly form; but it is no irreverence, since our

Lord Himself, its Author and Guardian, bore one also. . . It is externally what the Apostle calls an "earthen vessel," being the religion of men. And, considered as such, it grows "in wisdom and stature;" but the powers which it wields, and the words which proceed out of its mouth, attest its miraculous nativity.

Dev. 55-7.

2

As God rules the will, yet the will is free,—as He rules the course of the world, yet men conduct it,—so He has inspired the Bible, yet men have written it. Whatever else is true about it, this is true, that we may speak of the history or mode of its composition, as truly as of that of other books; we may speak of its writers having an object in view, being influenced by circumstances, being anxious, taking pains, purposely omitting or introducing matters, leaving things incomplete, or supplying what others had so left. Though the Bible be inspired, it has all such characteristics as might attach to a book uninspired, the characteristics of dialect and style, the distinct effects of times and places, youth and age, of moral and intellectual character; and I insist on this, lest in what I am going to say, I seem to forget (what I do not forget), that in spite of its human form, it has in it the Spirit and Mind of God. . .

[We have to do with] the writings of men who had already been introduced into a knowledge of the unseen world and the society of Angels, and who reported what they had seen and heard; and they are full of allusions to a system, a course of things, which was ever before their minds, which they felt both too awful and too familiar to them to be described minutely, which we do not know, and which these allusions, such as they are, but partially disclose to us. Try to make out the history of Rome from the extant letters of some of its great politicians, and from the fragments of ancient annals, histories, laws, inscriptions, and medals, and you will have something like the state of the case, viewed antecedently, as regards the structure of the Bible, and the task of deducing the true system of religion from it. . .

How confused is the course of the world, yet it is the working

70

out of a moral system, and is overruled in every point by God's Will! Or, take the structure of the earth; mankind are placed in fertile and good dwelling-places, with hills and valleys springs and fruitful fields, with metals and marbles, and coal and other minerals, with seas and forests; yet this beautiful and full-furnished surface is the result of (humanly speaking) a series of accidents, of gradual influences and sudden convulsions, of a long history of change and chance. . . Providence effects His great ends by apparent accidents. As in respect to this earth, we do not find minerals or plants arranged within it as in a cabinet,—as we do not find the materials for building laid out in order, stone, timber and iron—as metal is found in ore, and timber on the tree,—so we must not be surprised, but think it great gain, if we find revealed doctrines scattered about high and low in Scripture, in places expected and unexpected. It could not be otherwise, the same circumstances being opposed. Supposing fire, water and certain chemical and electrical agents in free operation, the earth's precious contents could not be found arranged in order and in the light of day without a miracle; and so without a miracle (which we are nowhere told to expect) we could not possibly find in Scripture all sacred truths in their place, each set forth clearly and fully, with its suitable prominence, its varied bearings, its developed meaning, supposing Scripture to be, what it is, the work of various independent minds, in various times and places, and under various circumstances.

D.A., 146-151.

3

There are two attributes of the Bible throughout . . . which, while at first sight in contrast, have a sort of necessary connexion, and set off each other—simplicity and depth. Simplicity leads a writer to say things without display; and depth obliges him to use inadequate words. Scripture then, treating of invisible things, at best must use words less than those things; and, as if from a feeling that no words can be worthy of them, it does not condescend to use even the strongest that exist, but often takes

71

the plainest. The deeper the thought, the plainer the word; the word and thought diverge from each other. Again, it is a property of depth to lead a writer into verbal contradictions; and it is a property of simplicity not to care to avoid them. Again, when a writer is deep, his half sentences, parentheses, clauses, nay his words, have a meaning in them independent of the context, and admit of exposition. There is nothing put in for ornament's sake, or for rhetoric; nothing put in for the mere sake of anything else, but all for its own sake; all as the expressions and shadows of great things, as seeds of thought, and with corresponding realities. Moreover, when a writer is deep, or again when he is simple, he does not set about exhausting his subject in his remarks upon it; he says so much as is in point, no more; he does not go out of his way to complete a view or to catch at collateral thoughts; he has something before him which he aims at, and while he cannot help including much in his meaning which he does not aim at, he does aim at one thing, not at another. . .

One of the most remarkable characteristics of Scripture narrative . . . is the absence of expressions by which the reader can judge whether the events recorded are presented for praise or blame. A plain bare series of facts is drawn out; and whether for imitation or warning, often cannot be decided except by the context, or by the event, or by our general notions of propriety— often not at all . . . no epithet, no turn of sentence which betrays the divine judgment. [They pass] in the Scripture narrative, as in God's daily providence, silently. . . They need a comment,—they are evidently but a text for a comment,—they have no comment; and as they stand, may be turned this way or that according to the accidental tone of mind in the reader. . .

Minds familiarized to supernatural things, minds set upon definite great objects, have no disposition, no time to indulge in embellishments, or to aim at impressiveness, or to consult for the weakness or ignorance of the hearer.

D.A., 173-9.

It is in point to notice also the structure and style of Scripture, a structure so unsystematic and various, and a style so figurative and indirect, that no one would presume at first sight to say what is in it and what is not. It cannot, as it were, be mapped, or its contents catalogued; but after all our diligence, to the end of our lives and to the end of the Church, it must be an unexplored and unsubdued land, with heights and valleys, forests and streams, on the right and left of our path and close about us, full of concealed wonders and choice treasures. Of no doctrine whatever, which does not actually contradict what has been delivered, can it be peremptorily asserted that it is not in Scripture; of no reader, whatever be his study of it, can it be said that he has mastered every doctrine which it contains.

Dev., 71.

5

I would not deny as an abstract proposition that a Christian may gain the whole truth from the Scriptures, but would maintain that the chances are very seriously against a given individual. I would not deny, rather I maintain that a religious, wise, and intellectually gifted man will succeed: but who answers to this description but the collective Church? There, indeed such qualifications might be supposed to exist; what is wanting in one member being supplied by another, and the opposite errors of individuals eliminated by their combination. . .

And this, by the way, may be taken as one remarkable test, or at least characteristic of error, in the various denominations of religion which surround us; none of them embraces the whole Bible, none of them is able to interpret the whole, none of them has a key which will revolve through the entire compass of the wards which lie within. Each has its favourite text, and neglects the rest. None can solve the great secret and utter the mystery of its pages. One makes trial, then another: but one and all in turn are foiled. They retire, as the sages of Babylon, and make way for Daniel. The Church Catholic, the true Prophet of God, alone is able to tell the dream and its interpretation.

V.M., *I*, 458-9.

6

I have been arguing, in respect to the revealed doctrine, given to us from above in Christianity, first, that, in consequence of its intellectual character, and as passing through the minds of so many generations of men, and as applied by them to so many purposes, and as investigated so curiously as to its capabilities, implications, and bearings, it could not but grow or develope, as time went on, into a large theological system;—next, that, if development must be, then, whereas Revelation is a heavenly gift, He who gave it virtually has not given it, unless He has also secured it from perversion and corruption, in all such development as comes upon it by the necessity of its nature, or, in other words, that that intellectual action through successive generations, which is the organ of development, must, so far forth as it can claim to have been put in charge of the Revelation, be in its determinations infallible. . .

There is nothing impossible in the notion of a revelation occurring without evidences that it is a revelation. . . The two ideas indeed are quite distinct, I grant, of revealing and of guaranteeing a truth, and they are often distinct in fact. . . There are various revelations all over the earth which do not carry with them the evidence of their divinity. Such are the inward suggestions and secret illuminations granted to so many individuals; such are the traditionary doctrines which are found among the heathen, that "vague and unconnected family of religious truths, originally from God, but sojourning, without the sanction of miracle or a definite home, as pilgrims up and down the world, and discernible and separable from the corrupt legends with which they are mixed, by the spiritual mind alone." . . .

But Christianity is not of this nature: it is a revelation which comes to us as a revelation, as a whole, objectively, and with a profession of infallibility . . . Christianity, unlike other revelations of God's will, except the Jewish, of which it is a continuation, is an objective religion, or a revelation with credentials; . . .

Surely, either an objective revelation has not been given, or it has been provided with means for impressing its objectiveness on the world. If Christianity be a social religion, as it certainly is, and if it be based on certain ideas acknowledged as divine or a creed, (which shall here be assumed,) and if these ideas have various aspects, and make distinct impressions on different minds, and issue in consequence in a multiplicity of developments, true, or false, or mixed, as has been shown, what power will suffice to meet and to do justice to these conflicting conditions, but a supreme authority ruling and reconciling individual judgments by a divine right and a recognized wisdom?

There can be no combination on the basis of truth without an organ of truth. . . If Christianity is both social and dogmatic, and intended for all ages, it must humanly speaking have an infallible expounder. Else you will secure unity of form at the loss of unity of doctrine, or unity of doctrine at the loss of unity of form; you will have to choose between a comprehension of opinions and a resolution into parties, between latitudinarian and sectarian error.

Dev., 92, 79-80, 89-90.

7

If the Author of Nature be the Author of Grace, it may be expected that, while the two systems of facts are distinct and independent, the principles displayed in them will be the same, and form a connecting link between them. In this identity of principle lies the Analogy of Natural and Revealed Religion. . .

The case then stands thus:—Revelation has introduced a new law of divine governance over and above those laws which appear in the natural course of the world; and in consequence we are able to argue for the existence of a standing authority in matters of faith on the analogy of Nature, and from the fact of Christianity. Preservation is involved in the idea of creation. As the Creator rested on the seventh day from the work which He had made, yet He "worketh hitherto;" so He gave the Creed once for all in the beginning, yet blesses its growth still, and provides for its increase. His word "shall not return unto Him void, but accomplish" His pleasure. As creation argues continual governance, so are Apostles harbingers of Popes.

Moreover, it must be borne in mind that, as the essence of all religion is authority and obedience, so the distinction between natural religion and revealed lies in this, that the one has a subjective authority, and the other an objective. Revelation consists in the manifestation of the Invisible Divine Power, or in the substitution of the voice of a Lawgiver for the voice of conscience. The supremacy of conscience is the essence of natural religion; the supremacy of Apostle, or Pope, or Church, or Bishop, is, the essence of revealed; and when such external authority is taken away, the mind falls back again of necessity upon that inward guide which it possessed even before Revelation was vouchsafed. Thus, what conscience is in the system of nature, such is the voice of Scripture, or of the Church, or of the Holy See, as we may determine it, in the system of Revelation. It may be objected, indeed, that conscience is not infallible; it is true, but still it is ever to be obeyed. . . And as obedience to conscience, even supposing conscience ill-informed, tends to the improvement of our moral nature, and ultimately of our knowledge, so obedience to our ecclesiastical superior may subserve our growth in illumination and sanctity, even though he should command what is extreme or inexpedient, or teach what is external to his legitimate province.

Dev., 85-7.

8

I am asking what must be the face-to-face antagonist, by which to withstand and baffle the fierce energy of passion and the all-corroding, all-dissolving scepticism of the intellect in religious inquiries? I have no intention at all of denying, that truth is the real object of our reason, and that, if it does not attain to truth, either the premiss or the process is in fault; but I am not speaking here of right reason, but of reason as it acts in fact and concretely in fallen man. I know that even the unaided reason, when correctly exercised, leads to a belief in God, in the immortality of the soul, and in a future retribution; but I am considering the faculty of reason actually and historically; and in this point of view, I do not think I am wrong in saying that its tendency is towards a simple unbelief in matters of religion. No truth, however sacred, can stand against it, in the long run; and hence it is that in the pagan world, when our Lord came, the last traces of the religious knowledge of former times were all but disappearing from those portions of the world in which the intellect had been active and had had a career.

And in these latter days, in like manner, outside the Catholic Church things are tending,—with far greater rapidity than in that old time from the circumstance of the age,—to atheism in one shape or other. . . Lovers of their country and of their race, religious men, external to the Catholic Church, have attempted various expedients to arrest fierce wilful human nature in its onward course, and to bring it into subjection. The necessity of some form of religion for the interests of humanity, has been generally acknowledged: but where was the concrete representative of things invisible, which would have the force and the toughness necessary to be a breakwater against the deluge? Three centuries ago the establishment of religion, material, legal, and social, was generally adopted as the best expedient for the purpose, in those countries which separated from the Catholic Church; and for a long time it was successful; but now the crevices of those establishments are admitting the enemy. Thirty years ago, education was relied upon: ten years ago there was a hope that wars would cease for ever, under the influence of commercial enterprise and the reign of the useful and fine arts; but will any one venture to say that there is any thing any where on this earth, which will afford a fulcrum for us, whereby to keep the earth from moving onwards?

The judgment, which experience passes whether on establishments or on education, as a means of maintaining religious truth in this anarchical world, must be extended even to Scripture, though Scripture be divine. Experience proves surely that the Bible does not answer a purpose for which it was never intended. It may be accidentally the means of the conversion of individuals; but a book, after all, cannot make a stand against the wild living intellect of man, and in this day it begins to testify, as regards its own structure and contents, to the power of that

77

universal solvent, which is so successfully acting upon religious establishments.

Supposing then it to be the Will of the Creator to interfere in human affairs, and to make provisions for retaining in the world a knowledge of Himself, so definite and distinct as to be proof against the energy of human scepticism, in such a case,—I am far from saying that there was no other way,—but there is nothing to surprise the mind, if He should think fit to introduce a power into the world, invested with the prerogative of infallibility in religious matters. Such a provision would be a direct, immediate, active, and prompt means of withstanding the difficulty; it would be an instrument suited to the need; and, when I find that this is the very claim of the Catholic Church, not only do I feel no difficulty in admitting the idea, but there is a fitness in it, which recommends it to my mind. And thus I am brought to speak of the Church's infallibility, as a provision, adapted by the mercy of the Creator, to preserve religion in the world, and to restrain that freedom of thought, which of course in itself is one of the greatest of our natural gifts, and to rescue it from its own suicidal excesses. And let it be observed that, neither here nor in what follows, shall I have occasion to speak directly of Revelation in its subject-matter, but in reference to the sanction which it gives to truths which may be known independently of it,—as it bears upon the defence of natural religion. I say, that a power, possessed of infallibility in religious teaching, is happily adapted to be a working instrument, in the course of human affairs, for smiting hard and throwing back the immense energy of the aggressive capricious, untrustworthy intellect.

Apo., 243-6.

9

It is the custom with Protestant writers to consider that, whereas there are two great principles in action in the history of religion, Authority and Private Judgment, they have all the Private Judgment to themselves, and we have the full inheritance and the superincumbent oppression of Authority. But this is not so; it is the vast Catholic body itself, and it only, which affords an arena for both combatants in that awful, never-dying duel. It is necessary for the very life of religion, viewed in its large operations and its history, that the warfare should be incessantly carried on. Every exercise of Infallibility is brought out into act by an intense and varied operation of the Reason, both as its ally and as its opponent, and provokes again, when it has done its work, a re-action of Reason against it; and, as in a civil polity the State exists and endures by means of the rivalry and collision, the encroachments and defeats of its constituent parts, so in like manner Catholic Christendom is no simple exhibition of religious absolutism, but presents a continuous picture of Authority and Private Judgment alternately advancing and retreating as the ebb and flow of the tide;—it is a vast assemblage of human beings with wilful intellects and wild passions, brought together into one by the beauty and the Majesty of a Super-human Power,—into what may be called a large reformatory or training-school, not as if into a hospital or into a prison, not in order to be sent to bed, not to be buried alive, but (if I may change my metaphor) brought together as if into some moral factory, for the melting, refining, and moulding, by an incessant, noisy process, of the raw material of human nature, so excellent, so dangerous, so capable of divine purposes.

Apo., 252.

10

And here another consideration presents itself to my thoughts. In reading ecclesiastical history, when I was an Anglican, it used to be forcibly brought home to me, how the initial error of what afterwards became heresy was the urging forward some truth against the prohibition of authority at an unseasonable time. There is a time for every thing, and many a man desires a reformation of an abuse, or the fuller development of a doctrine, or the adoption of a particular policy, but forgets to ask himself whether the right time for it is come; and, knowing that there is no one who will be doing any thing towards its accomplishment in his own lifetime unless he does it himself, he will not listen to the voice of authority, and he spoils a good work in his own century, in order that another man, as yet unborn, may not have the opportunity of bringing it happily to perfection in the next. He may seem to the world to be nothing else than a bold champion for the truth and a martyr to free opinion, when he is just one of those persons who the competent authority ought to silence; and, though the case may not fall within that subject-matter in which that authority is infallible, or the formal conditions of the exercise of that gift may be wanting, it is clearly the duty of authority to act vigorously in the case. Yet its act will go down to posterity as an instance of a tyrannical interference with private judgment, and of the silencing of a reformer, and of a base love of corruption or error; and it will show still less to advantage, if the ruling power happens in its proceedings to evince any defect of prudence or consideration. And all those who take the part of that ruling authority will be considered time-servers, or indifferent to the cause of uprightness and truth; while, on the other hand, the said authority may be accidentally supported by a violent ultra party, which exalts opinions into dogmas, and has it principally at heart to destroy every school of thought but its own.

Such a state of things may be provoking and discouraging at the time, in the case of two classes of persons; of moderate men who wish to make differences in religious opinion as little as they fairly can be made; and of such as keenly perceive, and are honestly eager to remedy, existing evils,—evils of which divines in this or that foreign country know nothing at all, and which even at home, where they exist, it is not every one who has the means of estimating. This is a state of things both of past time and of the present.

Apo., 259-60.

II

The Church ever begins with the beginning; and, as regards the multitude of her children, is never able to get beyond the beginning, but is continually employed in laying the foundation. She is engaged with what is essential, as previous and introductory, to the ornamental and attractive. She is curing men and keeping them clear of mortal sin; she is "treating of justice and chastity, and the judgment to come"; she is insisting on faith and hope, and devotion, and honesty, and the elements of charity; and has so much to do with precept, that she almost leaves it to inspirations from Heaven to suggest what is of counsel and perfection. She aims at what is necessary rather than at what is desirable. She is for the many as well as for the few. She is putting souls in the way of salvation, that they may then be in a condition, if they shall be called upon, to aspire to the heroic, and to attain the full proportions, as well as the rudiments, of the beautiful.

Idea, 203-4.

12

Thus, then, I would meet the difficulty of drawing the line between essentials and non-essentials. The Church asks for a dutiful and simple-hearted acceptance of her message growing into faith, and that variously, according to the circumstances or individuals. And, if this be the principle on which the Catholic Church anciently acted, we see how well it was adapted to try the humility of her children, without imposing any yoke upon them, or repressing the elastic or creative force of their minds. She makes her way by love, she does not force a way by violence. All she asks is their *confidence,* which will practically preserve them from all difference from her, except in minor matters. Thus, in the case of particular minds, she allows for a defect in the evidence they have received of her full doctrine, or in the impression of this or that part of her Creed. She is gentle, holds back, watches her time, and is persuasive according to the opportunity. She secures to herself the power of accommodating her communications to the circumstances, ranks, and ages of her children; of consulting for their ignorance, or even waywardness; of keeping silence when it would be inexpedient or unkind to urge truth in its fulness, or where men are unworthy of it; of letting the reason range freely, and then bringing it round. She exacts the great rudiments of the Gospel from all, she requires teachableness, she is severe with scepticism, but she is tender and considerate amid her zeal and loyalty towards God. She does not "strive nor cry," nor "quench the smoking flax"; but retires into the sanctuary, dispensing her message, not lavishly, or by necessity, but on those who care to follow her. She has that confidence in the truth of her doctrine and in the sovereignty of truth, that she can be long-suffering towards error; that faith in her spiritual powers, that she is slow to display them. She can within bounds bear with the froward or the obstinate, knowing her gift both in the word and in the sacraments, when the time comes for using it. She has too generous a temper to rule by engagements, but, like an absolute monarch, is familiar with her children without jealousy, because God is with her. But supposing they are hopelessly contumacious, resist her word, oppose and preach against her, she has no desire, nay, no warrant to retain them, and suffers or compels them to depart, lest the rest should be injured. Yet after all, even when she strips them of her glorious privileges, she does not thereby absolutely pronounce on their spiritual state in God's sight, or their future destiny. She is as little concerned with such questions as with the state of heathens.* She surrenders them to that Master "to whom they stand or fall"; doing her part and leaving the rest to Him.

V.M., i, 258-9.

II. THE LIVING CHURCH

13

Now there was this cardinal distinction between Christianity and the religions and philosophies by which it was surrounded, nay even the Judaism of the day, that it referred all truth and revelation to one source, and that the Supreme and Only God. Pagan rites which honoured one or other out of ten thousand deities; philosophies which scarcely taught any source of revelation at all; Gnostic heresies which were based on Dualism, adored angels, or ascribed the two Testaments to distinct authors,

---

*Written in 1837. The following footnote was added in 1877. "Nor is the Catholic Church, though she be infallible in her statements of doctrine. The whole paragraph is in the main true of her."

could not regard truth as one, unalterable, consistent, imperative, and saving. But Christianity started with the principle that there was but "one God and one Mediator," and that He, "who at sundry times and in divers manners spake in time past unto the fathers by the Prophets, had in these last days spoken unto us by His Son." He had never left Himself without witness, and now He had come, not to undo the past, but to fulfil and perfect it. His Apostles, and they alone, possessed, venerated, and protected a Divine Message, as both sacred and sanctifying; and, in the collision and conflict of opinions, in ancient times or modern, it was that Message, and not any vague or antagonist teaching, that was to succeed in purifying, assimilating, transmuting, and taking into itself the many-coloured beliefs, forms of worship, codes of duty, schools of thought, through which it was ever moving. It was Grace, and it was Truth. . .

[The Church] alone has succeeded in thus rejecting evil without sacrificing the good, and in holding together in one things which in all other schools are incompatible. Gnostic or Platonic words are found in the inspired theology of St. John; to the Platonists Unitarian writers trace the doctrine of our Lord's divinity; Gibbon the idea of the Incarnation to the Gnostics. The Gnostics too seem first to have systematically thrown the intellect upon matters of faith; and the very term "Gnostic" has been taken by Clement to express his perfect Christian. And, though ascetics existed from the beginning, the notion of a religion higher than the Christianity of the many, was first prominently brought forward by the Gnostics, Montanists, Novatians, and Manichees. And while the prophets of the Montanists prefigure the Church's Doctors, and their professed inspiration her infallibility, and their revelations her developments, and the heresiarch himself is the unsightly anticipation of St. Francis, in Novatian again we discern the aspiration of nature after such creations of grace as St. Benedict or St. Bruno. And so the effort of Sabellius to complete the enunciation of the mystery of the Ever-blessed Trinity failed: it became a heresy; grace would not be constrained; the course of thought could not be forced;—at length it was realized in the true Unitarianism of St. Augustine. . .

83

[Catholicism] has borne, and can bear, principles or doctrines, which in other systems of religion quickly degenerate into fanaticism or infidelity. This might be shown at great length in the history of the Aristotelic philosophy within and without the Church; or in the history of Monachism, or of Mysticism;—not that there has not been at first a conflict between these powerful and unruly elements and the Divine System into which they were entering, but that it ended in the victory of Catholicism. The theology of St. Thomas, nay of the Church of his period, is built on that very Aristotelism, which the early Fathers denounce as the source of all misbelief, and in particular of the Arian and Monophysite heresies. The exercises of asceticism, which are so graceful in St. Antony, so touching in St. Basil, and so awful in St. Germanus, do but become a melancholy and gloomy superstition even in the most pious persons who are cut off from Catholic communion. And while the highest devotion in the Church is the mystical, and contemplation has been the token of the most singularly favoured Saints, we need not look deeply into the history of modern sects, for evidence of the excesses in conduct, or the errors in doctrine, to which mystics have been commonly led, who have boasted of their possession of reformed truth, and have rejected what they called the corruptions of Catholicism. . .

There is in truth a certain virtue or grace in the Gospel which changes the quality of doctrines, opinions, usages, actions, and personal characters when incorporated with it, and makes them right and acceptable to its Divine Author, whereas before they were either infected with evil, or at best but shadows of the truth. This is the principle, above spoken of, which I have called the Sacramental. "We know that we are of God, and the whole world lieth in wickedness," is an enunciation of the principle;— or, the declaration of the Apostle of the Gentiles, "If any man be in Christ, he is a new creature; old things are passed away, behold all things are become new." Thus it is that outward rites, which are but worthless in themselves, lose their earthly character and become Sacraments under the Gospel. . .

Confiding then in the power of Christianity to resist the infec-

84

tion of evil, and to transmute the very instruments and appendages of demon-worship to an evangelical use, and feeling also that these usages had originally come from primitive revelations and from the instinct of nature, though they had been corrupted; and that they must invent what they needed, if they did not use what they found; and that they were moreover possessed of the very archetypes, of which paganism attempted the shadows; the rulers of the Church from early times were prepared, should the occasion arise, to adopt, or imitate, or sanction the existing rites and customs of the populace, as well as the philosophy of the educated class.

Dev., 356-7, 365, 443, 368, 371-2.

14

We prefer to say, and we think that Scripture bears us out in saying, that from the beginning the Moral Governor of the world has scattered the seeds of truth far and wide over its extent; that these have variously taken root, and grown up as in the wilderness, wild plants indeed but living; and hence that, as the inferior animals have tokens of an immaterial principle in them, yet have not souls, so the philosophies and religions of men have their life in certain true ideas, though they are not directly divine. What man is amid the brute creation, such is the Church among the schools of the world; and as Adam gave names to the animals about him, so has the Church from the first looked round upon the earth, noting and visiting the doctrines she found there. She began in Chaldea, and then sojourned among the Canaanites, and went down into Egypt, and thence passed into Arabia, till she rested in her own land. Next she encountered the merchants of Tyre, and the wisdom of the East country, and the luxury of Sheba. Then she was carried away to Babylon, and wandered to the schools of Greece. And wherever she went, in trouble or in triumph, still she was a living spirit, the mind and voice of the Most High, "sitting in the midst of the doctors, both hearing them and asking them questions"; claiming to herself what they said rightly, correcting their errors, supplying their defects, completing their beginnings, expanding

85

their surmises, and thus gradually by means of them enlarging the range and refining the sense of her own teaching. So far then from her creed being of doubtful credit because it resembles foreign theologies, we even hold that one special way in which Providence has imparted divine knowledge to us has been by enabling her to draw and collect it together out of the world, and in this sense, as in others "to suck the milk of the Gentiles and to suck the breast of kings. . ."

[There are two theories.] The advocates of the one imply that Revelation was a single, entire, solitary act, or nearly so, introducing a certain message; whereas we, who maintain the other, consider that Divine teaching has been in fact, what the analogy of nature would lead us to expect, "at sundry times and in divers manners," various, complex, progressive, and supplemental of itself. We consider the Christian doctrine, when analysed, to appear, like the human frame, "fearfully and wonderfully made"; but they think it some one tenet or certain principles given out at one time in their fulness, without gradual enlargement before Christ's coming or elucidation afterwards. They cast off all that they also find in Pharisee or heathen; we conceive that the Church, like Aaron's rod, devours the serpents of the magicians. They are ever hunting for a fabulous primitive simplicity; we repose in Catholic fulness. They seek what never has been found; we accept and use what even they acknowledge to be a substance. They are driven to maintain, on their part, that the Church's doctrine was never pure; we say that it never can be corrupt. We consider that a divine promise keeps the Church Catholic from doctrinal corruption; but on what promise, or on what encouragement they are seeking for their visionary purity does not appear.

Ess., ii, 231-34.

15

God who made the Prophet's ass speak, and thereby instructed the Prophet, might instruct His Church by means of heathen Babylon. . . *

* Note by Newman when he republished this Essay, "This principle seems here too broadly enunciated."

It does not therefore seem to me difficult, nay, nor even unlikely, that the prophets of Israel should, in the course of God's providence, have gained new truths from the heathen, among whom those truths lay corrupted. The Church of God in every age has been, as it were, on visitation through the earth, surveying, judging, sifting, selecting, and refining all matters of thought and practice; detecting what was precious amid what is ruined and refuse, and putting her seal upon it.

D.A., 211-12.

16

I observe, then, that, if the idea of Christianity, as originally given to us from heaven, cannot but contain much which will be only partially recognized by us as included in it and only held by us unconsciously; and if again, Christianity being from heaven, all that is necessarily involved in it, and is evolved from it, is from heaven, and if, on the other hand, large accretions actually do exist, professing to be its true and legitimate results, our first impression naturally is, that these must be the very developments which they profess to be. Moreover, the very scale on which they have been made, their high antiquity yet present promise, their gradual formation yet precision, their harmonious order, dispose the imagination most forcibly towards the belief that a teaching so consistent with itself, so well balanced, so young and so old, not obsolete after so many centuries, but vigorous and progressive still, is the very development contemplated in the Divine Scheme. These doctrines are members of one family, and suggestive, or correlative, or confirmatory, or illustrative of each other. One furnishes evidence to another, and all to each of them; if this is proved, that becomes probable; if this and that are both probable, but for different reasons, each adds to the other its own probability. The Incarnation is the antecedent of the doctrine of Mediation, and the archetype both of the Sacramental principle and of the merits of Saints. From the doctrine of Mediation follow the Atonement, the Mass, the merits of Martyrs and Saints, their invocation and *cultus*. From the Sacramental principle come the Sacraments properly so

87

called; the unity of the Church, and the Holy See as its type and centre; the authority of Councils; the sanctity of rites; the veneration of holy places, shrines, images, vessels, furniture, and vestments. Of the Sacraments, Baptism is developed into Confirmation on the one hand; into Penance, Purgatory, and Indulgences on the other; and the Eucharist into the Real Presence, adoration of the Host, Resurrection of the body, and the virtue of relics. Again, the doctrine of the Sacraments leads to the doctrine of Justification; Justification to that of Original Sin; Original Sin to the merit of Celibacy. Nor do these separate developments stand independent of each other, but by cross relations they are connected, and grow together while they grow from one. The Mass and Real Presence are parts of one; the veneration of Saints and their relics are parts of one; their intercessory power and the Purgatorial State, and again the Mass and that State are correlative; Celibacy is the characteristic mark of Monachism and of the Priesthood. You must accept the whole or reject the whole; attenuation does but enfeeble, and amputation mutilate. It is trifling to receive all but something which is as integral as any other portion; and, on the other hand, it is a solemn thing to accept any part, for, before you know where you are, you may be carried on by a stern logical necessity to accept the whole.

Dev., 93-4.

17

Sometimes an attempt is made to determine the "leading idea," as it has been called, of Christianity, an ambitious essay as employed on a supernatural work, when, even as regards the visible creation and the inventions of man, such a task is beyond us. Thus its one idea has been said by some to be the restoration of our fallen race, by others philanthropy, by others the tidings of immortality, or the spirituality of true religious service, or the salvation of the elect, or mental liberty, or the union of the soul with God. If, indeed, it is only thereby meant to use one or other of these as a central idea for convenience, in order to group others around it, no fault can be found with such a proceeding:

88

and in this sense I should myself call the Incarnation the central aspect of Christianity, out of which the three main aspects of its teaching take their rise, the sacramental, the hierarchical, and the ascetic.

. . . .

Here are nine specimens of Christian principles out of the many which might be enumerated, and will any one say that they have not been retained in vigorous action in the Church at all times . . . and [are] as patent and operative in the Latin and Greek Christianity of this day as they were in the beginning. . .

1. The principle of *dogma*, that is, supernatural truths irrevocably committed to human language, imperfect because it is human, but definitive and necessary because given from above.

2. The principal of *faith*, which is the correlative of dogma, being the absolute acceptance of the divine Word with an internal assent, in opposition to the informations, if such, of sight and reason.

3. Faith, being an act of the intellect, opens a way for inquiry, comparison and inference, that is, for science in religion, in subservience to itself; this is the principle of *theology*.

4. The doctrine of the Incarnation is the announcement of a divine gift conveyed in a material and visible medium, it being thus that heaven and earth are in the Incarnation united. That is, it establishes in the very idea of Christianity the *sacramental* principle as its characteristic.

5. Another principle involved in the doctrine of the Incarnation, viewed as taught or as dogmatic, is the necessary use of language, e.g., of the text of Scripture, in a second or *mystical sense*. Words must be made to express new ideas, and are invested with a sacramental office.

6. It is our Lord's intention in His Incarnation to make us what He is Himself; this is the principle of *grace*, which is not only holy but sanctifying.

7. It cannot elevate and change us without mortifying our lower nature:—here is the principle of *asceticism*.

8. And, involved in this death of the natural man, is neces-

89

sarily a revelation of the *malignity of sin,* in corroboration of the forebodings of conscience.

9. Also by the fact of an Incarnation we are taught that matter is an essential part of us, and, as well as mind, is *capable of sanctification.*

. . . .

But one aspect of Revelation must not be allowed to exclude or to obscure another; and Christianity is dogmatical, devotional, practical all at once; it is esoteric and exoteric; it is indulgent and strict; it is light and dark; it is love, and it is fear.

Dev., 36, 326, 325-6, 36.

18

Let us quit this survey of the general system, and descend to the history of the formation of any Catholic dogma. What a remarkable sight it is, as almost all unprejudiced persons will admit, to trace the course of the controversy, from its first disorders to its exact and determinate issue. Full of deep interest, to see how the great idea takes hold of a thousand minds by its living force, and will not be ruled or stinted, but is "like a burning fire," as the Prophet speaks, "shut up" within them, till they are "weary of forbearing, and cannot stay," and grows in them, and at length is born through them, perhaps in a long course of years, and even successive generations; so that the doctrine may rather be said to use the minds of Christians, than to be used by them. Wonderful it is to see with what effort, hesitation, suspense, interruption,—with how many swayings to the right and to the left—with how many reverses, yet with what certainty of advance, with what precision in its march, and with what ultimate completeness, it has been evolved; till the whole truth "self-balanced on its centre hung," part answering to part, one absolute, integral, indissoluble, while the world lasts! Wonderful, to see how heresy has but thrown that idea into fresh forms, and drawn out from it farther developments, with an exuberance which exceeded all questioning, and a harmony which baffled all criticism, like Him, its Divine Author, who, when put on trial by the Evil One, was but fortified by the assault, and is ever justified in His sayings, and overcomes when He is judged.

U.S., 316-17.

19

This is a phenomenon proper to the Gospel, and a note of divinity. Its half sentences, its overflowings of language, admit of development; they have a life in them which shows itself in progress; a truth, which has the token of consistency; a reality, which is fruitful in resources; a depth, which extends into mystery: for they are representations of what is actual, and has a definite location and necessary bearings and a meaning in the great system of things, and a harmony in what it is, and a compatibility in what it involves. What form of Paganism can furnish a parallel? What philosopher has left his words to posterity as a talent which could be put to usury, as a mine which could be wrought? Here, too, is the badge of heresy; its dogmas are unfruitful; it has no theology; so far forth as it is heresy, it has none. Deduct its remnant of Catholic theology, and what remains? Polemics, explanations, protests. It turns to Biblical Criticism, or to the Evidences of Religion, for want of a province. Its *formulæ* end in themselves, without development, because they are words; they are barren, because they are dead. If they had life, they would increase and multiply; or, if they do live and bear fruit, it is but as "sin, when it is finished, bringeth forth death." It develops into dissolution; but it creates nothing, it tends to no system, its resultant dogma is but the denial of all dogmas, any theology, under the Gospel. No wonder it denies what it cannot attain.

U.S., 317-18.

20

It is a great evidence of truth, in the case of revealed teaching, that it is so consistent, that it so hangs together, that one thing springs out of another, that each part requires and is required by the rest. . .

The great truths of Revelation are all connected together and form a whole. Everyone can see this in a measure even at a glance, but to understand the full consistency and harmony of Catholic teaching requires study and meditation. Hence, as philosophers of this world bury themselves in museums and laboratories, descend into mines, or wander among woods or on the sea-shore, so the enquirer into heavenly truths dwells in the cell and the oratory, pouring forth his heart in prayer, collecting his thoughts in meditation . . . till before his mental sight arises the hidden wisdom of the perfect, "which God predestined before the world unto our glory," and which He "reveals unto them by His Spirit."

Mix., 343, 360-1.

III. THE ROCK

21

It [Christianity] alone has a definite message addressed to all mankind. As far as I know, the religion of Mahomet has brought into the world no new doctrine whatever, except, indeed, that of its own divine origin; and the character of its teaching is too exact a reflection of the race, time, place, and climate in which it arose, to admit of its becoming universal. The same dependence on external circumstances is characteristic, so far as I know, of the religions of the far East; nor am I sure of any definite message from God to man which they convey and protect, though they may have sacred books. Christianity, on the other hand, is in its idea an announcement, a preaching; it is the depository of truths beyond human discovery, momentous, practical, maintained one and the same in substance in every age from its first, and addressed to all mankind. And it has actually been embraced and is found in all parts of the world, in all climates, among all races, in all ranks of society, under every degree of civilization, from barbarism to the highest cultivation of mind. Coming to set right and to govern the world, it has ever been, as it ought to be, in conflict with large masses of men, with the civil power, with physical force, with adverse philosophies; it has had successes, it has had reverses; but it has had a grand history, and has effected great things, and is as vigorous in its age as in its youth. In all these respects it has a distinction in the world and a pre-eminence of its own; it has upon it *primâ facie* signs of divinity; I do not know what can be advanced by rival religions to match prerogatives so special; so that I feel myself justified in saying either Christianity is from God, or a revelation has not yet been given to us.

G.A., 430-1.

22

Look around, my brethren, at the forms of religion now in the world, and you will find that one, and one only, has this note of a divine origin. The Catholic Church has accompanied human society through one revolution of its great year; and is now beginning a second. She has passed through the full cycle of changes, in order to show us that she is independent of them all. She has had trial of East and West, of monarchy and democracy, of peace and war, of imperial and of feudal tyranny, of times of darkness and times of philosophy, of barbarousness and luxury, of slaves and freemen, of cities and nations, of marts of commerce and seats of manufacture, of old countries and young, of metropolis and colonies. . .

And so I might proceed, going to and fro, and telling of her political successes since, and of her intellectual victories from the beginning, and of her social improvements, and of her encounters with those other circumstances of human nature or combinations of human kind, which I just now enumerated; all which prove to us, with a cogency as great as that of a physical demonstration, that she comes not of earth, that she holds not of earth, that she is no servant of man, else he who made could have destroyed her. . .

There is but one form of Christianity, my brethren, possessed of that real internal unity which is the primary condition of independence. Whether you look to Russia, England, or Germany, this note of divinity is wanting. In this country, especially, there is nothing broader than class religions; the established form itself is but the religion of a class. There is one persuasion for the rich, and another for the poor; men are born in this or that

93

sect; the enthusiastic go here, and the sober-minded and rational go there. They make money, and rise in the world, and then they profess to belong to the Establishment. This body lives in the world's smile, that in its frown; the one would perish of cold in the world's winter, and the other would melt away in the summer. Not one of them undertakes human nature: none compasses the whole man; none places all men on a level; none addresses the intellect and the heart, fear and love, the active and the contemplative. It is considered, and justly, as an evidence for Christianity, that the ablest men have been Christians; not that all sagacious or profound minds have taken up its profession, but that it has gained victories among them, such and so many, as to show that it is not the mere fact of ability or learning which is the reason why all are not converted. Such, too, is the characteristic of Catholicity; not the highest in rank, not the meanest, not the most refined, not the rudest, is beyond the influence of the Church; she includes specimens of every class among her children. She is the solace of the forlorn, the chastener of the prosperous, and the guide of the wayward. She keeps a mother's eye for the innocent, bears with a heavy hand upon the wanton, and has a voice of majesty for the proud. She opens the mind of the ignorant, and she prostrates the intellect of even the most gifted. These are not words; she has done it, she does it still, she undertakes to do it. All she asks is an open field and freedom to act. She asks no patronage from the civil power: in former times and places she indeed has asked it; and, as Protestantism also, has availed herself of the civil sword. It is true she did so, because in certain ages it has been the acknowledged mode of acting, the most expeditious, and open at the time to no objection, and because, where she has done so, the people clamoured for it and did it in advance of her; but her history shows that she needed it not, for she has extended and flourished without it. She is ready for any service which occurs : she will take the world as it comes; nothing but force can repress her. . .

She is the same as she was three centuries ago, ere the present religions of the country existed ; you know her to be the same;

94

it is the charge brought against her that she does not change ; time and place affect her not, because she has her source where there is neither place nor time, because she comes from the throne of the Illimitable, Eternal God. . .

The question lies between the Church and no divine messenger at all; there is no revelation given us unless she is the organ of it, for where else is there a Prophet to be found.

Mix., 247-254, 278.

23

There is a religious communion claiming a divine commission, and holding all other religious bodies around it heretical or infidel; it is a well-organized, well-disciplined body; it is a sort of secret society, binding together its members by influences and by engagements which it is difficult for strangers to ascertain. It is spread over the known world; it may be weak or insignificant locally, but it is strong on the whole from its continuity; it may be smaller than all other religious bodies together, but is larger than each separately. It is a natural enemy to governments external to itself; it is intolerant and engrossing, and tends to a new modelling of society; it breaks laws, it divides families. It is a gross superstition; it is charged with the foulest crimes; it is despised by the intellect of the day; it is frightful to the imagination of the many. And there is but one communion such.

Place this description before Pliny or Julian; place it before Frederick the Second or Guizot. "Apparent diræ facies." Each knows at once, without asking a question, who is meant by it. One object, and only one, absorbs each item of the detail of the delineation.

. . . .

(1)

If there is a form of Christianity now in the world which is accused of gross superstition, of borrowing its rites and customs from the heathen, and of ascribing to forms and ceremonies an occult virtue;—a religion which is considered to burden and enslave the mind by its requisitions, to address itself to the weak-minded and ignorant, to be supported by sophistry and imposture, and to contradict reason and exalt mere irrational faith;—a religion which impresses on the serious mind very distressing views of the guilt and consequences of sin, sets upon the minute acts of the day, one by one, their definite value for praise or blame, and thus casts a grave shadow over the future;—a religion which holds up to admiration the surrender of wealth, and disables serious persons from enjoying it if they would;—a religion, the doctrines of which, be they good or bad, are to the generality of men unknown; which is considered to bear on its very surface signs of folly and falsehood so distinct that a glance suffices to judge of it, and that careful examination is preposterous; which is felt to be so simply bad, that it may be calumniated at hazard and at pleasure, it being nothing but absurdity to stand upon the accurate distribution of its guilt among its particular acts, or painfully to determine how far this or that story concerning it is literally true, or what has to be allowed in candour, or what is improbable, or what cuts two ways, or what is not proved, or what may be plausibly defended;—a religion such, that men look at a convert to it with a feeling which no other denomination raises except Judaism, Socialism, or Mormonism, viz. with curiosity, suspicion, fear, disgust, as the case may be, as if something strange had befallen him, as if he had had an initiation into a mystery, and had come into communion with dreadful influences, as if he were now one of a confederacy which claimed him, absorbed him, stripped him of his personality, reduced him to a mere organ or instrument of a whole;—a religion which men hate as proselytizing, anti-social, revolutionary, as dividing families, separating chief friends, corrupting the maxims of government, making a mock at law, dissolving the empire, the enemy of human nature, and a "conspirator against its rights and privileges;"—a religion which they consider the champion and instrument of darkness, and a pollution calling down upon the land the anger of heaven;—a religion which they associate with intrigue and conspiracy, which they speak about in whispers, which they detect by anticipation in whatever goes wrong, and to which they impute whatever is unaccountable; a religion, the very name of which they cast out as evil, and use simply as a bad epithet, and which from the impulse of self-preservation they would persecute if they could;—if there be such a religion now in the world, it is not unlike Christianity as that same world viewed it, when first it came forth from its Divine Author.

(2)

On the whole, then, we have reason to say, that if there be a form of Christianity at this day distinguished for its careful organization, and its consequent power; if it is spread over the world; if it is conspicuous for zealous maintenance of its own creed; if it is intolerant towards what it considers error; if it is engaged in ceaseless war with all other bodies called Christian; if it, and it alone, is called "Catholic" by the world, nay, by those very bodies, and if it makes much of the title, if it names them heretics, and warns them of coming woe, and calls on them one by one, to come over to itself, overlooking every other tie; and if they, on the other hand, call it seducer, harlot, apostate, Anti-Christ, devil; if, however much they differ one with another, they consider it their common enemy; if they strive to unite together against it, and cannot; if they are but local; if they continually subdivide; and it remains one; if they fall one after another, and make way for new sects, and it remains the same, such a religious communion is not unlike historical Christianity, as it comes before us at the Nicene Era.

(3)

If then there is now a form of Christianity such, that it extends throughout the world, though with varying measures of prominence or prosperity in separate places;—that it lies under the power of sovereigns and magistrates, in various ways alien to its faith;—that flourishing nations and great empires, professing or tolerating the Christian name, lie over against it as antagonists; —that schools of philosophy and learning are supporting theories, and following out conclusions, hostile to it, and establishing an exegetical system subversive of its Scriptures;—that it has lost whole Churches by schism, and is now opposed by powerful communions once part of itself;—that it has been altogether or almost driven from some countries;—that in others its line of teachers is overlaid, its flocks oppressed, its Churches occupied, its property held by what may be called a duplicate succession;— that in others its members are degenerate and corrupt, and are surpassed in conscientiousness and in virtue, as in gifts of intellect, by the very heretics whom it condemns;—that heresies are rife and bishops negligent within its own pale;—and that amid its disorders and its fears there is but one Voice for whose decisions the peoples wait with trust, one Name and one See to which they look with hope, and that name Peter, and that See Rome;— such a religion is not unlike the Christianity of the fifth and sixth Centuries.

Dev., 208, 245-7, 272-3, 321-2.

24

When we consider the succession of ages during which the Catholic system has endured, the severity of the trials it has undergone, the sudden and wonderful changes without and within which have befallen it, the incessant mental activity and the intellectual gifts of its maintainers, the enthusiasm which it has kindled, the fury of the controversies which have been carried on among its professors, the impetuosity of the assaults made upon it, the ever-increasing responsibilities to which it has been committed by the continuous development of its dogmas, it is quite inconceivable that it should not have been broken up and lost, were it a corruption of Christianity. Yet it is still living, if there be a living religion or philosophy in the world; vigorous, energetic, persuasive, progressive; *vires acquirit eundo;* it grows and is not overgrown; it spreads out, yet is not enfeebled; it is ever germinating, yet ever consistent with itself. . .

It is true, there have been seasons when, from the operation of external or internal causes, the Church has been thrown into what was almost a state of *deliquium;* but her wonderful revivals, while the world was triumphing over her, is a further evidence of the absence of corruption in the system of doctrine and worship into which she has developed. If corruption be an incipient disorganization, surely an abrupt and absolute recurrence to the former state of vigour after an interval, is even less conceivable than a corruption that is permanent. Now this is the case with the revivals I speak of. After violent exertion men are exhausted and fall asleep; they wake the same as before, refreshed by the temporary cessation of their activity; and such has been the slumber and such the restoration of the Church. She pauses in her course, and almost suspends her functions; she rises again, and she is herself once more; all things are in their place and ready for action. Doctrine is where it was, and usage and precedence, and principle, and policy; there may be changes, but they are consolidations or adaptations; all is unequivocal and determinate, with an identity which there is no disputing.

Dev., 437-8, 447.

25

But in truth the whole course of Christianity from the first, when we come to examine it, is but one series of troubles and disorders. Every century is like every other and to those who live in it seems worse than all times before it. The Church is ever ailing, and lingers on in weakness, "always bearing about in the body the dying of the Lord Jesus, that the life also of Jesus might be made manifest in her body." Religion seems ever expiring, schisms dominant, the light of Truth dim, its adherents scattered. The cause of Christ is ever in its last agony, as though it were but a question of time whether it fails finally this day or another. The Saints are ever all but failing from the earth, and Christ all but coming; and thus the Day of Judgment is literally ever at hand; and it is our duty ever to be looking out for it, not disappointed that we have so often said, "now is the moment," and that at the last, contrary to our expectation, Truth has somewhat rallied. Such is God's will, gathering in His elect, first one and then another, by little and little, in the intervals of sunshine between storm and storm, or snatching them from the surge of evil, even when the waters rage most furiously. Well may prophets cry out, "How long will it be, O Lord, to the end of these wonders?" how long will this mystery proceed? how long will

99

this perishing world be sustained by the feeble lights which struggle for existence in its unhealthy atmosphere? God alone knows the day and the hour when that will at length be, which He is ever threatening; meanwhile, thus much of comfort do we gain from what has been hitherto,—not to despond, not to be dismayed, not to be anxious, at the troubles which encompass us. They have ever been; they ever shall be; they are our portion. "The floods are risen, the floods have lift up their voice, the floods lift up their waves. The waves of the sea are mighty, and rage horribly; but yet the Lord, who dwelleth on high, is mightier."

V.M., i, 354-5.

VI: FAITH

ANALYTICAL SUMMARY

Man, then, has learned by his obedience to conscience to submit his individual judgment and his self-will to God's voice and guidance, as manifested in his conscience, and is prepared to follow the same voice by surrender to the authority of the Speaker.

The man of "the Fullness of Time" recognises in Christ and Christianity at once the witness and the content of such a revelation.

He recognises God's immediate intervention; he recognises that this intervention witnesses to God's revealing voice; because, and only because, this Speaker is the Eternal Truth he accepts His Word as indubitably true.

Not because the content of this revelation or the evidence for the fact of revelation compels the assent of his private judgment, nor because the beauty of the Church fascinates his bodily vision, nor because life in her bosom inherited from others has become endeared to him by custom;
neither with the intellectual nor the bodily eye;
nor yet with the vision of the heart or of custom and inheritance;
nor with his own vision does he behold the truth of revelation;
but with the vision of God, inasmuch as he believes what God sees.

(Nos. 1-4.)

Faith, therefore, is at once the creature's homage to his Creator's eternal Truth and the elevation of the Creature to participate in this eternal Truth: the submission of the Creature in its obedience, the condescension of God in His grace, from the outset the grace which is a "partaking of the Divine Nature":

Thus the "I believe" is a consequence of "I will believe"; this "I will believe," in turn, "being drawn by the Father."

Understanding of the evidence for the fact of revelation produces the conclusion "*I may and must believe,*" and thus provides the sufficient rational basis for the determination "*I will believe;*"

but the will is free to utter or to refrain from uttering its "*I will,*" and God is free to "*draw*" or not to draw.

(Nos. 5-10.)

Therefore, though the evidence is a necessary condition if the determination to believe is to be morally justified, nevertheless the determination is in the last resort independent of that evidence.

Hence dimness and obscurity in the evidence is tolerable, if only there be sufficient certitude on which to base the duty of faith, and no degree of clearness in the evidence is a guarantee that the act of faith will actually be made.

Dimness and obscurity—as opposed to the light of personal perception— accompany faith from the beginning to the end, until it issues in the beatific vision in which the intellectual wedding of creature and creator is consummated.

But from beginning to end there is one luminous certitude—the duty of faith.

But from beginning to end in face of this duty man is free to surrender himself to God by the homage of his understanding; free to persevere in this intellectual homage of faith—his freedom assured because God's grace never "*forsakes him, if he does not forsake God*" (*Vat. Sess. 3, cap. 3*).

Faith, therefore, "*which constitutes the beginning of salvation . . . is a supernatural virtue, whereby we, incited and assisted by God's grace, accept as true whatsoever He has revealed, not because our intellect by its natural light perceives in its own evidence the truth of the objects of revelation, but on the authority of God, who reveals them, who can neither be deceived nor deceive. For as the apostle testifies, faith is the foundation of that which is hoped for, the evidence of what is unseen*" (*Vat. Sess. cap. 3*).

(Nos. 11-17.)

FAITH

I

THERE is a large floating body of Catholic truth in the world; it comes down by tradition from age to age; it is carried forward by preaching and profession from one generation to another, and is poured about into all quarters of the world. It is found in fulness and purity in the Church alone, but portions of it, larger or smaller, escape far and wide, and penetrate into places which have never been blest with her presence and ministration. Now men may take up and profess these scattered truths, merely because they fall in with them; these fragments of Revelation, such as the doctrine of the Holy Trinity, or the Atonement, are the religion which they have been taught in their childhood; and therefore they may retain them, and profess them, and repeat them, without really seeing them, as the Catholic sees them, but as receiving them merely by word of mouth, from imitation of others. And in this way it often happens that a man external to the Catholic Church writes sermons and instructions, draws up and arranges devotions, or composes hymns, which are faultless, or nearly so; which are the fruit, not of his own illuminated mind, but of his careful study, sometimes of his accurate translation of Catholic originals. Then, again, Catholic truths and rites are so beautiful, so great, so consolatory, that they draw one on to love and admire them with a natural love, as a prospect might attract us, or a skilful piece of mechanism. Hence men of lively imagination may profess this doctrine or that, or adopt this or that ceremony or usage, for its very beauty-sake, not asking themselves whether it be true, and having no real perception or mental hold of it. Thus, too, they will decorate their churches, stretch and strain their ritual, introduce candles, vestments, flowers, incense, and processions, not from faith, but from poetical feeling. And, moreover, the Catholic Creed, as coming from God, is so harmonious, so consistent with itself, holds together so perfectly, so corresponds part to part, that an acute mind, knowing one portion of it, would often infer another portion, merely as a matter of just reasoning. Thus a correct thinker might be sure, that if God is infinite and man finite, there must be mysteries in religion. It is not that he really feels the mysteriousness of religion, but he infers it; he is led to it as a matter of necessity, and from mere clearness of mind and love of consistency, he maintains it. Again, a man may say, "Since this or that doctrine has so much historical evidence in its favour, I must accept it"; he has no real sight or direct perception of it, but he takes up the profession of it, because he feels it would be absurd, under the conditions with which he starts, to do otherwise. He does no more than load himself with a form of words instead of contemplating, with the eye of the soul, God Himself, the source of all truth, and this doctrine as proceeding from His mouth.

Mix., 174-5.

2

Why do not blind men see the sun? because they have no eyes; in like manner it is vain to discourse upon the beauty, the sanctity, the sublimity of the Catholic doctrine and worship, where men have no faith to accept it as Divine. They may confess its beauty, sublimity, and sanctity, without believing it; they may acknowledge that the Catholic religion is noble and majestic; they may be struck with its wisdom, they may admire its adaptation to human nature, they may be penetrated by its tender and winning bearing, they may be awed by its consistency. But to commit themselves to it, that is another matter; to choose it for their portion, to say with the favoured Moabitess, "Whithersoever thou shalt go, I will go! and where thou shalt dwell, I will dwell; thy people shall be my people, and thy God my God," this is the language of faith. A man may revere, a man may extol, who has no tendency whatever to obey, no notion whatever of professing. And this often happens in fact: men are respectful to the Catholic religion; they acknowledge its services to mankind, they encourage it and its professors; they like to know them, they are interested in hearing of their movements, but they are not, and never will be, Catholics. They will die as they have lived, out of the Church, because they have not possessed themselves of that faculty by which the Church is to be approached. Catholics who have not studied them or human nature will wonder they remain where they are; nay, they themselves, alas for them! will sometimes lament they cannot become Catholics. They will feel so intimately the blessedness of being a Catholic that they will cry out, "Oh, what would I give to be a Catholic! Oh, that I could believe what I admire! but I do not, and I can no more believe merely because I wish to do so, than I can leap over a mountain. I should be much happier were I a Catholic; but I am not; it is no use deceiving myself; I am what I am; I revere, I cannot accept."

Mix., 207-8.

3

Truth has two attributes—beauty and power. . . . Pursue it, either as beauty or power, to its furthest extent and its true limit, and you are led by either road to the Eternal and Infinite, to the intimations of conscience and the announcements of the Church. Satisfy yourself with what is only visibly or intelligibly excellent, as you are likely to do, and you will make present utility and natural beauty the practical test of truth, and the sufficient object of the intellect. It is not that you will at once reject Catholicism, but you will measure and proportion it by an earthly standard. You will throw its highest and most momentous disclosures into the background, you will deny its principles, explain away its doctrines, re-arrange its precepts, and make light of its practices, even while you profess it. Knowledge, viewed as knowledge, exerts a subtle influence in throwing us back on ourselves, and making us our own centre, and our own minds the measure of all things. This is [its] tendency . . . . to view Revealed Religion from an aspect of its own,—to fuse and recast it,—to tune it, as it were, to a different key, and to reset its harmonies,—to circumscribe it by a circle which unwarrantably amputates here, and unduly develops there ; and all under the notion, conscious or unconscious, that the human intellect, self-educated and self-supported, is more true and perfect in its ideas and judgments than that of Prophets and Apostles, to whom the sights and sounds of Heaven were immediately conveyed. A sense of propriety, order, consistency, and completeness gives birth to a rebellious stirring against miracle and mystery, against the severe and the terrible.

. . . Catholicism, as it has come down to us from the first, seems to be mean and illiberal; it is a mere popular religion; it is the religion of illiterate ages or servile populations or barbarous warriors; it must be treated with discrimination and delicacy, corrected, softened, improved, if it is to satisfy an enlightened generation. It must be stereotyped as the patron of arts, or the pupil of speculation, or the protégé of science; it must play the literary academician, or the empirical philanthropist, or the political partisan; it must keep up with the age; some or other expedient it must devise, in order to explain away, or to hide, tenets under which the intellect labours and of which it is ashamed—its doctrine, for instance, of grace, its mystery of the Godhead, its preaching of the Cross, its devotion to the Queen of Saints, or its loyalty to the Apostolic See.

Let this spirit be freely evolved out of . . . . [a] philosophical condition of mind . . . . and it is impossible but, first indifference, then laxity of belief, then even heresy will be the successive results.

Idea, 217-8.

4

Faith is, in its very nature, the acceptance of what our reason cannot reach, simply and absolutely upon testimony.

There is, of course, a multitude of cases in which we allowably and rightly accept statements as true, partly on reason, and partly on testimony. We supplement the information of others by our own knowledge, by our own judgment of probabilities; and, if it be very strange and extravagant, we suspend our assent. This is undeniable; still, after all, there are truths which are incapable of reaching us except on testimony, and there is testimony which, by and in itself, has an imperative claim on our acceptance.

As regards Revealed Truth, it is not Rationalism to set about to ascertain, by the exercise of reason, what things are attainable by reason, and what are not; nor, in the absence of an express Revelation, to inquire into the truths of Religion, as they come to us by nature; nor to determine what proofs are necessary for the acceptance of a Revelation, if it be given; nor to reject a Revelation on the plea of insufficient proof; nor, after recognizing it as divine, to investigate the meaning of its declarations, and to interpret its language ; nor to use its doctrines, as far as they can be fairly used, in inquiring into its divinity; nor to compare and connect them with our previous knowledge, with a view of making them parts of a whole; nor to bring them into dependence on each other, to trace their mutual relations, and to pursue them to their legitimate issues. This is not Rationalism; but it is Rationalism to accept the Revelation, and then to explain it away; to speak of it as the Word of God, and to treat it as the word of man ; to refuse to let it speak for itself; to claim to be told the *why* and the *how* of God's dealings with us, as therein described, and to assign to Him a motive and a scope of our own; to stumble at the partial knowledge which He may give us of them; to put aside what is obscure, as if it had not been said at all; to accept one half of what has been told us, and not the other half; to assume that the contents of Revelation are also its proof; to frame some gratuitous hypothesis about them, and then to garble, gloss and colour them, to trim, clip, and pare away, and twist them, in order to bring them into conformity with the idea to which we have subjected them.

. . . .

The Rationalist makes himself his own centre, not His Maker; he does not go to God, but he implies that God must come to him.

Ess., 31-32, 33.

5

Faith is "the substance," or the realizing of what as yet is not here, but only "hoped for"; it is the making present what is future. Again: it is "the evidence" of what is not seen, that is, the

107

ground or medium of proof, on or through which the unseen is accepted as really existing. In the way of nature, we ascertain the things around and before us by sight ; and things which are to be by reason ; but faith is our informant about things present which we do not see, and things future which we cannot forecast. And as sight contemplates form and colour, and reason the processes of argument, so faith rests on the divine word as the token and criterion of truth. And as the mind trusts to sense and reason, by a natural instinct, which it freely uses prior to experience, so in a parallel way, a moral instinct, independent of experience, is its impelling and assuring principle in assenting to revelation as divine. By faith then is meant the mind's perception or apprehension of heavenly things, arising from an instinctive trust in the divinity or truth of the external word, informing it concerning them.

Jfc., 252-3.

6

Faith is the correlative, the natural instrument of the things of the Spirit. While Christ was present in the flesh, He might be seen by the eye; but His more perfect and powerful presence which we now enjoy, being invisible, can be discerned, and used by faith only. Thus faith is a mysterious means of gaining gifts from God, which cannot otherwise be gained; according to the text, "If thou canst believe, all things are possible to him that believeth." If it was necessary for our justification that Christ should become a quickening Spirit and so be invisible; therefore it was as necessary for the same, in God's providence, that we should believe; as necessary a condition, in St. Paul's language, for "the heart to *believe* unto *righteousness*" as any one thing is a necessary condition of another, as (in this world) eating and drinking are necessary for animal life, or the sun for ripening the fruits of the earth, or the air for transmitting sounds. . . As the Spirit is the only justifier, so faith is the only recipient of justification. The eye sees what is material; the mind alone can embrace what is spiritual.

Jfc., 214-216.

Now, in the first place, what is faith? it is assenting to a doctrine as true, which we do not see, which we cannot prove, because God says it is true, who cannot lie. And further than this, since God says it is true, not with His own voice, but by the voice of His messengers, it is assenting to what man says, not simply viewed as a man, but to what he is commissioned to declare, as a messenger, prophet, or ambassador from God. In the ordinary course of this world we account things true either because we see them, or because we can perceive that they follow and are deducible from what we do see; that is, we gain truth by sight or by reason, not by faith. You will say indeed, that we accept a number of things which we cannot prove or see, on the word of others; certainly, but then we accept what they say only as the word of man; and we have not commonly that absolute and unreserved confidence in them, which nothing can shake. We know that man is open to mistake, and we are always glad to find some confirmation of what he says, from other quarters, in any important matter; or we receive his information with negligence and unconcern, as something of little consequence, as a matter of opinion; or, if we act upon it, it is as a matter of prudence, thinking it best and safest to do so. We take his word for what it is worth, and we use it either according to our necessity, or its probability. We keep the decision in our own hands, and reserve to ourselves the right of re-opening the question whenever we please. This is very different from divine faith; he who believes that God is true, and that this is His word, which He has committed to man, has no doubt at all. He is as certain that the doctrine taught is true as that God is true; and he is certain, *because* God is true, *because* God has spoken, not because he sees its truth or can prove its truth. That is, faith has two peculiarities;—it is most certain, decided, positive, immovable in its assent, not because it sees with the eye, or sees with the reason, but because it receives the tidings from one who comes from God.

Mix., 194-6.

8

Faith is the gift of God, and not a mere act of our own, which we are free to exert when we will. It is quite distinct from an exercise of reason, though it follows upon it. I may feel the force of the argument for the divine origin of the Church; I may see that I ought to believe; and yet I may be unable to believe. This is no imaginary case; there is many a man who has ground enough to believe, who wishes to believe, but who cannot believe. It is always indeed his own fault, for God gives grace to all who ask for it, and use it, but still such is the fact, that conviction is not faith. Take the parallel case of obedience: many a man knows he ought to obey God, and does not and cannot,—through his own fault, indeed,—but still he cannot; for through grace alone can he obey. Now, faith is not a mere conviction in reason, it is a firm assent, it is a clear certainty greater than any other certainty; and this is wrought in the mind by the grace of God, and by it alone. As then men may be convinced, and not act according to their conviction, so may they be convinced, and not believe according to their conviction. They may confess that the argument is against them, that they have nothing to say for themselves, and that to believe is to be happy; and yet, after all, they avow they cannot believe, they do not know why, but they cannot; they acquiesce in unbelief, and they turn away from God and His Church. Their reason is convinced, and their doubts are moral ones, arising in their root from a fault of the will. In a word, the arguments for religion do not compel any one to believe, just as arguments for good conduct do not compel any one to obey. Obedience is the consequence of willing to obey, and faith is the consequence of willing to believe; we may see what is right, whether in matters of faith or obedience, of ourselves, but we cannot will what is right without the grace of God. Here is the difference between other exercises of reason, and arguments for the truth of religion. It requires no act of faith to assent to the truth that two and two make four; we cannot help assenting to it; and hence there is no merit in assenting to it; but there is merit in believing that the Church is from God; for though there are abundant reasons to prove it to us, yet we can, without an absurdity, quarrel with the conclusion; we may complain that it is not clearer, we may suspend our assent, we may doubt about it, if we will, and grace alone can turn a bad will into a good one. . . .

There are, to be sure, many cogent arguments to lead one to join the Catholic Church, but they do not force the will. We may know them, and not be moved to act upon them. We may be convinced without being persuaded. The two things are quite distinct from each other, seeing you ought to believe, and believing; reason, if left to itself, will bring you to the conclusion that you have sufficient grounds for believing, but belief is the gift of grace. You are then what you are, not from any excellence or merit of your own, but by the grace of God who has chosen you to believe.

Mix., 211, 224-5.

9

It is the very characteristic of the profession of faith made by numbers of educated Protestants, and it is the utmost extent to which they are able to go in believing, to hold, not that Christian doctrine is certainly true, but that it has such a semblance of truth, it has such considerable marks of probability upon it, that it is their duty to accept and act upon it, as if it were true beyond all question or doubt: and they justify themselves, and with much reason, by the authority of Bishop Butler. Undoubtedly, a religious man will be led to go as far as this, if he cannot go farther; but unless he can go farther, he is no catechumen of the Catholic Church. We wish all men to believe that her creed is true; but till they do so believe, we do not wish, we have no permission, to make them her members. Such a faith . . . . does not rise to the level of the *sine qua non*, which is the condition prescribed for becoming a Catholic. Unless a convert so believes that he can sincerely say, "After all, in spite of all difficulties, objections, obscurities, mysteries, the creed of the Church undoubtedly comes from God, and is true, because He who gave it is the Truth," such a man, though he be outwardly received into her fold, will receive no grace from the sacraments, no sanctifica-

tion in baptism, no pardon in penance, no life in communion . . . .
if our doctrine is true, it must be received as such; if a man cannot
so receive it, he must wait till he can. It would be better, indeed,
if he now believed; but since he does not as yet, to wait is the best
he can do under the circumstances.

D.A., 391-2.

10

Be convinced in your reason that the Catholic Church is a
teacher sent to you from God, and it is enough. I do not wish
you to join her, till you are. If you are half convinced, pray for a
full conviction, and wait till you have it. It is better indeed to
come quickly, but better slowly than carelessly; and sometimes,
as the proverb goes, the more haste, the worse speed. Only make
yourselves sure that the delay is not from any fault of yours
which you can remedy. God deals with us very differently;
conviction comes slowly to some men, quickly to others; in some
it is the result of much thought and many reasonings, in others of
a sudden illumination. One man is convinced at once, as in the
instance described by St. Paul: "If all prophesy," he says, speaking of exposition of doctrine, "and there come in one that
believeth not, or one unlearned, he is convinced of all, he is
judged of all. The secrets of his heart are made manifest; and
so, falling down on his face, he will worship God, and say that
God is among you of a truth." The case is the same now: some
men are converted merely by entering a Catholic Church; others
are converted by reading one book; others by one doctrine.
They feel the weight of their sins, and they see that that religion
must come from God which alone has the means of forgiving
them. Or they are touched and overcome by the evident sanctity, beauty, and (as I may say) fragrance of the Catholic Religion. Or they long for a guide amid the strife of tongues; and
the very doctrine of the Church about faith, which is so hard to
many, is conviction to them. Others, again, hear many
objections to the Church, and follow out the whole subject
far and wide; conviction can scarcely come to them except as at
the end of a long inquiry. As in a court of justice, one man's

112

innocence may be proved at once, another's is the result of a careful investigation; one has nothing in his conduct or character to explain, against another there are many unfavourable presumptions at first sight; so Holy Church presents herself very differently to different minds who are contemplating her from without. God deals with them differently; but, if they are faithful to their light, at last, in their own time, though it may be a different time to each, He brings them to that one and the same state of mind, very definite and not to be mistaken, which we call *conviction*. They will have no doubt, whatever difficulties may still attach to the subject, that the Church is from God; they may not be able to answer this objection or that, but they will be certain in spite of it. . . .

In such a case it is his duty to join the Church at once; he must not delay; let him be cautious in counsel, but prompt in execution.

Mix., 233-4, 235.

II

We have reason to believe that God, our Maker and Governor, has spoken to us by Revelation; yet why has He not spoken more distinctly? He has given us doctrines which are but obscurely gathered from Scripture, and a Scripture which is but obscurely gathered from history. . . . The Jews were left in the same uncertainty about Christ, in which we are about His doctrine. . . . The Old Testament certainly does speak about the Messiah as a temporal monarch, and a conqueror of this world. *We* are accustomed to say that the prophecies must be taken spiritually; and rightly do we say so. True: yet does not this look like an evasion to a Jew? Is it not much more like an evasion, though it be not, than to say (what the Church does say and rightly) that rites remain, *though* Jewish rites are done away, because *our* rites are not Jewish, but spiritual, gifted with the Spirit, channels of grace? . . . The doctrines of the Church are not hidden so deep in the New Testament as the Gospel doctrines are hidden in the Old; but they are hidden; and I am persuaded that were men but consistent, who oppose the Church doctrines as being

113

unscriptural, they would vindicate the Jews for rejecting the Gospel? . . .

"Then came the Jews round about Him, and said unto Him, how long dost Thou make us to doubt?" or more literally, "How long dost Thou keep our soul in suspense? If thou be the Christ, *tell us plainly?*" Christ answers by referring to His works, and by declaring that His sheep do hear and know Him, and follow Him. If any one will seriously consider the intercourse between our Lord and the Pharisees, he will see that, not denying their immorality and miserable pride, still they had reason for complaining (as men now speak) that "the Gospel was not preached to them,"—that the Truth was not placed before them clearly, and fully, and uncompromisingly, and intelligibly, and logically,— that they were bid to believe on weak arguments, and fanciful deductions.*

This then, I say, is certainly a most striking coincidence in addition. Whatever perplexity any one of us may feel about the evidence of Scripture, or the evidence of Church doctrine, we see that such a perplexity is represented in Scripture as the lot of the Jews, too; and this circumstance, while it shows that it is a sort of law of God's providence, and thereby affords an additional evidence of the truth of the Revealed system by showing its harmony, also serves to quiet and console, and moreover to awe and warn us. Doubt and difficulty, as regards evidence, seem our lot ; the simple question is—What is our duty under it? . . .

Scripture is quite aware of those difficulties . . . . it knows them all; it has provided against them by recognising them. It says, "Believe."

Ess., 244-49.

12

What is faith itself but an acceptance of things unseen, from the love of them *beyond* the determinations of calculation and experience? Faith outstrips argument. If there is only a fair chance that the Bible is true, that heaven is the reward of obe-

* Note by Newman when he re-published this Tract : "This is said too strongly."

114

dience, and hell of wilful sin, it is worth while—it is safe—to sacrifice this world to the next. It were worth while, though Christ told us to sell all that we have and follow Him, and to pass our time here in poverty and contempt—it were worth while on that chance to do it. This, then, is what is meant by faith going against reason, that it cares not for the measure of probabilities; it does not ask whether a thing is more or less likely; but if there is a fair and clear likelihood what God's will is, it acts upon it. If Scripture were not true, we should in the next world be left where we were; we should, in the event, be no worse off than before; but if it be true, then we shall be infinitely worse off for not believing it than if we had believed it. . . .

Faith does not regard *degrees* of evidence. You might lay it down as a rule, speaking in the way of reason, that we ought to have faith according to the evidence. But this is not the case as regards religious faith,—which accepts the Word of God as firmly on the evidence which it is vouchsafed as if that evidence were doubled. This, indeed, we see to be the case as regards things of earth; and surely what we do towards men we may bear to do towards God. If any one whom we trust and revere told us any news, which he had perfect means of knowing, we should believe him; we should not believe it more thoroughly because presently another told it to us also. And in like manner, though it is quite certain that Almighty God might have given us greater evidence than we possess, that He speaks to us in the Bible; yet since He has given us enough, faith does not ask for more, but is satisfied, and acts upon what *is* enough; whereas unbelief is ever asking for signs, more and greater, before it will yield to the Divine Word.

P.S., *vi*, 258-60.

13

Love of heaven is the only *way* to heaven. Sight will not move us; else why did Judas persist in covetousness in the very presence of Christ? why did Balaam, whose "eyes were opened," remain with a closed heart? why did Satan fall, when he was a bright Archangel? Nor will reason subdue us; else why was the Gospel, in the beginning, "to the Greeks foolishness?" Nor will excited feelings convert us; for there is one who "heareth the word, and anon with joy receiveth it"; yet "hath no root in himself," and "dureth" only "for a while." Nor will self-interest prevail with us; or the rich man would have been more prudent, whose "ground brought forth plentifully," and would have recollected that "that night his soul" might be "required of him." Let us understand that nothing but the love of God can make us believe in Him or obey Him; and let us pray Him, who has "prepared for them that love Him, such good things as pass man's understanding, to pour into our hearts such love towards Him, that we, loving Him above all things, may obtain His promises, which exceed all that we can desire."

P.S., *viii*, 89-90.

14

Our difficulty and its religious solution are contained in the sixth chapter of St. John. After our Lord had declared what all who heard seemed to feel to be a hard doctrine, some in surprise and offence left Him. Our Lord said to the Twelve most tenderly, "Will ye also go away?" St. Peter promptly answered No: but observe on what ground He put it: "Lord, *to whom* shall we go?" He did not bring forward evidences of our Lord's mission, though He knew of such in abundance, in the miracles which our Lord wrought: but, still, questions might be raised about the so-called miracles of others, such as of Simon the sorcerer, or of vagabond Jews, or about the force of the evidence from miracles itself. This was not the evidence on which he rested personally, but this,—that if Christ were not to be trusted, there was nothing in the world to be trusted; and this was a conclusion repugnant both to his reason and to his heart. He had within him ideas of greatness and goodness, holiness and eternity—he had a love of them—he had an instinctive hope and longing after their possession. Nothing could convince him that this unknown good was a dream. Divine life, eternal life, was the object which his soul, as far as it had learned to realize and express its wishes, supremely longed for. In Christ he found what he wanted. He says, "Lord to whom *shall* we go?" implying he must go somewhere. Christ had asked "Will ye also go *away?*" He only asked about Peter's leaving *Himself*; but in Peter's thought to leave Him was to go somewhere else. He only thought of leaving Him by taking another god. That negative state of neither believing or disbelieving, neither acting this way nor that, which is so much in esteem now, did not occur to his mind as possible. The fervent Apostle ignored the existence of scepticism. With him his course was at best but *a choice of difficulties*—of difficulties perhaps, but still a choice. He knew of no course without a choice,—choice he must make. Somewhither he must go: whither else? If Christ could deceive him, to whom should he go? Christ's ways might be dark, His words often perplexing, but still he found in Him what He found nowhere else,—amid difficulties a realization of his inward longings. "Thou hast the words of eternal life."

So far he saw. He might have misgivings at times; He might have permanent and in themselves insuperable objections; still in spite of such objections, in spite of the assaults of unbelief, on the whole, he saw that in Christ which was positive, real and satisfying. He saw it nowhere else. "Thou," he says, "hast the words of eternal life; and we *have believed* and *have* known that thou art the Christ, the Son of the Living God." As if he said, "We will stand by what we believed and knew yesterday—what we believed and knew the day before. A sudden gust of new doctrines, a sudden inroad of new perplexities, shall not unsettle us. We *have* believed, we *have* known: we cannot collect together all the evidence, but this is the abiding deep conviction of our minds. We feel that it is better, safer, truer, more pleasant, more blessed to cling to Thy feet, O merciful Saviour, than to leave Thee, Thou *canst not* deceive us: it is impossible. We will hope in Thee against hope, and believe in Thee against doubt, and obey Thee in spite of gloom."

Now what are the feelings I have described but the love of Christ? Thus love is the parent of faith.* . . . Love of God led

*The following note, part of which is embodied by Fr. P. in the text, was appended by Newman in 1872: "To say that 'love is the parent of faith';—is true, if by 'love' is meant, not evangelical charity, the theological virtue, but that desire for the knowledge and drawing towards the service of our Maker

117

St. Peter to follow Christ, and love of Christ leads men now to love and follow the Church, as His representative and voice.

Ess., 249-52.

15

"Do you mean," said Charles with a beating heart, "that before conversion one can attain to a present abiding actual conviction of this truth . . . . that the Catholic Church, and none other, is the voice of God?"

"I do not know," answered the other; "but, at least, he may have habitual *moral certainty*, I mean, a conviction, and one only, steady, without rival conviction, or even reasonable doubt, present to him when he is most composed and in his hours of solitude, and flashing on him from time to time, as through clouds, when he is in the world;—a conviction to this effect, 'The Roman Catholic Church is the one only voice of God, the one only way of salvation.'"

"Then you mean to say," said Charles, while his heart beat faster, "that such a person is under no duty to wait for a clearer light."

"He will not have, he cannot expect, clearer light before conversion. Certainty, in its highest sense, is the reward of those who, by an act of the will, and at the dictate of reason and prudence, embrace the truth, when nature, like a coward, shrinks. You must make a venture; faith is a venture before a man is a Catholic; it is a gift after it. You approach the Church in the way of reason, you enter into it in the light of the Spirit."

L.G., 384-5.

16

Faith is not a conclusion from premises, but the result of an

which precedes religious conversion. Such is the main outline, personally and historically, of the inward reception of Revelation on the part of individuals, and does not at all exclude, but actually requires, the exercise of Reason, and the presence of grounds for believing, as an incidental and necessary part of the process. The preliminary called in the text 'love,' but more exactly a 'pia affectio' or 'pia voluntas,' does not stand in antagonism or in contrast to Reason, but is a sovereign condition without which Reason cannot be brought to bear upon the great work in hand."

act of the *will*, following upon a conviction that to believe is a *duty*. The simple question you have to ask yourself is, "Have I a *conviction* that I *ought* to accept the (Roman) Catholic Faith as God's word?" If not, at least, "do I *tend* to such a *conviction?*" or "am I *near* upon it?" For directly you have a conviction that you ought to believe, reason has done its part, and what is wanted for faith is, not proof, but will. . . . We are answerable for what we choose to believe; if we believe lightly, or if we are hard of belief, in either case we do wrong.

Ward, i, 242.

17

She says there are persons who are *certain* of the Christian religion *because* they have strictly proved it—no one is certain for this reason. Every one believes by an act of will, more or less ruling his intellect (as a matter of duty) to believe absolutely *beyond* the evidence. . . .

"How can any human testimony make me *quite certain* that I am hearing a message from God?" None can, but human testimony may be such as to make me see it is my *duty* to be certain. Action is distinct [from] a conclusion—yet a conclusion may be such as to make me see that action is a *duty*—And so *belief* is not a conclusion—yet [a conclusion] may be such as to make me see that belief is a duty—And as I cannot act merely because I ought to act, so I cannot believe merely because I ought to believe.

I may wish both to act and believe—though I can do neither—and, as I ask God for grace to enable me to act, so I ask Him for grace to enable me to believe.

"It is the gift of God—why does He not give it me?" Because you do not come to him perseveringly for the gift, and do your part by putting aside all those untrue and unreal and superfluous arguings.

"To see and touch the supernatural with the eye of my soul, with its *own experience*, this is what I want to do." Yes, it is—You wish to "walk *not* by faith, *but* by sight." If you had *experience*, how would it be faith?

Ward, ii, 276-7.

VII: FROM FAITH TO SIGHT

ANALYTICAL SUMMARY

Faith, however, once introduced into our life by the free surrender of the understanding, is incorporated, by a life lived in loyal obedience to its precepts, ever more fully into our individual thought will and feeling, until it becomes the sap of our most personal and interior life, as indubitable as that life itself.

(NOS. 1-12.)

Thus from our life of faith there blossoms and unfolds ever more fully a matured insight into the internal connection which binds the truth of faith into one fabric—part adheres to part and with a delicious sense of free "enlargement" we catch sight of a self-complete organism of truth.

(NOS. 13-18.)

No doubt—and this is the other aspect of this development—we realise ever more powerfully the obscurity of the mysteries of faith, that even the light of faith does nothing to remove it, that "we dwell in a dark place until the day star arise;"

that even the knowledge of faith is still knowledge "through a mirror darkly" and not yet "face to face";

that the keenest insight of faith and the ripest wisdom of faith is still only "in part" as compared with that knowledge to come when "I shall know, even as I am known";

121

that all revelation in this life is but the carnest-money of that complete marriage portion with which God shall endow his bride in the beatific vision. But the humble believer does not presume "to be wiser than it behoveth." He accepts with thankfulness what he is given, that he may thereby become worthy to receive more;

patiently abides "in umbris et imaginibus" amid veils and symbols till the hour when the bud of faith shall open as the unfading flower of vision.

(Nos. 19-22.)

I. LIVING BY FAITH

I

THE convert comes, not only to believe the Church but also to trust and obey her priests, and to conform himself in charity to her people. It would never do for him to resolve that he never would say a Hail Mary, never avail himself of an indulgence, never kiss a crucifix, never accept the Lent dispensations, never mention a venial sin in confession. All this would not only be unreal, but would be dangerous too, as arguing a wrong state of mind, which could not look to receive the divine blessing. Moreover he comes to the ceremonial, and the moral theology, and the ecclesiastical regulations, which he finds on the spot where his lot is cast. And again, as regards matters of politics, of education, of general expedience, of taste, he does not criticize or controvert. And thus surrendering himself to the influences of his new religion, and not risking the loss of revealed truth altogether by attempting by a private rule to discriminate every moment its substance from its accidents, he is gradually so indoctrinated in Catholicism, as at length to have a right to speak as well as to hear.

Diff., *ii*, 18, 19.

2

Belief, in any true sense of the word, requires a certain familiarity or intimacy of the mind with the thing believed. Till it is in some way brought home to us and made our own, we cannot properly say we believe it, even when our reason receives it. . . . Belief implies an habitual presence and abidance of the matter believed in, in our thoughts, and a familiar acquaintance with the ideas it involves. . . . Here we see the use of reading and studying the Gospels in order to true belief in our Lord; and, again, of acting upon His words in order to true belief in them.

Mir., 259.

3

Faith and devotion are as distinct in fact as they are in idea.
We cannot, indeed, be devout without faith, but we may believe
without feeling devotion. Of this phenomenon every one has
experience both in himself and in others; and we bear witness to
it as often as we speak of realizing a truth or not realizing it. . . .
It is like the distinction between objective and subjective truth.
The sun in the spring-time will have to shine many days before
he is able to melt the frost, open the soil, and bring out the leaves;
yet he shines out from the first notwithstanding, though he
makes his power but felt gradually. It is one and the same sun,
though his influence day by day becomes greater.

Diff., *ii*, 26, 28.

4

[Faith lives in works.] It is not (as it were) a shadow or phantom, which flits about without voice or power, but it is faith
developed into height and depth and breadth, as if in a bodily
form, not as a picture but as an image, with a right side and a
left, a without and a within; not a mere impression or sudden
gleam of light upon the soul, not knowledge, or emotion, or conviction, which ends with itself, but the beginning of that which
is eternal, the operation of the Indwelling Power which acts
from within us, outwards and round about us; works in us mightily,
so intimately with our will as to be in a true sense one with it;
pours itself out into our whole mind; runs over into our thoughts,
desires, feelings, purposes, attempts, and works, combines them
all together into one, makes the whole man its one instrument,
and justifies him into one holy and gracious ministry, one
embodied lifelong act of faith, one "sacrifice, holy, acceptable to
God, which is his reasonable service." Such is faith, springing
up out of the immortal seed of love, and ever budding forth in
new blossoms and maturing new fruit, existing indeed in feelings
but passing on into acts, into victories of whatever kind over self,
being the power of the will over the whole soul for Christ's sake,
constraining the reason to accept mysteries, the heart to acquiesce
in suffering, the hand to work, the feet to run, the voice to bear

witness, as the case may be. These acts we sometimes call labours, sometimes endurances, sometimes confessions, sometimes devotions, sometimes services; but they are all instances of self-command, arising from Faith seeing the invisible world, and Love choosing it.

Jfc., 302-3.

5

When a friend dies, we cannot believe him taken from us at first;—we cannot believe ourselves to be in any new place when we are just come to it. When we are told a thing, we assent to it, we do not doubt it, but we do not feel it to be true, we do not understand it as a fact which must take up a position or station in our thoughts, and must be acted from and acted towards, must be dealt with *as* existing: that is, we do not realize it. . . .

At first children do not know that they are responsible beings; but by degrees they not only feel that they are, but reflect on the great truth, and on what it implies. Some persons recollect a time as children when it fell on them to reflect what they were, whence they came, whither they tended, why they lived, what was required of them. The thought fell upon them long after they had heard and spoken of God; but at length they began to realize what they had heard, and they began to muse about themselves. So, too, it is in matters of this world. As our minds open, we gradually understand where we are in human society. We have a notion of ranks and classes, of nations, of countries. We begin to see how we stand relatively to others. Thus a man differs from a boy; he has a general view of things; he sees their bearings on each other; he sees his own position, sees what is becoming, what is expected of him, what his duty is in the community, what his rights. He understands his place in the world, and, in a word, he is at home in it. . . .

[In like manner] we are born almost into the fulness of Christian blessings, long before we have reason. We could not apprehend them at all, and that without our own fault, when we were baptized; for we were infants. As, then, we acquire reason itself but gradually, so we acquire the knowledge of what we are but

125

gradually also; and as it is no fault in us, but a blessing to us, that we were baptized so early, so from the nature of the case, and not from any fault of ours, do we but slowly enter into the privileges of our baptism. . . . We begin our Catechism by confessing that we are risen [to a supernatural condition], but it takes a long life to apprehend what we confess. We are like people waking from sleep, who cannot collect their thoughts at once, or understand where they are. By little and little the truth breaks upon us. Such are we in the present world: sons of light, gradually waking to a knowledge of ourselves. For this let us meditate, let us pray, let us work,—gradually to attain to a real apprehension of what we are. Thus, as time goes on, we shall gain first one thing, then another. By little and little we shall give up shadows and find the substance. Waiting on God day by day we shall make progress day by day, and approach to the true and clear view of what He has made us to be in Christ.

P.S., vi, 97, 98, 99.

6

The most unlearned Christian may have a very real and substantial argument, an intimate token, of the truth of the Gospel, quite independent of the authority of his parents and teachers; nay, that were all the world, even were his teachers to tell him that religion was a dream, still he would have a good reason for believing it true.

This reason, I say, is contained in the text—"I have more understanding than the aged, *because* I keep Thy commandments" By obeying the commands of Scripture, we learn that these commands really come from God; by trying we make proof; by doing we come to know. Now how comes this to pass? It happens in several ways.

1. Consider the Bible tells us to be meek, humble, single-hearted, and teachable. Now, it is plain that humility and teachableness are qualities of mind necessary for arriving at the truth in any subject, and in religious matters as well as others. By obeying Scripture, then, in practising humility and teachableness, it is evident we are at least *in the way* to arrive at the know-

126

ledge of God. On the other hand, impatient, proud, self-confident obstinate men are generally wrong in the opinions they form of persons and things. Prejudice and self-conceit blind the eyes and mislead the judgment, whatever be the subject inquired into. . . . When I see a person hasty and violent, harsh and high-minded, careless of what others feel, and disdainful of what they think; —when I see such a one proceeding to inquire into religious subjects, I am sure beforehand he cannot go right—he will not be led into all the truth—it is contrary to the nature of things and the experience of the world that he should find what he is seeking. I should say the same were he seeking to find out what to believe or do in any other matter not religious,—but especially in any such important and solemn inquiry; for the *fear* of the Lord (humbleness, teachableness, reverence towards Him) is the very *beginning* of wisdom, as Solomon tells us; it leads us to think over things modestly and honestly, to examine patiently, to bear doubt and uncertainty, to wait perseveringly for an increase of light, to be slow to speak, and to be deliberate in deciding.

2. Consider, in the next place, that those who are trained carefully according to the precepts of Scripture, gain an elevation, a delicacy, refinement, and sanctity of mind, which is most necessary for judging fairly of the truth of Scripture.

A man who loves sin does not wish the Gospel to be true, and therefore is not a fair judge of it; a mere man of the world, a selfish and covetous man, or a drunkard, or an extortioner, is, from a sense of interest, against that Bible which condemns him, and would account that man indeed a messenger of good tidings of peace who could prove to him that Christ's doctrine was not from God. "Every one that doeth evil hateth the light, neither cometh to the light, lest his deeds should be reproved." I do not mean to say that such men necessarily reject the word of God, as if we could dare to conclude that all who do not reject it are therefore sure to be not covetous, drunkards, extortioners, and the like; for it is often a man's interest not openly to reject it, though it be against him; and the bulk of men are inconsistent, and have some good feelings left, even amid their sins and vices, which keep them from going all lengths. But, while they still

127

profess to honour, at least they try to pervert and misinterpret Scripture, and that comes to the same thing. They try to persuade themselves that Christ will save them, though they continue in sin; or they wish to believe that future punishment will not last for ever; or they conceive that their good deeds or habits, few and miserable as they are at best, will make up for the sins of which they are too conscious. Whereas such men as have been taught betimes to work with God their Saviour,—in ruling their hearts, and curbing their sinful passions, and changing their wills,— though they are still sinners, have not within them that treacherous enemy of the truth which misleads the judgments of irreligious men.

. . . .

But to proceed. Consider, moreover, that those who try to obey God evidently gain a knowledge of themselves at least; and this may be shown to be the first and principal step towards knowing God. For let us suppose a child, under God's blessing, profiting by his teacher's guidance, and trying to do his duty and please God. He will perceive that there is much in him which ought not to be in him. His own natural sense of right and wrong tells him that peevishness, sullenness, deceit, and self-will, are tempers and principles of which he has cause to be ashamed, and he feels that these bad tempers and principles are in his heart. As he grows older, he will understand this more and more. Wishing, then, and striving to act up to the law of conscience, he will yet find that, with his utmost efforts, and after his most earnest prayers, he still falls short of what he knows to be right, and what he aims at. Conscience, however, being respected, will become a more powerful and enlightened guide than before; it will become more refined and hard to please, and he will understand and perceive more clearly the distance that exists between his own conduct and thoughts, and perfection. He will admire and take pleasure in the holy law of God, of which he reads in Scripture; but he will be humbled withal, as understanding himself to be a continual transgressor against it. Thus he will learn from experience the doctrine of original sin, before he knows the actual name of it. He will, in fact, say to himself, what St. Paul describes all beginners in religion as saying, "What I would, that do I not; but what I hate, that do I. I delight in the law of God after the inward man, but I see another law in my members, warring against the law of my mind, and bringing me into captivity. I know that in my flesh dwelleth no good thing." The effect of this experience will be to make him take it for granted, as an elementary truth, that he cannot gain heaven for himself; to make him feel himself guilty before God; and to feel, moreover, that even were he admitted into the Divine presence, yet, till his heart be (so to say) made over again, he cannot perfectly enjoy God. This, surely, is the state of self-knowledge; these are the convictions to which every one is brought on, who attempts honestly to obey the precepts of God. I do not mean that all that I have been saying will necessarily pass through his mind, and in the same order, or that he will be conscious of it, or be able to speak of it, but that on the whole thus he will feel.

When, then, even an unlearned person thus trained—from his own heart, from the action of his mind upon itself, from struggles with self, from an attempt to follow those impulses of his own nature which he feels to be highest and noblest, from a vivid natural perception (natural, though cherished and strengthened by prayer; natural, though unfolded and diversified by practice; natural, though of that new and second nature which God the Holy Ghost gives), from an innate, though supernatural perception of the great vision of Truth which is external to him (a perception of it, not indeed in its fulness, but in glimpses, and by fits and seasons, and in its persuasive influences, and through a courageous following on after it, as a man in the dark might follow after some dim and distant light)—I say, when a person thus trained from his own heart, reads the declarations and promises of the Gospel, are we to be told that he believes in them merely because he has been bid believe in them? Do we not see he has besides this a something in his own breast which bears a confirming testimony to their truth? He reads that the heart is "deceitful above all things and desperately wicked," and that he inherits an evil nature from Adam, and that he is still under its power, except so far as he has been renewed. Here is a mystery; but his own actual and too bitter experience bears witness to the truth of the declaration; he feels the mystery of iniquity within him. He reads, that "without holiness no man shall see the Lord"; and his own love of what is true and lovely and pure approves and embraces the doctrine as coming from God. He reads that God is angry at sin, and will punish the sinner, and that it is a hard matter, nay, an impossibility, for us to appease His wrath. Here, again, is a mystery: but here, too, his conscience anticipates the mystery, and convicts him; his mouth is stopped. And when he goes on to read that the Son of God has Himself come into the world in our flesh, and died upon the Cross for us, does he not, amid the awful mysteriousness of the doctrine, find those words fulfilled in him which that gracious Saviour uttered, "And I, if I be lifted up from the earth, will draw all men unto Me!" He cannot choose but believe in Him. He says, "O Lord, Thou art stronger than I, and hast prevailed."

P.S., *viii*, 112-17.

7

In spite of the great differences in God's dealings with man and man, there is this one thing the same in all cases, that He *has* dealt with each. I mean that religion is a personal, private, and individual matter, that it consists in a communion between God and the soul, and that its true evidences belong to the soul that believes, are its property, and not something common to it and the whole world. God vouchsafes to speak to us one by one, to manifest Himself to us one by one, to lead us forward one by one; He gives us something to rely upon which others do not experience, which we cannot convey to others, which we can but use for ourselves.

Now that there is much in Scripture agreeable to this statement, no one I suppose will deny; but the question arises . . . . whether the Gospel Dispensation does not, even more than the Law, in one respect modify it, or even run counter to it and reverse it? For if there be a distinction of the Gospel plainly laid down in Scripture, it is that it is a social religion, and addresses individuals as parts of a whole. . . . And, further, if it is social, it must be a public religion, "a city set upon a hill"; and its evidences will be in a measure public. Nay, further, its great note, as announced by the Prophets, is not only that it is social, that it is public, but that it is both social and public in the very highest sense, because it is Catholic, universal every where; and this note is insisted on as something special in itself, of a nature to dazzle and subdue the mind, like a miracle, or like the sun's light in the heavens. It was to be the characteristic gift of the Christian Church, that she herself was to be a great public evidence of her mission, that she was to be her own evidence. Her very look, her bearing, her voice, were to be her credentials. As Adam had sovereignty over brute animals on his creation, or as the second Adam, her Lord and Maker, "spake as one having authority, and not as the Scribes," so she was to win or to awe the souls of men generally, not this one or that, but all, though variously, by the manifest royalty of her very presence. She received this gift from her Lord in the beginning—to claim and command obedience when she spoke, because she spoke; and that not from any thing special in the mind of the hearer, but from the voice and tone of the speaker.

Never must we disguise this great truth. . . Yet in spite of these tokens, outward, visible, common to all, St. Paul. . . when about to die and contemplating the judgment, speaks, not of them, of an evidence not outward, not visible, not common, but inward, private, incommunicable. "I know,"he says, "whom I have believed." I bear about me "the marks of the Lord Jesus" in my own person; I have assurance that He has "stood by me," because He has "strengthened me"; His tabernacle is not only "with men," but "the grace of Christ tabernacles upon me." In other words (could we doubt it?), in his instance the general had become particular; the external had flowed into his secret soul; the universal gift had been appropriated; the visible glory had kindled a light in his own breast; and thus, just as we need not read a friend's writing when we hear his voice, so, though Christ had gone forth into the wide world, and had been lifted up aloft to draw men to Him, and had lodged among them the power

131

and the presence of His Atonement, yet the blessed Apostle needed not seek Him abroad, who had graciously condescended to "come under his roof" and manifest Himself unto him.

. . . .

I observe, then, this: that the public notes of the Church, which are the common property of all men, are rather a sign to unbelievers than to the faithful, and to the world than to Christians; and a sign to members of the Church in proportion as they are without, and till they gain those truer and more precious tokens, to which the external notes lead, and by which they are practically superseded. . . [It is] their very gift, as Christians, to know the Lord, personally, individually, inwardly; and hence the Apostle says, "I know *whom* I have believed, and am persuaded that He is able to keep that which I have committed unto Him against that day."

O.S., 325-28, 330.

8

Religious men have, in their own religiousness, an evidence of the truth of their religion. That religion is true which has power, and so far as it has power; nothing but what is divine can renew the heart. And this is the secret reason *why* religious men believe, whether they are adequately conscious of it or no, whether they can put it into words or no; viz. their past experience that the doctrine which they hold is a reality in their minds, not a mere opinion, and has come to them, "not in word, but in power." And in this sense the presence of religion in us is its own evidence. I am not at all denying the use of either of those arguments for religion which are external to us . . . . but still so it is, we go by external reasons, before we have, or so far as we have not, inward ones; and we rest upon our logical proofs only when we get perplexed with objections, or are in doubt, or otherwise troubled in mind. . . . . .

Would you know why holy men believe even in an age of miracles? Hear St. Polycarp's words, when the heathen magistrate urged him to blaspheme Christ: "Eighty and six years," said he, "have I served Him, and *He hath never wronged me;* and

132

how can I blaspheme my King, who hath saved me?" Or, as St. Paul said, "I know whom I have believed." It is these inward effects (I speak of the matter of fact), according to the degree in which they are realized, which guarantee to a man the divinity of his form of religion, which make him willing to risk his salvation upon it; as is expressed, in another form, by the Samaritans in the text, when they say to their countrywoman, 'Now we believe, not because of thy saying, for we have heard Him ourselves, and know that this is indeed the Christ, the Saviour of the world."

You will observe that neither the blessed Martyr, who had served Christ so long, nor the ignorant Samaritans, who were beginning to acknowledge Him, stated *what* their reasons were, though they had reasons. And, in truth, it is very difficult to draw out our reasons for our religious convictions, and that on many accounts. It is very painful to a man of devout mind to do so; for it implies, or even involves, a steadfast and almost curious gaze at God's wonder-working presence within and over him, from which he shrinks, as savouring of a high-minded and critical temper. And much more is it painful, not to say impossible, to put these reasons forth in explicit statements, because they are so very personal and private. Yet, as in order to the relief of his own perplexity, a religious man may at times try to ascertain them, so again for the service of others he will try, as best he may, to state them.

O.S., 346-8.

9

I suppose a religious man is conscious that God has been with him, and given him whatever he has of good within him. He knows quite enough of himself to know how fallen he is from original righteousness, and he has a conviction, which nothing can shake, that without the aid of his Lord and Saviour, he can do nothing aright. I do not say he need recollect any definite season when he turned to God and gave up the service of sin and Satan; but in one sense every season, every year is such a time of turning. I mean, he ever has experience, just as if he had hitherto been living to the world, of a continual conversion; he is ever taking advantage of holy seasons and new providences, and beginning again. The elements of sin are still alive within him; they still tempt and influence him, and threaten when they do no more; and it is only by a continual fight against them that he prevails; and what shall persuade him that his power to fight is his own, and not from above? And this conviction of a Divine Presence with him is stronger according to the length of time during which he has served God, and to his advance in holiness. The multitude of men—nay, a great number of those who think themselves religous—do not aim at holiness, and do not advance in holiness; but consider what a great evidence it is that God is with us, so far as we have it. Religious men, really such, cannot but recollect in the course of years, that they have become very different from what they were. I say "in the course of years": this it is, among other things, which makes young persons less settled in their religion. They have not given it a trial; they have not had time to do so; but in the course of years a religious person finds that a mysterious unseen influence has been upon him and has changed him. He is indeed very different from what he was. His tastes, his views, his judgments are different. You will say that time changes a man as a matter of course; advancing age, outward circumstances, trials, experience of life. It is true; and yet I think a religious man would feel it little less than sacrilege, and almost blasphemy, to impute the improvement in his heart and conduct, in his moral being, with which he has been favoured in a certain sufficient period, to outward or merely natural causes. He will be unable to force himself to do so: that is to say, he has a conviction, which it is a point of religion with him not to doubt, which it is a sin to deny, that God has been with him . . . . that God is present with him to an extent, with a fulness, in a depth, which he knows not.

S.D., 343-5-6.

10

Is it not undeniable that the very life of personal religion among Catholics lies in a knowledge of the Gospels? It is the character and conduct of our Lord, His words, His deeds, His sufferings, His work, which are the very food of our devotion and rule of our life.. . . . "The life that I now live in the flesh, I live in the faith of the Son of God, who loved me, and delivered Himself for me." As the Psalms have ever been the manual of our prayer, so have the Gospels been the subject-matter of our meditation. In these latter times especially, since St. Ignatius, they have been divided into portions, and arranged in a scientific order, not unlike that which the Psalms have received in the Breviary. To contemplate our Lord in His person and his History, is with us the exercise of every retreat and the devotion of every morning.

D.A., 387.

11

To be *spiritually-minded* is to see by faith all those good and holy beings who actually surround us, though we see them not with our bodily eyes; to see them by faith as vividly as we see the things of earth—the green country, the blue sky, and the brilliant sunshine. Hence it is that, when saintly souls are favoured with heavenly visions, these visions are but the extraordinary continuations and the crown, by a divine intuition, of objects which, by the ordinary operation of grace, are ever before their minds.

M.D., 78.

12

Make me like Thyself O my God, since in spite of myself, such Thou canst make me. . . . Thou hast shown it to be possible in the face of the whole world by the most overwhelming proof, by taking our created nature on Thyself and exalting it to Thee. Let me have in my own person what in Jesus Thou has given to my nature. Let me be partaker of that Divine Nature in all the riches of Its attributes, which in fulness of substance and in personal presence became the Son of Mary. . . Enter my heart substantially and personally . . . filling it with Thee. Thou alone canst fill the soul of man, and Thou hast promised to do so.

M.D., 596, 597, 599.

135

13

Mary is our pattern of Faith, both in the reception and in the study of Divine Truth. She does not think it enough to accept, she dwells upon it; not enough to possess, she uses it; not enough to assent, she develops it; not enough to submit the Reason, she reasons upon it; not indeed reasoning first, and believing afterwards, with Zacharius, yet first believing without reasoning, next from love and reverence, reasoning after believing.*

U.S., 313.

14

When the Divine Voice quickens us from the dust in which we lie, it is to call us to a dignity higher even than that which was ours in the beginnng; but it restores us by degrees. At first, we emerge from the state of slaves into that of children and of children only, and not yet men. We are exercised by faith; it is our education. And in like manner children are exercised at school; they are taught the rudiments of knowledge upon faith; they do not begin with philosophy. But, as in the natural order, we mount up to philosophical largeness of mind from lessons learned by rote and the schoolmaster's rod, so, too, in the order supernatural, even in this life, and far more truly in the life to come, we pass on from faith and penance to contemplation. Such is the loving-kindness of the Everlasting Father, "suscitans a terra inopem, et de stercore erigens pauperem." To those who have begun with faith, He adds, in course of time, a higher gift, the gift of Wisdom, which, not superseding, but presupposing, Faith, gives us so broad and deep a view of things revealed, that their very consistency is evidence of their Author, and like the visible world, persuades us to adore His Majesty. . . .

"I will not call you servants," He says, "for the servant knoweth not what his Lord doth; but I have called you friends, because all things, whatsoever I have heard from my Father, I have made known to you."

Idea, 184-186.

* "But Mary kept all these things, and pondered them in her heart."— Luke ii, 19.

Religion has its own enlargement, and an enlargement, not of tumult, but of peace. It is often remarked of uneducated persons, who have hitherto thought little of the unseen world, that, on their turning to God, looking into themselves, regulating their hearts, reforming their conduct, and meditating on death and judgment, heaven and hell, they seem to become, in point of intellect, different beings from what they were. Before, they took things as they came, and thought no more of one thing than another. But now every event has a meaning; they have their own estimate of whatever happens to them; they are mindful of times and seasons, compare the present with the past; and the world no longer dull, monotonous, unprofitable, and hopeless, is a various complicated drama, with parts and an object and an awful moral. . . .

[Such an] enlargement consists, not merely in the passive reception into the mind of a number of ideas hitherto unknown to it, but in the mind's energetic and simultaneous action upon and towards and among these new ideas, which are rushing in upon it. It is the action of a formative power, reducing to order and meaning the matter of our acquirements; it is a making the objects of our knowledge subjectively our own, or, to use a familiar word, it is a digestion of what we receive into the substance of our previous state of thought; and without this no enlargement is said to follow. There is no enlargement unless there be a comparison of ideas one with another, as they come before the mind, and a systematizing of them. We feel our minds to be growing and expanding *then*, when we not only learn, but refer what we learn to what we know already. It is not the mere addition to our knowledge, which is illumination; but the locomotion, the movement onwards, of that moral centre, to which both what we know, and what we are learning, the accumulating mass of our acquirements, gravitate. And therefore a truly great intellect, and recognised to be such by the common opinion of mankind . . . . is one which takes a connected view of old and new, past and present, far and near, and which has an insight into the influence of all these one on another; without which there is no whole, and no centre. It possesses the knowledge, not only of things, but also of their mutual and true relations; knowledge, not merely considered as acquirement, but as philosophy.

Idea, 133-4.

16

Just as our bodily organs, when mentioned, recall their function in the body, as the word "creation" suggests the Creator, and "subjects" a sovereign, so in the mind of the Philosopher, as we are abstractedly conceiving of him, the elements of the physical and moral world, sciences, arts, pursuits, ranks, offices, events, opinions, individualities, are all viewed as one, with correlative functions, and as gradually by successive combinations converging, one and all, to the true centre.

To have even a portion of this illuminative reason and true philosophy is the highest state to which nature can aspire, in the way of intellect; it puts the mind above the influences of chance and necessity, above anxiety, suspense, unsettlement, and superstition which are the lot of the many. Men, whose minds are possessed with some one object, take exaggerated views of its importance, are feverish in the pursuit of it, make it the measure of things which are utterly foreign to it, and are startled and despond if it happens to fail them. They are ever in alarm or in transport. Those on the other hand who have no object or principle whatever to hold by, lose their way every step they take. They are thrown out, and do not know what to think or say, at every fresh juncture; they have no view of persons, or occurrences, or facts, which come suddenly upon them, and they rely upon the opinion of others for want of internal resources. But the intellect which has been disciplined to the perfection of its powers, which knows, and thinks while it knows, which has learned to leaven the dense mass of facts and events with the elastic force of reason,—such an intellect cannot be partial, cannot be exclusive, cannot be impetuous, cannot be at a loss, cannot but be patient, collected, and majestically calm, because it discerns the end in every beginning, the origin in every end, the law in every interruption, the limit in each delay; because it ever knows where it stands, and how its path lies from one point to another. . . . It is almost prophetic from its knowledge of history; it is almost heart-searching from its knowledge of human nature; it has almost supernatural charity from its freedom from littleness and prejudice; it has almost the repose of faith, because nothing can startle it; it has almost the beauty and harmony of heavenly contemplation, so intimate is it with the eternal order of things and the music of the spheres.

Idea, 137-39.

17

Wisdom is the clear, calm, accurate vision and comprehension of the whole course, the whole work of God; and though there is none who has it in its fulness but He who "searcheth all things, yea, the deep things of" the Creator, yet "by that Spirit" they are, in a measure, "revealed unto us." And thus, according to that measure, is the text fulfilled, that "he that is spiritual judgeth all things, yet he himself is judged by no man." Others understand him not, master not his ideas, fail to combine, harmonize, or make consistent, those distinct views and principles which come to him from the Infinite Light, and are inspirations of the breath of God. He, on the contrary, compasses others, and locates them, and anticipates their acts, and fathoms their thoughts, for, in the Apostle's language, he "hath the mind of Christ," and all things are his, "whether Paul, or Apollos, or Cephas, or the world or life, or death, or things present, or things to come." Such is the marvellousness of the Pentecostal gift, whereby we "have an unction from the Holy One, and know all things."

U.S., 293.

18

Such are the two gifts which will be found to lie at the beginning and at the end of our new life, both intellectual in their nature, and both divinely imparted; Faith being an exercise of the Reason, so spontaneous, unconscious, and unargumentative, as to seem at first sight even to be a moral act, and Wisdom

139

being that orderly and mature development of thought, which in earthly language goes by the name of science and philosophy.

U.S., 279.

III.   FAITH, NOT YET SIGHT

19

Again, the various terms and figures which are used in the doctrine of the Holy Trinity or of the Incarnation, surely may by their combination create ideas which will be altogether new, though they are still of an earthly character. And further, when it is said that such figures convey no knowledge of the Divine Nature itself, beyond those figures, whatever they are, it should be considered whether our senses can be proved to suggest any real idea of matter. All that we know, strictly speaking, is the existence of the impressions our senses make on us; and yet we scruple not to speak as if they conveyed to us the knowledge of material substances. Let, then, the Catholic dogmas, as such, be freely admitted to convey no true idea of Almighty God, but only an earthly one, gained from earthly figures, provided it be allowed, on the other hand, that the senses do not convey to us any true idea of matter, but only an idea commensurate with sensible impressions.

Nor is there any reason why this should not be fully granted. Still there may be a certain correspondence between the idea, though earthly, and its heavenly archetype, such, that that idea belongs to the archetype, in a sense in which no other earthly idea belongs to it, as being the nearest approach to it which our present state allows. Indeed Scripture itself intimates the earthly nature of our present ideas of Sacred Objects, when it speaks of our now "seeing in a glass *darkly*, ἐν αἰνίγματι, but then face to face"; and it has ever been the doctrine of divines that the Beatific Vision, or true sight of Almighty God, is reserved for the world to come. Meanwhile we are allowed such an approximation to the truth as earthly images and figures may supply us.

U.S., 339-40.

20

It is as strange that, after an eternal rest, He should begin to create, as that, when He once created, He should take on Himself a created nature; it is as strange that man should be allowed to fall so low, as we see before our eyes in so many dreadful instances as that Angels and Saints should be exalted even to religious honours; it is as strange that such large families in the animal world should be created without souls and subject to vanity as that one creature, the Blessed Mother of God, should be exalted over all the rest; as strange that the book of nature should sometimes seem to vary from the rule of conscience or the conclusions of reason as that the Church's Scriptures should admit of being interpreted in opposition to her Tradition. And if it shocks a religious mind to doubt of the being of the All-wise and All-good God on the ground of the mysteries in Nature, why may it not shrink also from using the revealed mysteries as an argument against Revelation? . . .

If God exists in spite of the difficulties attending the doctrine, so the Church may be of divine origin, though that truth also has its difficulties;—nay, I might even say, the Church is divine, *because* of those difficulties; for the difficulties which exist in the doctrine that there is a Divine Being, do but give countenance and protection to parallel difficulties in the doctrine that there is a Catholic Church. If there be mysteriousness in her teaching, this does but show that she proceeds from Him, who is Himself Mystery, in the most simple and elementary ideas which we have of Him, whom we cannot contemplate at all except as One who is absolutely greater than our reason, and utterly strange to our imagination.

Mix., 264, 275-6.

. . . . That internal concentration of His Attributes in self-contemplation, which took place on the seventh day, when He rested from all the work which He had made . . . since this everlasting and unchangeable quiescence is the simplest and truest notion we can form of the Deity, it seems to follow that, strictly speaking, all those so-called Economies or dispensations, which display His character in action, are but condescensions to the infirmity and peculiarity of our minds, shadowy representations of realities which are incomprehensible to creatures such as ourselves. . . [*Ari.*]

I understood these passages* to mean that the exterior world, physical and historical, was but the manifestation to our senses of realities greater than itself. Nature was a parable; Scripture was an allegory; pagan literature, philosophy, and mythology, properly understood, were but a preparation for the Gospel. The Greek poets and sages were in a certain sense prophets; for "thoughts beyond their thoughts to those high bards were given." There had been a directly divine dispensation granted to the Jews; but there had been in some sense a dispensation carried on in favour of the Gentiles. He who had taken the seed of Jacob for his elect people had not, therefore, cast the rest of mankind out of His sight. In the fulness of time both Judaism and Paganism had come to nought; the outward framework, which concealed yet suggested the Living Truth, had never been intended to last, and it was dissolving under the beams of the Sun of Justice which shone behind it and through it. The process of change had been slow; it had been done not rashly, but by rule and measure, "at sundry times and in divers measures," first one disclosure and then another, till the whole evangelical doctrine was brought into full manifestation. And thus room was made for the anticipation of further and deeper disclosures of truth, still under the veil of the letter, and in their season to be revealed. The visible world still remains without its divine interpretation. Holy Church in her sacraments and her hierarchial appointments, will remain, even to the end of the world, after all but a symbol of those heavenly facts which fill eternity. Her mysteries are but the expressions in human language of truths to which the human mind is unequal. . . [*Apo.*]

Whatever is told us from heaven, is true in so full and substantial a sense, that no possible mistake can arise practically from

* He is referring to his reading of Clement of Alexandria and Origen before 1833.

following it. And it may be added, on the other hand, that the greatest risk will result from attempting to be wiser than God has made us, and to outstep in the least degree the circle which is prescribed as the limit of our range. This is but the duty of implicit faith in Him who knows what is good for us, and who has ordained that in our practical concerns intellectual ability should do no more than enlighten us in the difficulties of our situation, not in the solution of them. [*Ari.*]

Ari., 75-6; *Apo.*, 26-7.

22

On the other hand, it must be recollected that not even the Catholic reasonings and conclusions, as contained in Confessions, and most thoroughly received by us, are worthy of the Divine Verities which they represent, but are the truth only in as full a measure as our minds can admit it; the truth as far as they go, and under the conditions of thought which human feebleness imposes. It is true that God is without beginning, if eternity may worthily be considered to imply succession; in every place, if He who is a Spirit can have relations with space. It is right to speak of His Being and Attributes, if He be not rather super-essential; it is true to say that He is wise or powerful, if we may consider Him as other than the most simple Unity. He is truly Three, if He is truly One; He is truly One, if the idea of Him falls under earthly number. He has a triple Personality, in the sense in which the Infinite can be understood to have Personality at all. If we know anything of Him,—if we may speak of Him in any way,— if we may emerge from Atheism or Pantheism into religious faith,—if we would have any saving hope, any life of truth and holiness within us,—this only do we know, with this only confession, we must begin and end our worship—that the Father is the One God, the Son the One God, and the Holy Ghost the One God; and that the Father is not the Son, the Son not the Holy Ghost, and the Holy Ghost not the Father.

U.S., 350-51.

143

VIII: THE WORLD OF FAITH

ANALYTICAL SUMMARY

So at last the true wisdom of faith in the full grown man sees in its unity the glorious picture of Christianity as the restitution of all things lost by the fall;

the whole of Christianity nothing but the One Christ.

Christ as the crucified Redeemer living on in the Church, the dispenser of the graces of redemption;

the redeeming death of Christ daily renewed in the Church's Eucharistic Sacrifice "one and the same victim" (Trent. Sess. 22, cap. 2).

Christ Himself the One sacrificing and administering High Priest in His priests as his representatives;

Christ Himself the gift of redemption, not through a merely external imputation of His righteousness, but through the inner reality of His divine inhabitation. "Participation of the Divine Nature";

Christ therefore the One Life of His Church, which is Christianity: *He the Head, we the members growing in Him to His Maturity, "The fullness of Him who filleth all in all."*

(Nos. 1-14.)

But in the One Christ—"Head and Body one Christ"—God revealed in the greatness of His Infinity as "Strength in weakness, God in flesh, Life in death."

(Nos. 15-18.)

And the one God shining in "the countenance of Jesus Christ, whose body is the Church" now known as the undreamed-of fulfilment of that presentiment of His Majesty which the voice of conscience awoke at the entrance of the path whose conclusion has now been reached;

(Nos. 19-20.)

restored Unity in the One God.

Beginning and End of the path meet in Him who is "Alpha and Omega," "the First and the Last."

I CHRISTIANITY IS CHRIST

I

NATURAL RELIGION is based upon the sense of sin; it recognises the disease, but it cannot find, it does but look out for the remedy. That remedy, both for guilt and for moral impotence, is found in the central doctrine of Revelation, the Mediation of Christ. . .

Thus it is that Christianity is the fulfilment of the promise made to Abraham, and of the Mosaic revelations; this is how it has been able from the first to occupy the world and gain a hold on every class of human society to which its preachers reached; this is why the Roman power and the multitude of religions which it embraced could not stand against it; this is the secret of its sustained energy, and its never-flagging martyrdoms; this is how at present it is so mysteriously potent, in spite of the new and fearful adversaries which beset its path. It has with it that gift of staunching and healing the one deep wound of human nature, which avails more for its success than a full encyclopædia of scientific knowledge and a whole library of controversy, and therefore it must last while human nature lasts. It is a living truth which never can grow old.

Some persons speak of it as if it were a thing of history, with only indirect bearings upon modern times; I cannot allow that it is a mere historical religion. Certainly it has its foundations in past and glorious memories, but its power is in the present. It is no dreary matter of antiquarianism; we do not contemplate it in conclusions drawn from dumb documents and dead events, but by faith exercised in ever-living objects, and by the appropriation and use of ever-recurring gifts.

Our communion with it is in the unseen, not in the obsolete. At this very day its rites and ordinances are continually eliciting the active interposition of that Omnipotence in which the Reli-

147

gion long ago began. First and above all is the Holy Mass, in which He who once died for us upon the Cross brings back and perpetuates, by His literal presence in it, that one and the same sacrifice which cannot be repeated. Next, there is the actual entrance of Himself, soul and body, and divinity, into the soul and body of every worshipper who comes to Him for the gift, a privilege more intimate than if we lived with Him during His long-past sojourn upon earth. And then, moreover, there is His personal abidance in our churches, raising earthly service into a foretaste of heaven. . . .

He has given us Saints and Angels for our protection. He has taught us how by our prayers and services to benefit our departed friends, and to keep up a memorial of ourselves when we are gone. He has created a visible hierarchy and a succession of sacraments to be the channels of His mercies, and the Crucifix secures the thought of Him in every house and chamber. In all these ways He brings Himself before us. I am not here speaking of His gifts as gifts, but as memorials; not as what Christians know they convey, but in their visible character; and I say, that, as human nature itself is still in life and action as much as ever it was, so He too lives, to our imaginations, by His visible symbols, as if He were on earth, with a practical efficacy which even unbelievers cannot deny, so as to be the corrective of that nature, and its strength day by day,—and that this power of perpetuating His Image, being altogether singular and special, and the prerogative of Him and Him alone, is a grand evidence how well He fulfils to this day that Sovereign Mission which, from the first beginning of the world's history, has been in prophecy assigned to Him.

G.A., 487-89.

2

Christ who promised to make all His disciples one in God with Him, who promised that we should be in God and God in us, has made us so. . . . It would seem . . . . that He has done so by ascending to the Father; that His ascent bodily is His descent spiritually; that His taking our nature up to God, is the descent of God into us. . . Thus . . . our life is hid with Him in God . . . we ascend into Him, he descends into us; we are in Him, He in us; Christ being the one Mediator, the way, the truth, and the life, joining earth with heaven . . .

"Touch me not," He says to St. Mary Magdalen, "I am not yet ascended to my Father. . . *Why* might not our Lord be touched *before* His ascension, and how *could* He be touched *after* it? But Christ speaks, it would seem, thus (if, as before, we might venture to paraphrase His sacred words)—"Hitherto you have only known Me after the flesh. I have lived among you as a man. You have been permitted to approach Me sensibly, to kiss and embrace My feet, to pour ointment upon My head. But all this is at an end, now that I have died and risen again in the power of the Spirit. A glorified state of existence is begun in Me, and will soon be perfected. At present, though I bid you at one moment handle Me as possessed of flesh and bones, I vanish like a spirit at another; though I let one follower embrace My feet, and say, 'Fear not,' I repel another with the words, 'Touch Me not.' Touch Me not, for I am fast passing for your great benefit from earth to heaven, from flesh and blood into glory, from a natural body to a spiritual body. When I am ascended, then the change will be completed. To pass hence to the Father in My bodily presence, is to descend from the Father to you in spirit. When I am thus changed, when I am thus present to you, more really present than now, though invisibly, then you may touch Me,—may touch Me, more really though invisibly, by faith, in reverence, through such outward approaches as I shall assign. Now you but see Me from time to time; when you see most of Me I am at best but 'going in and out among you.' Thou hast seen Me, Mary, but couldst not hold Me; thou hast approached Me, but only to embrace My feet, or to be touched by My hand; and thou sayest, 'O that I knew where I might find Him, that I might come even to His seat! O that I might hold Him and not let Him go!' Henceforth this shall be; when I am ascended, thou shalt see nothing, thou shalt have everything. Thou shalt 'sit down under My shadow with great delight, and My fruit shall be sweet to thy taste.' Thou shalt have Me whole and entire. I will be near thee, I will be in thee; I will come into thy heart a whole Saviour, a whole Christ,—in all My fulness as God and man,—in the awful virtue of that Body and Blood, which has been taken into the Divine Person of the Word, and is indivisible from it, and has atoned for the sins of the world,—not by external contact, not by partial possession, not by momentary approaches, not by a barren manifestation, but inward in presence, and intimate in fruition, a principle of life and a seed of immortality, that thou mayest 'bring forth fruit unto God.' "

Jfc., 216-17, 218-19.

3

Though Christ now sits on the right hand of God, He has, in one sense, never left the world since He first entered it. . . . Even when visibly on earth He, the Son of Man, was still "in heaven"; and now, though He is ascended on high, He is still on earth. . . . Time and space have no portion in the spiritual Kingdom which He has founded; and the rites of His Church are as mysterious spells by which He annuls them both. . . Christ shines through them, as through transparent bodies, without impediment. He is the Light and Life of the Church, acting through it, dispensing of His fulness, knitting and compacting together every part of it; and these its Mysteries are not mere outward signs, but (as it were) effluences of His grace developing themselves in external forms, as Angels might do when they appeared to men. . . . Once for all He hung upon the cross, and blood and water issued from His pierced side, but by the Spirit's ministration, the blood and water are ever flowing, as though His cross were really set up among us. . . .

To view Christ as all but visibly revealed—to look upon His ordinances, not in themselves, but as signs of His presence and power, as the accents of His love, the very form and countenance of Him who ever beholds us, ever cherishes us—to see Him thus revealed in glory day by day—is not this to those who believe it an unspeakable privilege? Is it not so great that a man might well wish it true from the excellence of it, and count them happy who are able to receive it? And when this is all plainly revealed in Scripture, when we are expressly told that Christ washes us by Water to change us into a glorious Church, that the consecrated bread is His flesh, that He is present with His ministers, and is in the midst of His Church, why should we draw back like Thomas doubting of our Lord's resurrection? "Blessed are they that have not seen and yet have believed!"

P.S., iii, 277-8, 285.

4

Christ is the only Ruler and Priest in His Church, dispensing gifts, and has appointed none to supersede Him, because He is departed only for a brief season. Aaron took the place of Christ, and had a priesthood of His own; but Christ's priests have no priesthood but His. They are merely His shadows and organs, they are His outward signs; and what they do, He does; when they baptize, He is baptizing; when they bless, He is blessing. He is in all acts of His Church, and one of its acts is not more truly His act than another, for all are His. Thus we are, in all times of the Gospel, brought close to His Cross. We stand, as it were, under it, and receive its blessings fresh from it; only that since, historically speaking, time has gone on, and the Holy One is away, certain outward forms are necessary, by way of bringing us again under His shadow; and we enjoy those blessings through a mystery, or sacramentally, in order to enjoy them really. All this witnesses to the duty both of remembering and of looking out for Christ, teaching us to neglect the present, to rely on no plans, to form no expectations, for the future, but so to live in faith, as if He had not left us, so in hope, as if He had returned to us. We must try to live as if the Apostles were living, and we must try to muse upon our Lord's life in the Gospels, not as a history, but as if a recollection.

P.S., vi, 242-43

5

The Mass is not a mere form of words,—it is a great action, the greatest action that can be on earth. It is not the invocation merely, but, if I dare use the word, the evocation of the Eternal

151

He becomes present on the altar in flesh and blood, before whom Angels bow and devils tremble. This is that awful event which is the scope, and is the interpretation, of every part of the solemnity. Words are necessary, but as means, not as ends; they are not mere addresses to the throne of grace, they are instruments of what is far higher, of consecration, of sacrifice. They hurry on as if impatient to fulfil their mission. Quickly they go, the whole is quick; for they are all parts of one integral action. Quickly they go; for they are awful words of sacrifice, they are a work too great to delay upon; as when it was said in the beginning: "What thou doest do quickly." Quickly they pass; for the Lord Jesus goes with them, as He passed along the lake in the days of His flesh, quickly calling first one and then another. Quickly they pass; because as the lightning which shineth from one part of heaven unto the other, so is the coming of the Son of Man. Quickly they pass; for they are the words of Moses, when the Lord came down in the cloud, calling on the Name of the Lord, as He passed by, "the Lord, the Lord God, merciful and gracious, long-suffering, and abundant in goodness and truth." And as Moses on the mountain, so we, too, make haste and "bow our heads to the earth and adore." So we all around, each in his place, look out for the great Advent, "waiting for the movement of the water." Each in his place, with his own heart, with his own wants, with his own thoughts, his own intention, with his own prayers, separate but concordant, watching what is going on, watching its progress, uniting in its consummation;—not painfully and hopelessly following a hard form of prayer from beginning to end, but, like a concert of musical instruments, each different but concurring in a sweet harmony, we take our part with God's priest, supporting him, yet guided by him. There are little children there, and old men, and simple labourers and students in seminaries, priests preparing for Mass, priests making their thanksgiving; there are innocent maidens, and there are penitent sinners; but out of these many minds rises one eucharistic hymn, and the great Action is the measure and scope of it.

L.G., 327-29.

6

Because the Brazen Serpent in the wilderness healed by being looked at, men consider that Christ's Sacrifice saves by the mind's contemplating it. This is what they call casting themselves upon Christ,—coming before Him simply and without self-trust, and being saved by faith. Surely we ought so to *come* to Christ; surely we must believe; surely we must look; but the question is, in what form and manner He *gives* Himself to us; and it will be found that, when He enters into us, glorious as He is Himself, pain and self-denial are His attendants. Gazing on the Brazen Serpent did not heal; but God's invisible communication of the gift of health to those who gazed. So also justification is wholly the work of God; it comes from God to us; it is a power exerted on our souls by Him, as the healing of the Israelites was a power exerted on their bodies. The gift must be brought *near* to us; it is not like the Brazen Serpent, a mere external, material, local sign; it is a spiritual gift, and, as being such, admits of being applied to us individually. Christ's Cross does not justify by being looked at, but by being applied; not by as merely beheld by faith, but by being actually set up within us, and that not by our act, but by God's invisible grace. . . . The Cross must be brought home to us, not in word, but in power, and this is the work of the Spirit. . . .

As, then, the Cross, in which St. Paul gloried, was not the *material* cross on which Christ suffered,—so neither is it simply the Sacrifice on the cross, but it is that Sacrifice coming in power to him who has faith in it, and converting body and soul into a sacrifice. It is the Cross, realized, present, living in him, sealing him, separating him from the world, sanctifying him, afflicting him. Thus the great Apostle clasped it to his heart, though it pierced it through like a sword; held it fast in his hands, though it cut them; reared it aloft, preached it, exulted in it.

Jfc., 174-75, 178.

7

Christ Himself vouchsafes to repeat in each of us in figure and mystery all that He did and suffered in the flesh. He is formed

153

in us, born in us, suffers in us, rises again in us, lives in us; and this not by a succession of events, but all at once: for He comes to us as a Spirit, all dying, all rising again, all living. We are ever receiving our birth, our justification, our renewal, ever dying to sin, ever rising to righteousness. His whole economy in all its parts is ever in us all at once; and this divine presence constitutes the title of each of us to heaven; this is what He will acknowledge and accept at the last day. He will acknowledge Himself,—His image in us,—as though we reflected Him, and He, on looking round about, discerned at once who were His; those, namely, who gave back to Him His image.

P.S., v, 139-40.

8

Christ, who is the Well-beloved, All-powerful Son of God, is possessed by every Christian as a Saviour in the full meaning of that title, or becomes to us righteousness; and in and after so becoming, really communicates a measure, and a continually increasing measure, of what He is Himself. In the words of the Apostle, "We are *complete* in Him," and again, of the Evangelist, "Of His fulness have all we *received,* and *grace for grace.*" He makes us gradually and eventually to be in our own persons, what He has been from eternity in Himself, what He is from our Baptism towards us, righteous. . . . "As by one man's disobedience many were made sinners, so by the obedience of One shall many be made righteous". . . . By Christ's righteousness we are made righteous; made, not accounted merely. . . .

He is the Well-beloved Son, in whom the Father is well pleased, as being "the Brightness of His glory, and the express Image of His Person," "the unspotted Mirror of the power of God, and the Image of His goodness." Nothing can He absolutely delight in, but what is like Himself; hence he is said to "put no trust even in His servants, and to charge His Angels with folly." None but the Eternal Son, who is incommunicably like the Father, can be infinitely acceptable to Him or simply righteous. Yet in proportion as rational beings are like the Son, or partake of His excellence, so are they really righteous; in proportion as God sees His Son in them, He is well pleased with them.

Jfc., 104, 107.

9

Is justification *remission of sins?* the Gift of the Spirit conveys it, as is evident from the Scripture doctrine about Baptism: "One Baptism for the remission of sins." Is justification *adoption* into the family of God? in like manner the Spirit is expressly called the Spirit of adoption, "the Spirit whereby we cry, Abba, Father." Is justification *reconciliation* with God? St. Paul says, "Jesus Christ is in you, unless ye be reprobates." Is justification *life?* the same Apostle says, "Christ liveth in me." Is justification given to *faith?* it is his prayer "that *Christ* may dwell in" Christian "hearts by faith." Does justification lead to holy *obedience?* Our Lord assures us that "he that abideth in Him and He in him, the same bringeth forth much fruit." Is it through justification that we rejoice *in hope of the glory* of God? In like manner "Christ in us" is said to be "the hope of glory." Christ then is our Righteousness by dwelling in us by the Spirit: He justifies us by entering into us, He continues to justify us by remaining in us. *This* is really and truly our justification, not faith, not holiness, not (much less) a mere imputation; but through God's mercy, the very Presence of Christ.

Jfc., 149-50.

10

This is to be justified, to receive the Divine Presence within us, and be made a Temple of the Holy Ghost.

God is everywhere as absolutely and entirely as if He were nowhere else; and it seems to be essential to the existence of every creature, rational and irrational, good and evil, in heaven and hell, that in some sense or other He should be present with it and be its life. Thus we are told concerning mankind, that "in Him we live, and move, and have our being." And He who lives in all creatures on earth in order to their mortal life, lives in Christians in a more divine way in order to their life immortal;

155

and as we do not know how the creation exists and lives in Him as a Creator, and use words about it beyond our comprehension, so much more (were not comparison out of the question) are we ignorant of the mode or nature of that life of God in the soul, which is the wellspring of the Christian's sanctity, and the seed of everlasting happiness.

Jfc., 144-5.

11

This is what it is to be one of Christ's little ones. . . to be possessed by His presence as our life, our strength, our merit, our hope, our crown; to become in a wonderful way His members, the instruments, or visible form, or sacramental sign, of the One Invisible Ever-Present Son of God, mystically reiterating in each of us all the acts of His earthly life, His birth, consecration, fasting, temptation, conflicts, victories, sufferings, agony, passion, death, resurrection, and ascension;—He being all in all,—we, with as little power in ourselves, as little excellence or merit, as the water in Baptism, or the bread and wine in Holy Communion; yet strong in the Lord and in the power of His might.

P.S., *vi*, 3.

12

He left His Father's courts, He was manifested, He spake; and His voice went out into all lands. He has taken to Himself His great power and reigned; and, whereas an enemy is the god and tyrant of this world, as Adam made it, so, as far as He occupies it, does He restore it to His Father. Henceforth He is the one principle of life in all His servants, who are but His organs. The Jewish Church looked towards Him; the Christian speaks and acts from Him. What is prior to Him is dark, but all that comes after Him is illuminated. The Church, before His manifestation, offered to Him material elements "which perish with the using;" but now He has sent His Spirit to fill such elements with Himself, and to make them living and availing sacrifices to the Father. Figures have become means of grace, shadows are substances, types are Sacraments in Him. What

156

before were decent ordinances and pious observances, have now not only a meaning but a virtue. Water could but wash the Body in the way of nature; but now it acts towards the cleansing of the soul. "Wine which maketh glad the heart of man," and "bread which strengthens man's heart," nay, the "oil which maketh him a cheerful countenance," henceforth are more than means of animal life, and savour of Him. Hands raised in blessing, the accents of the voice of man, which before could but symbolize the yearnings of human nature, or avail for lower benefits, have now become the "unutterable intercessions" of the Spirit, and the touch, and the breath of the Incarnate Son. The Church has become His Body, her priests His delegates, her people His members.

This is what Christ has done by His coming; but observe, *while* He did all this for His Church, He claimed all He did *as* His own. Henceforth whatever is done is His doing, and it is called what it is. As He is the unseen Source, so must He be acknowledged as the Agent, the present Object of worship and thanksgiving in all that is done; and His instruments are not even so much as instruments, but only the outward lineaments of Him. All is superseded by Him, and transmuted into Him. Before He came there were many masters, but henceforth only One; before He came many Fathers, but He is the One Father of the coming age, as the Prophet styles Him; before He came, all to whom the word of God came were called gods, but He is the One God manifested in the flesh; before He came, there were many angelic appearances with the name of God on them, but now the great Angel of the Covenant is alone to be worshipped; before He came, there were many priests who had infirmity, offering sacrifices year by year continually, but now there is but One High Priest, "who is set on the right hand of the throne of the majesty in the heavens, a minister of the sanctuary, and of the true tabernacle, which the Lord pitched, and not man"; before, there were innumerable sacrifices of bulls and calves which could never perfect the worshippers, now One Immaculate Lamb who taketh away the sin of the world; before, there were judges, kings, and rulers of various ranks, but now there is but

157

One King of kings, and Lord of lords, in His kingdom. . . .There were mediators many, and prophets many, and atonements many. But now all is superseded by One, in whom all offices merge, who has absorbed into Himself all principality, power, might, and dominion, and every name that is named; who has put His holy and fearful Name upon all, who is in and through all things, and without whom nothing is good. He is the sole self-existing principle in the Christian Church, and everything else is but a portion or declaration of Him. Not that now, as then, we may not speak of prophets, and rulers, and priests, and sacrifices, and altars, and saints, and that in a far higher and more spiritual sense than before, but that they are not any of them such of themselves; it is not they, but the grace of God that is in them. There is under the Gospel but One proper Priest, Prophet, and King, Altar Sacrifice, and House of God.* Unity is its characteristic sacrament; all grace flows from One Head, and all life circulates in the members of One Body. . . . Far better surely than Solomon in all his glory, is that chosen generation, that royal priesthood, that holy nation, that peculiar people, whose life is hid with Christ in God, who live because He lives in them, who are blessed because He is blessed, who are the fragrance of His breath, the myrrh, aloes, and cassia from His garments; nay, are one spirit with Him as His dove, "His undefiled one," "His sister and spouse, coming up from the wilderness leaning upon her Beloved."

Jfc., 195-9.

13

From the day of Pentecost to this hour there has been in the Church but One Holy One, the King of kings, and Lord of lords Himself, who is in all believers, and through whom they are what they are; their separate persons being but as separate developments, vessels, instruments, and works of Him who is

*[It is true that there is but one Priest and one Sacrifice under the Gospel, but this is because the Priests of the Gospel are *one* with Christ, not because they are only *improperly* called Priests. "Christus et Sacerdotes sunt *unus Sacerdos.*"—*Catech. Roman.* ii, 84. "Profiteor in Missa offerri Deo verum, *proprium*, et propitiatorium sacrificium pro vivis et defunctis."—*Profess. Fid. Trident.*] Added by Newman in 1874.

invisible. . . . They are all the organs as if of one invisible, governing Soul, the hands, or the tongues, or the feet, or the eyes of one and the same directing Mind, the types, tokens, beginnings, and glimpses of the Eternal Son of God.

P.S., *iv*, 170-71.

14

Christ came . . . to gather together in one all the elements of good dispersed throughout the world, to make them His own, to illuminate them with Himself, to reform and refashion them into Himself. He came to make a new and better beginning of all things than Adam had been, and to be a fountain-head from which all good henceforth might flow. Hence it is said that "in the dispensation of the fulness of times" Almighty God "gathered together in one all things in Christ, both which are in heaven, and which are on earth." How He became a new commencement to things in heaven, we know not; nor know we adequately in what way He recapitulated or ordered anew things on earth. But this we know, that, the world being under the dominion of Satan, and truth and goodness in it being but as gems in the mine, or rather as metal in the ore, He came to elicit, to disengage, to combine, to purify, to perfect. And, further than this, He came to new-create,—to begin a new line, and construct a new kingdom on the earth: that what had as yet lain in sin, might become what it was at the first, and more than that. . . He took on Him our nature, that in God that nature might revive and be restored; that it might be new born, and, after being perfected on the Cross, might impart that which itself was, as an incorruptible seed, for the life of all who receive it in faith, till the end of time. Hence He is called in Scripture the Beginning of the Creation of God, the First-begotten of the dead, the First-fruits of the Resurrection.

Jfc., 193-4.

15

Christ came to make a new world. He came into the world to regenerate it in Himself, to make a new beginning, to be the beginning of the creation of God, to gather together in one, and recapitulate all things in Himself. The rays of His glory were scattered through the world; one state of life had some of them, another others. The world was like some fair mirror, broken in pieces, and giving back no one uniform image of its Maker. But He came to combine what was dissipated, to recast what was shattered in Himself. He began all excellence, and of His fulness have all we received.

S.D., 61.

II. GOD, THE INCOMPREHENSIBLE, MANIFESTED IN CHRIST

16

He is above us, my brethren, we feel He is; how little can we understand Him! We fall in even with men upon earth, whose ways are so different from our own, that we cannot understand them. . . we call them strange and incomprehensible; but what are they compared with the all-marvellousness of the Everlasting God? He alone indeed is incomprehensible, who has not only lived an eternity without beginning, but who has lived through a whole eternity by Himself, and has not wearied of the solitude. . . . He was from eternity ever in action, though ever at rest; ever surely in rest and peace profound and ineffable, yet with a living, present mind, self-possessed, and all-conscious, comprehending Himself and sustaining the comprehension. He rested ever, but He rested in Himself; His own resource, His own end, His own contemplation, His own blessedness.

Yet so it be in us; and if it is incomprehensible that He should have existed solitary through an eternity, is it not incomprehensible too, that He should have ever given up that solitariness, and have willed to surround Himself with creatures? Why was He not content to be as He had been? Why did He bring into existence those who could not add to His blessedness and were not secure of their own? Why did He give them that gift which we see they possess, of doing right or wrong as they please, and of working out their ruin as well as their salvation? Why did He create a world like that which is before our eyes, which at best so dimly shows forth His glory, and at worst is a scene of sin and sorrow? He might have made a far more excellent world than this; He might have excluded sin; but, oh, wonderful mystery, He has surrounded Himself with the cries of fallen souls, and has created and opened the great pit. He has willed, after an eternity of peace, to allow of everlasting anarchy, of pride, and blasphemy, and guilt and hatred of Himself, and the worm that dieth not. . .

He is everywhere on earth, and sees every crime committed, whether under the sun or in the gloom of night; He is even the sustaining power of those who sin; He is most close to every, the most polluted, soul; He is in the midst of the eternal prison; but . . . nothing touches Him, though He touches all things. The sun's rays penetrate into the most hideous recesses, yet keep their brightness and their perfection; and so the Almighty witnesses and suffers evil, yet is not touched or tried by the creature's wilfulness, pride, uncleanness, or unbelief. The lusts of earth and the blasphemies of hell neither sully His purity nor impair His majesty. . . . in persecution, or in triumph, or in peace, whether His enemies hold out or are routed, when the innocent sin, when the just are falling, when good Angels weep, when souls are hardened, He is one and the same. He is in His blessedness still, and not even the surface is ruffled of His everlasting rest. He neither hopes nor fears, nor desires, nor sorrows, nor repents. All around Him seems full of agitation and confusion, but in His eternal decrees and infallible foreknowledge there is nothing contingent, nothing uncertain, nothing which is not part of one vast plan, as fixed in its issue, and as unchangeable, as His own Essence. Such is the great God, so all-sufficient, so all-blessed, so separate from creatures, so inscrutable, so unapproachable. Who can see Him? who can fathom Him? who can move Him? who can change Him? who can even speak of Him? . . . You say that God and man never can be one, that man cannot bear the sight and touch of his Creator, nor the Creator condescend to the feebleness of the creature; but blush and be confounded to hear, oh, peevish, restless hearts, that He has come down from His high throne and humbled Himself to the creature, in order that the creature might be inspired and strengthened to rise to Him. . .

It became Him who is higher than the highest, to act as if even humility, if this dare be said, was in the number of His attributes, by taking Adam's nature upon Himself, and manifesting Himself to men and Angels in it. It became Him, of whom are all things, and who is in all things, not to create new natures, which had not been before, inconstant spirit and corruptible matter, without taking them to Himself and absorbing them into a personal union with God. . . . The manifold attributes of the Infinite are to be poured out before your eyes through material channels and the operations of a human soul, since He, whose contemplation did but trouble you in Nature, is coming to take you captive by a manifestation, which is both intelligible to you and a pledge that He loves you one by one, raise high your expectations, for surely they cannot suffer disappointment. . . . At fault when he speculated on the height of God, and now again at fault when he tries to sound the depth, man thinks that a royal glory is the note of His presence upon earth. Lift up your eyes and answer whether he has guessed aright. Oh, incomprehensible in eternity and in time! Solitary in heaven and solitary upon earth. . . . The Maker of man, the Wisdom of God, has come, not in strength, but in weakness. . . . Instead of wealth, He has come poor; instead of honour, He has come in ignominy; instead of blessedness, He has come to suffer . . . . Out of the infinitude of His greatness, He has defaced His own glory, and wounded and deformed His own beauty,—not indeed as it is in itself, for He is ever the same, transcendently perfect and unchangeable, but in the contemplation of His creatures,—by the unutterable condescension of His incarnation. . . . When in fact He has taken flesh for those, who might have been saved without it, though more suitably to His glorious majesty with it, and moreover has shed His whole blood in satisfaction, when a drop might have sufficed, shall we think such teaching strange and hard to receive, and not rather consider it consistent and merely consistent, with that great truth, which we all start with admitting, that He is infinite? . . . .

Oh, wayward man! discontented first that thy God is far from thee, discontented again when He has drawn near,—complaining first that He is high, complaining next that He is low!—unhumbled being, when wilt thou cease to make thyself thine own centre, and learn that God is infinite in all He does, infinite when He reigns in heaven, infinite when He serves on earth, exacting our homage in the midst of His Angels, and winning homage from us in the midst of sinners? Adorable He is in His eternal rest, adorable in the glory of His court, adorable in the beauty of His works, most adorable of all, most royal, most persuasive in His deformity. . . . Better for me that Thou shouldst come thus abject and dishonourable, than hadst Thou put on a body fair as Adam's when he came out of Thy Hand. . . . The gentle and tender expression of that Countenance is no new beauty, or created grace; it is but the manifestation, in a human form, of Attributes which have been from everlasting. Thou canst not change, O Jesus; and, as Thou art still Mystery, so wast Thou always Love. I cannot comprehend Thee more than I did, before I saw Thee on the Cross; but I have gained my lesson. I have before me the proof, that in spite of Thy awful nature, and the clouds and darkness which surround it, Thou canst think of me with a personal affection. Thou hast died that I might live. "Let us love God," says Thy Apostle, "because He first hath loved us." I can love Thee now from first to last, though from first to last I cannot understand Thee. As I adore Thee, O Lover of souls, in Thy humiliation, so will I admire Thee and embrace Thee in Thy infinite and everlasting power.

Mix., 288-92, 298, 299, 301, 302-4, 311, 315.

17

"His head and hairs are white like white wool, and as snow"— Thy hair is white, O Jesus, because Thou art the Ancient of Days, as the Prophet Daniel speaks. From everlasting to everlasting Thou art God. Thou didst come indeed to us as a little child—Thou didst hang upon the Cross at an age of life before as yet grey hairs come—but, O my dear Lord, there was always something mysterious about Thee, so that men were not quite sure of thy age. The Pharisees talked of Thee as near fifty. For Thou hadst lived millions upon millions of years, and Thy face as fully showed it. And even when Thou wast a child, Thy hair shone so bright that people said, "It is snow." O my Lord Thou art ever old, and ever young. Thou hast all perfection, and old age in Thee is ten thousand times more beautiful than the most beautiful youth. Thy white hair is an ornament, not a sign of decay. It is as dazzling as the sun, as white as the light, and as glorious as gold.

Jesus may I ever love Thee, not with human eyes, but with the eyes of the Spirit, which sees not as man sees.

M.D., 313-4.

18

Christianity, then, is at once a philosophy, a political power, and a religious rite: as a religion, it is Holy; as a philosophy, it is Apostolic; as a political power, it is imperial, that is, One and Catholic. As a religion, its special centre of action is pastor and flock; as a philosophy, the Schools; as a rule, the Papacy and its Curia.

Though it has exercised these three functions in substance from the first, they were developed in their full proportions one after another, in a succession of centuries; first, in the primitive time it was recognized as a worship, springing up and spreading in the lower ranks of society, and among the ignorant and dependent, and making its power felt by the heroism of its Martyrs and confessors. Then it seized upon the intellectual and cultivated class, and created a theology and schools of learning. Lastly it seated itself, as an ecclesiastical polity, among princes, and chose Rome for its centre.

Truth is the guiding principle of theology and theological inquiries; devotion and edification, of worship; and of government, expedience. The instrument of theology is reasoning; of worship, our emotional nature; of rule, command and coercion. Further, in man as he is, reasoning tends to rationalism; devotion to superstition and enthusiasm; and power to ambition and tyranny.

Arduous as are the duties involved in these three offices to discharge one by one, much more arduous are they to administer when taken in combination. Each of the three has its separate scope and direction; each has its own interests to promote and further; each has to find room for the claims of the other two; and each will find its own line of action influenced and modified by the others, nay, sometimes in a particular case the necessity of the others converted into a rule of duty for itself.

. . . .

To conclude:—whatever is great refuses to be reduced to human rule and to be made consistent in its many aspects with itself. Who shall reconcile with each other the various attributes of the Infinite God? and, as He is, such in their several degrees are His works. This living world to which we belong, how self-contradictory it is when we attempt to measure and master its meaning and scope! And how full of incongruities, that is, of mysteries, in its higher and finer specimens, is the soul of man, viewed in its assemblage of opinions, tastes, habits, powers, aims, and doings! We need not feel surprise then, if Holy Church too, the supernatural creation of God, is an instance of the same law, presenting to us an admirable consistency and unity in word and deed, as her general characteristic, but crossed and discredited now and then by apparent anomalies which need, and which claim, at our hands an exercise of faith.

V.M. i, xl, xli, xciv, xl, xli, xciv.

19

When we confess God as Omnipotent only, we have gained but a half-knowledge of Him: His is an Omnipotence which can at the same time swathe itself in infirmity and can become the captive of Its own creatures. He has, if I may so speak, the incomprehensible power of even making Himself weak. We must know Him by His Names, Emmanuel and Jesus, to know Him perfectly.

O.S., 87-88.

165

*Callista loq.** "I feel that God within my heart, I feel myself in His presence. He says to me 'Do this: don't do that.' You may tell me that this dictate is a mere law of my nature, as is to joy or to grieve. I cannot understand this. No, it is the echo of a person speaking to me. Nothing shall persuade me that it does not ultimately proceed from a person external to me. It carries with it its proof of its divine origin. My nature feels towards it as towards a person. When I obey it, I feel a satisfaction; when I disobey, a soreness—just like that which I feel in pleasing or offending some revered friend. So you see, Polemo, I believe in what is more than a mere 'something.' I believe in what is more real to me than sun, moon, stars, and the fair earth, and the voice of friends. You will say, Who is He? Has He ever told you anything about Himself. Alas! no!—the more's the pity! But I will not give up what I have, because I have not more. An echo implies a voice; a voice a speaker. That speaker I love and I fear. . . ."

"O that I could find Him. . . . On the right hand and on the left I grope, but touch Him not. Why dost Thou fight against me?—why dost Thou scare and perplex me, O First and Only Fair? I have Thee not, and I need Thee. . . ."

[*In prison, after the interview with Polemo, Callista reads the Gospel of St. Luke entrusted to her by St. Cyprian, here called Caeciluis.*]

[The Gospel] opened a view of a new state and community of beings, which only seemed too beautiful to be possible. But not into a new state of things alone, but into the presence of One who was simply distinct and removed from any thing that she had, in her most imaginative moments, ever depicted to her mind as ideal perfection. Here was that to which her intellect tended, though that intellect could not frame it. It could approve and acknowledge, when set before it, what it could not originate. Here was He who spake to her in her conscience; whose voice she heard, whose Person she was seeking for. . . .

*Polemo was the philosopher who was interviewing Callista in prison. She had previously asked him, "Do you believe in one God?" His answer was that he believed "in one eternal, self-existing something." (ED.)

[St. Cyprian and a deacon visit Callista in prison. The former has warned her of what she will have to endure if she turns Christian.]

"Give me my place at the feet of Jesus, Son of Mary, my God. I wish to love Him. I think I can love Him. Make me His." "He has loved you from eternity," said Cæcilius, "and, therefore, you are beginning to love Him." She covered her face with her hands, and remained in profound meditation. "I am very ignorant—very sinful," she said at length; "but one thing I know, that there is but One to love in the whole world, and I wish to love Him. I surrender myself to Him if He will take me; and He shall teach me about Himself."

Call., 314-5, 326, 346-7.

21

I am a Catholic by virtue of my believing in a God; and if I am asked why I believe in a God, I answer that it is because I believe in myself, for I feel it impossible to believe in my own existence (and of that fact I am quite sure) without believing also in the existence of Him, who lives as a Personal, All-seeing, All-judging Being in my conscience.

Apo., 198.

IX: THE GOD OF THE SOUL

ANALYTICAL SUMMARY

Our interior life is based on two facts: the fact of the creature elevated by grace, the fact of the pardoned sinner.

The fact of the creature elevated by grace renders an interior life an indescribable "through and with and in God;"

a life with and in Him the One-Reality, and the immutable Reality, compared with which every other reality is but a shadow imprint and image;

(Nos. 1-7.)

a life with and in Him who in most intimate presence is "the God of my life" who counts our heart-beats and listens to our thoughts: He, the friend;

(Nos. 8-11.)

a life with and in Him, who alone is the answer to our questioning, the plenitude which fills our emptiness, but an answer which fades into the divine incomprehensibility and a plenitude which knows no bounds;

(Nos. 12-15.)

a life with and in Him in such wise that we feel, see, do, and love all else in Him, and in all things feel, see, and love Him and act for Him alone in reverent service of the Divine Majesty.

(Nos. 16-19.)

169

I. THE ONE REALITY

I

INDEED, it is a very difficult thing to bring home to us, and to feel that we have souls; and there cannot be a more fatal mistake than to suppose we see what the doctrine means as soon as we can use the words which signify it. . . . To understand that we have souls, is to feel our separation from things visible, our independence of them, our distinct existence in ourselves, our individuality, our power of acting for ourselves this way or that way, our accountableness for what we do. . . . Indeed none of us (of course) are entirely loosened from this world. We all use words, in speaking of our duties, higher and fuller than we really understand. No one entirely realizes what is meant by his having a soul; even the best of men is but in a state of progress towards the simple truth; and the most weak and ignorant of those who seek after it cannot but be in progress.

P.S., i, 17, 19-25.

2

We are from our birth apparently dependent on things about us. We see and feel that we could not live or go forward without the aid of man. To a child this world is everything: he seems to himself a part of this world,—a part of this world in the same sense in which a branch is part of a tree; he has little notion of his own separate and independent existence, that is, he has no just idea he has a soul. And if he goes through life with his notions unchanged, he has no just notion, even to the end of life, that he has a soul. He views himself merely in his connection with this world, which is his all; he looks to this world for his good as to an idol; and when he tries to look beyond this life, he is able to discern nothing in prospect, because he has no idea of anything, nor can fancy anything, *but* this life. And if he is obliged to fancy something, he fancies this life over again; just as the heathen, when they reflected on those traditions of another life, which were floating among them, could but fancy the happiness of the blessed to consist in the enjoyment of the sun, and the sky, and the earth, as before, only as if these were to be more splendid than they are now. . . .

Such is our state,—a depending for support on the reeds which are no stay, and overlooking our real strength,—at the time when God begins His process of reclaiming us to a truer view of our place in His great system of providence. And when He visits us, then in a little while there is a stirring within us. The unprofitableness and feebleness of the things of this world are forced upon our minds; they promise but cannot perform, they disappoint us. Or, if they do perform what they promise, still (so it is) they do not satisfy us. We still crave for something, we do not well know what; but we are sure it is something which the world has not given us. And then its changes are so many, so sudden, so silent, so continual. It never leaves changing; it goes on to change, till we are quite sick at heart:—then it is that our reliance on it is broken. It is plain we cannot continue to depend upon it unless we keep pace with it and go on changing too; but this we cannot do. We feel that, while it changes, we are one and the same; and thus, under God's blessing, we come to have some glimpse of the meaning of our independence of things temporal, and our immortality. And should it so happen that misfortunes come upon us (as they often do), then still more are we led to understand the nothingness of this world; then still more are we led to distrust it, and are weaned from the love of it, till at length it floats before our eyes merely as some idle veil, which, notwithstanding its many tints, cannot hide the view of what is beyond it;—and we begin, by degrees, to perceive that there are but two beings in the whole universe, our own soul, and the God who made it.

P.S., i, 13-20.

3

To every one of us there are but two beings in the whole

world, himself and God; for, as to this outward scene, its pleasures and pursuits, its honours and cares, its contrivances, its personages, its kingdoms, its multitude of busy slaves, what are they to us? nothing—no more than a show:—"The world passeth away and the lust thereof." And as to those others nearer to us, who are not to be classed with the vain world—I mean our friends and relations, whom we are right in loving—these, too, after all, are nothing to us here. They cannot really help or profit us; we see them, and they act upon us, only (as it were) at a distance, through the medium of sense; they cannot get at our souls; they cannot enter into our thoughts, or really be companions to us. In the next world it will, through God's mercy, be otherwise; but here we enjoy, not their presence, but the anticipation of what one day shall be; so that, after all, they vanish before the clear vision we have, first, of our own existence, next, of the presence of the great God in us, and over us, as our Governor and Judge, who dwells in us by our conscience, which is His representative.

P.S., i, 20-23.

4

All below heaven changes: spring, summer, autumn, each has its turn. The fortunes of the world change; what was high, lies low; what was low, rises high. Riches take wing and flee away; bereavements happen. Friends become enemies, and enemies friends. Our wishes, aims, and plans change. There is nothing stable but Thou, O my God! And Thou art the centre and life of all who change, who trust Thee as their Father, who look to Thee, and who are content to put themselves into Thy hands.

M.D., 507-8.

5

"The love," cried Cæcilius, "which He inspires lasts, for it is the love of the Unchangeable. It satisfies, for He is inexhaustible. The nearer we draw to Him, the more triumphantly does He enter into us; the longer He dwells in us, the more intimately have we possession of Him. It is an espousal for eternity. This

173

is why it is so easy for us to die for our faith, at which the world marvels."

Call., 222.

6

O my God, whatever is nearer to me than Thou, things of this earth, and things more naturally pleasing to me, will be sure to interrupt the sight of Thee, unless Thy grace interfere. Keep Thou my eyes, my ears, my heart, from any such miserable tyranny. Break my bonds—raise my heart. Keep my whole being fixed on Thee. Let me never lose sight of Thee; and, while I gaze on Thee, let my love of Thee grow more and more every day.

M.D., 450-51.

7

Let me ever hold communion with Thee, my hidden, but my living God. Thou art in my innermost heart. Thou art the life of my life. Every breath I breathe, every thought of my mind, every good desire of my heart, is from the presence within me of the unseen God. . . . I see Thee not in the material world except dimly, but I recognise Thy voice in my own intimate consciousness. I turn round and say Rabboni. O be ever thus with me; and if I am tempted to leave *Thee*, do not Thou, O my God, leave *me*.

M.D., 496-7.

II. THE GOD OF MY LIFE

8

His Providence manifests itself in general laws, it moves forward upon the lines of truth and justice; it has no respect of persons, rewarding the good and punishing the bad, not as individuals, but according to their character. How shall He who is Most Holy direct His love to this man or that for the sake of each, contemplating us one by one, without infringing on His own perfections? Or even were the Supreme Being a God of unmixed benevolence, how, even then, shall the thought of Him come home to our minds with that constraining power which the kindness of a human friend exerts over us? . . . [But] He has met and aided it in that same Dispensation by which He redeemed our souls. In order that we may understand that in spite of His mysterious perfections He has a separate knowledge and regard for individuals, He has taken upon Him the thoughts and feelings of our own nature, which we all understand *is* capable of such personal attachments. By becoming man, He has cut short the perplexities and the discussions of our reason on the subject, as if He would grant our objections for argument's sake, and supersede them by taking our own ground.

P.S., iii, 119-20.

9

How gracious is this revelation of God's particular providence to those who seek Him! how gracious to those who have discovered that this world is but vanity, and who are solitary and isolated in themselves, whatever shadows of power and happiness surround them! The multitude, indeed, go on without these thoughts, either from insensibility, as not understanding their own wants, or changing from one idol to another, as each successively fails. But men of keener hearts would be overpowered by despondency, and would even loathe existence, did they suppose themselves under the mere operation of fixed laws, powerless to excite the pity or the attention of Him who has appointed them. What should they do especially, who are cast among persons unable to enter into their feelings, and thus strangers to them, though by long custom ever so much friends! or who have perplexities of mind they cannot explain to themselves, much less remove, and no one to help them; or who have affections and aspirations pent up within them, because they have not met with objects to which to devote them; or who are misunderstood by those around them, and find they have no words to set themselves right with them, or no principles in common by way of appeal; or who seem to themselves to be without place or purpose in the world, or to be in the way of others; or who have to follow their own sense of duty without advisers or supporters, nay, to resist the wishes and solicitations of superiors or relatives; or who have the burden of some painful secret, or of some incommunicable solitary grief! In all such cases the Gospel narrative supplies our very need, not simply presenting to us an unchangeable Creator to rely upon, but a compassionate Guardian, a discriminating Judge and Helper.

P.S., v, 123-4.

10

God beholds thee individually, whoever thou art. He "calls thee by thy name." He sees thee, and understands thee, as He made thee. He knows what is in thee, all thy own peculiar feelings and thoughts, thy dispositions and likings, thy strength and thy weakness. He views thee in thy day of rejoicing and thy day of sorrow. He sympathizes in thy hopes and thy temptations. He interests Himself in all thy anxieties and remembrances, all the risings and fallings of thy spirit. He has numbered the very hairs of thy head and the cubits of thy stature. He compasses thee round and bears thee in His arms; He takes thee up and sets thee down. He notes thy very countenance, whether smiling or in tears, whether healthful or sickly. He looks tenderly upon thy hands and thy feet; He hears thy voice, the beating of thy heart, and thy very breathing. Thou dost not love thyself better than He loves thee. Thou canst not shrink from pain more than He dislikes thy bearing it; and if He puts it on thee, it is as thou wilt put it on thyself, if thou art wise, for a greater good afterwards.

P.S., v, 124-5.

11

O dearest Lord, Thou art more fully man than the Holy Baptist, than St. John, Apostle and Evangelist, than Thy own sweet mother. As in Divine knowledge of me Thou art beyond them all, so also in experience and personal knowledge of my nature. Thou art my elder brother. How can I fear, how should I not repose my whole heart on one so gentle, so tender, so familiar, so unpretending, so modest, so natural, so humble? Thou art now, though in heaven, just the same as Thou wast on earth: the mighty God, yet the little child—the all-holy, yet the all sensitive, all human.

M.D., 493.

III. LIFE IN GOD

12

The happiness of the soul consists in the exercise of the affections; not in sensual pleasures, not in activity, not in excitement, not in self-esteem, not in the consciousness of power, not in knowledge. . . This is our real and true bliss, not to know, or to affect, or to pursue; but to love, to hope, to joy, to admire, to revere, to adore. Our real and true bliss lies in the possession of those objects on which our hearts may rest and be satisfied. . . . Here is at once a reason for saying that the thought of God, and nothing short of it, is the happiness of man; for though there is much besides to serve as subject of knowledge, or motive for action, or means of excitement, yet the affections require a something more vast and more enduring than anything created. What is novel and sudden excites, but does not influence; what is pleasurable or useful raises no awe; self moves no reverence, and mere knowledge kindles no love. He alone is sufficient for the heart who made it. . .

We gain much for a time from fellowship with each other. It is a relief to us, as fresh air to the fainting, or meat and drink to the hungry, or a flood of tears to the heavy in mind. It is a soothing comfort to have those whom we may make our confidants; a comfort to have those to whom we may confess our faults; a comfort to have those to whom we may look for sympathy. Love of home and family in these and other ways is sufficient to make this life tolerable to the multitude of men, which otherwise it would not be; but still, after all, our affections exceed such exercise of them, and demand what is more stable. Do not all men die? are they not taken from us? are they not as uncertain as the grass of the field? We do not give our hearts to things irrational, because these have no permanence in them. We do not place our affections in sun, moon, and stars, or this rich and fair earth, because all things material come to nought, and vanish like day and night. Man, too, though he has an intelligence within him, yet in his best estate he is altogether vanity. If our happiness consists in our affections being employed and recompensed, "man that is born of a woman" cannot be our happiness; for how can he stay another who "continueth not in one stay" himself?

But there is another reason why God alone is the happiness of our souls—the contemplation of Him, and nothing but it, is able fully to open and relieve the mind, to unlock, occupy, and fix our affections. We may indeed love things created with great intenseness, but such affection, when disjoined from the love of the Creator, is like a stream running in a narrow channel, impetuous, vehement, turbid. The heart runs out, as it were, only at one door; it is not an expanding of the whole man. Created natures cannot open us, or elicit the ten thousand mental senses which belong to us, and through which we really live. None but the presence of our Maker can enter us; for to none besides can the whole heart in all its thoughts and feelings be unlocked and subjected. . . .

We know that even our nearest friends enter into us but partially, and hold intercourse with us only at times; whereas the consciousness of a perfect and enduring Presence, and it alone, keeps the heart open. Withdraw the Object on which it rests, and it will relapse again into its state of confinement and constraint; and in proportion as it is limited, either to certain seasons or to certain affections, the heart is straitened and distressed. If it be not overbold to say it, He who is infinite can alone be its measure; He alone can answer to the mysterious assemblage of feelings and thoughts which it has within it. . . .

Life passes, riches fly away, popularity is fickle, the senses decay, the world changes, friends die. One alone is constant; One alone is true to us; One alone can be true; One alone can be all things to us; One alone can supply our needs; One alone can train us up to our full perfection; One alone can give a meaning

178

to our complex and intricate nature; One alone can give us tune and harmony; One alone can form and possess us.

P.S., v, 315-319, 326.

13

That mysterious Presence of God which encompasses us, which is in us, and around us, which is in our heart, which enfolds us as though with a robe of light, hiding our scarred and discoloured souls from the sight of Divine Purity, and making them shining as the Angels; and which flows in upon us too by means of all forms of beauty and grace which this visible world contains, in a starry host or (if I may so say) a milky way of divine companions, the inhabitants of Mount Zion where we dwell.

P.S., iv, 277.

14

[My God], I am to live for ever, not for a time—and I have no power over my being; I cannot destroy myself, even though I were so wicked as to wish to do so. I must live on with intellect and consciousness for ever, in spite of myself. Without Thee eternity would be another name for eternal misery. In Thee alone have I that which can stay me up for ever: Thou alone art the food of my soul. Thou alone art inexhaustible, and ever offerest to me something new to know, something new to love.... At the end of millions of years I shall find in Thee, the same, or rather, greater sweetness than at first, and shall seem then only to be beginning to enjoy Thee; and so on for eternity I shall ever be a little child beginning to be taught the rudiments of Thy Infinite Divine Nature.

M.D., vi, 2.

15

O mighty God, strengthen me with Thy strength, console me with Thy everlasting peace, soothe me with the beauty of Thy countenance; enlighten me with Thy uncreated brightness; purify me with the fragrance of Thy ineffable holiness. Bathe me

179

in Thyself, and give me to drink, as far as mortal man may ask, of the rivers of grace which flow from the Father and the Son, the grace of Thy consubstantial, co-eternal Love.

M.D., 504.

IV.   ALL IN GOD AND GOD IN ALL

16

The aim of most men esteemed conscientious and religious, or who are what is called honourable, upright men, is, to all appearance, not how to please God, but how to please themselves without displeasing Him. I say confidently,—that is, if we may judge of men in general by what we see,—that they make this world the first object in their minds, and use religion as a corrective, a restraint, upon *too much* attachment to the world. They think that religion is a negative thing, a sort of moderate love of the world, a moderate luxury, a moderate avarice, a moderate ambition, and a moderate selfishness. You see this in numberless ways. You see it in the course of trade, of public life, of literature, in all matters where men have objects to pursue. Nay, you see it in religious exertions; of which it too commonly happens that the chief aim is, to attain *anyhow* a certain definite end, religious indeed, but of man's own choosing; not, to please God, and *next*, if possible, to attain it; not, to attain it religiously, or not at all.

P.S., iv, 29.

17

In one shape or other, we see daily on all sides of us . . . . men living to the world, yet not without a certain sense of religion, which acts as a restraint on them. They pursue ends of this world, but not to the full; they are checked, and go a certain way only, because they dare not go further. This external restraint acts with various degrees of strength on various persons. They all live to this world, and act from the love of it; they all allow their love of the world a certain range; but at some particular point, which is often quite arbitrary, this man stops, and that man stops. Each stops at a different point in the course of the world, and thinks every one else profane who goes further, and superstitious who does not go so far,—laughs at the latter, is shocked at the former. And hence those few who are miserable enough to have rid themselves of all scruples, look with great contempt on such of their companions as have any, be those scruples more or less, as being inconsistent and absurd. They scoff at the principle of mere fear as a capricious and fanciful principle; proceeding on no rule, and having no evidence of its authority, no claim on our respect; as a weakness in our nature, rather than an essential portion of that nature, viewed in its perfection and entireness. And this being all the notion which their experience gives them of religion, as not knowing really religious men, they think of religion only as a principle which interferes with our enjoyments unintelligibly and irrationally. Man is made to love. So far is plain. They see that clearly and truly; but religion, as far as they conceive of it, is a system destitute of objects of love; a system of fear. It repels and forbids, and thus seems to destroy the proper function of man, or, in other words, to be unnatural. And it is true that this sort of fear of God, or rather slavish dread, as it may more truly be called, *is* unnatural; but then it is not religion, which really consists, not in the mere fear of God, but in His love; or if it be religion, it is but the religion of devils, who believe and tremble; or of idolaters, whom devils have seduced, and whose worship is superstition,— the attempt to appease beings whom they love not; and, in a word, the religion of the children of this world, who would, if possible, serve God and Mammon, and, whereas religion consists of love *and* fear, give to God their fear, and to Mammon their love.

P.S., v, 321-2

18

Man cannot really be religious one hour and not religious the next. We might as well say he could be in a state of good health one hour and in bad health the next. A man who is religious, is religious morning, noon, and night; his religion is a certain character, a mould in which his thoughts, words, and actions are cast, all forming parts of one and the same whole. He sees God in all things; every course of action he directs towards those spiritual objects which God has revealed to him; every occurrence of the day, every event, every person met with, all news which he hears, he measures by the standard of God's will. And a person who does this may be said almost literally to pray without ceasing; for, knowing himself to be in God's presence, he is continually led to address Him reverently, whom he sets always before him, in the inward language of prayer and praise, of humble confession and joyful trust.

All this, I say, any thoughtful man acknowledges from mere natural reason. To be religious is, in other words, to have the habit of prayer, or to pray always. This is what Scripture means by doing all things to God's glory; that is, so placing God's presence and will before us, and so consistently acting with a reference to Him, that all we do becomes one body and course of obedience, witnessing without ceasing to Him who made us, and whose servants we are; and in its separate parts promoting more or less directly His glory, according as each particular thing we happen to be doing admits more or less of a religious character. Thus religious obedience is, as it were, a spirit dwelling in us, extending its influence to every motion of the soul; and just as healthy men and strong men show their health and strength in all they do (not indeed equally in all things, but in some things more than in others, because all actions do not require or betoken the presence of that health and strength, and yet even in their step, and their voice, and their gestures, and their countenance, showing in due measure their vigour of body), so they who have the true health and strength of the soul, a clear, sober, and deep faith in Him in whom they have their being, will in all they do, nay (as St. Paul says), even whether they "eat or drink," be living in God's sight, or, in the words of the same Apostle in the text, live in ceaseless prayer. . . . Our spiritual "life" (as St. Paul says) "is *hid* with Christ in God." But as our bodily life discovers itself by its activity, so is the presence of the Holy Spirit in us discovered by a spiritual activity; and this activity is the spirit of continual prayer. Prayer is to spiritual life what the beating of the pulse and the drawing of the breath are to the life of the body. . .

Thus the true Christian pierces through the veil of this world and sees the next. He holds intercourse with it; he addresses God as a child might address his parent, with as clear a view of Him, and with as unmixed a confidence in Him; with deep reverence indeed, and godly fear and awe, but still with certainty and exactness: as St. Paul says, "I know whom I have believed," with the prospect of judgment to come to sober him, and the assurance of present grace to cheer him.

P.S., vii, 205-11.

19

To rush into His presence, to address Him familiarly, to urge Him, to strive to make our duty lie in one direction when it lies in another, to handle rudely and practise upon His holy Word, to trifle with truth, to treat conscience lightly, to take liberties (as it may be called) with anything that is God's, all irreverence, profaneness, unscrupulousness, wantonness, is represented in Scripture not only as a sin, but as felt, noticed, quickly returned on God's part (if I may dare use such human words of the Almighty and All-holy God, without transgressing the rule I am myself laying down,—but He vouchsafes in Scripture to represent Himself to us in that only way in which we can attain to the knowledge of Him), I say all irreverence towards God is represented as being jealously and instantly and fearfully noticed and visited, as friend or stranger among men might resent an insult shown him. This should be carefully considered; we are apt to act towards God and the things of God as towards a mere system, a law, a name, a religion, a principle, not as against a Person, a living, watchful, present, prompt, and powerful Eye and Arm.

P.S., iv, 31.

X: THE SINNER'S GOD

ANALYTICAL SUMMARY

But the fact of the pardoned sinner necessitates the uninterrupted kneeling of the returned Prodigal at the feet of his outraged Father;

a searchlight directed unrelentingly upon the depths of our sinfulness, so that with the Prodigal Son "we return to ourselves" and plant the roots of our life in "a contrite heart;"

(Nos. 1-6.)

a gaze fixed ever more steadily upon the radiant light of God's holiness, so that the nearer we approach Him, the deeper the realisation of our own sinfulness, that we may finally have open eyes whereby to see Him—not the blind eyes to which Heaven itself would be Hell;

(Nos. 7-11.)

a perception increasingly profound that our entire life is full of sin, weakness and deformity—the cry of the publican in the temple: "Lord be merciful to me a sinner;"

(Nos. 12-14.)

and therefore in the presence of God's Holiness Justice and Mercy the unconditional "Do unto me according to Thy Will."

(Nos. 15-20.)

I. A CONTRITE HEART

1

All teaching about duty and obedience, about attaining heaven and about the office of Christ towards us, is hollow and unsubstantial, which is not built *here*, in the doctrine of our original corruption and helplessness; and, in consequence, of original guilt and sin. Christ Himself indeed is the foundation, but a broken, self-abased, self-renouncing heart is (as it were) the ground and soil in which the foundation must be laid; and it is but building on the sand to profess to believe in Christ, yet not to acknowledge that without Him we can do nothing.

P.S., *v*, 134-5.

2

Could men come nearer to God than when they seized Him, struck Him, spit on Him, hurried Him along, stripped Him, stretched out His limbs upon the cross, nailed Him to it, raised it up, stood gazing on Him, jeered Him, gave Him vinegar, looked close whether He was dead, and then pierced Him with a spear? O dreadful thought, that the nearest approaches man has made to God upon earth have been in blasphemy! Whether of the two came closer to Him, St. Thomas, who was allowed to reach forth his hand and reverently touch His wounds, and St. John, who rested on His bosom, or the brutal soldiers who profaned Him limb by limb, and tortured Him nerve by nerve? . . . . So it is with sinners: they would walk close to the throne of God; they would stupidly gaze at it; they would touch it; they would meddle with the holiest things; they would go on intruding and prying, not meaning any thing wrong by it, but with a sort of brute curiosity, till the avenging lightnings destroyed them;—all because they have no *senses* to guide them in the matter. . . . Let us suppose the sinner could remain in heaven unblasted, yet it would seem that at least he would not know that he was there. He would see nothing wonderful there. . . .

Our bodily senses tell us of the approach of good or evil on earth. By sound, by scent, by feeling we know what is happening to us. We know when we are exposing ourselves to the weather, when we are exerting ourselves too much. We have warnings, and feel we must not neglect them. Now, sinners have no spiritual senses; they can presage nothing; they do not know what is going to happen the next moment to them. So they go fearlessly further and further among precipices, till on a sudden they fall, or are smitten and perish. Miserable beings! and this is what sin does for immortal souls; that they should be like the cattle which are slaughtered at the shambles, yet touch and smell the very weapons which are to destroy them!

P.S., iv, 226-248.

3

Unless we have some just idea of our hearts and of sin, we can have no right idea of a Moral Governor, a Saviour or a Sanctifier. . . . Thus self-knowledge is at the root of all real religious knowledge; and it is in vain,—worse than vain,—it is a deceit and a mischief, to think to understand the Christian doctrines as a matter of course, merely by being taught by books, or by attending sermons, or by any outward means, however excellent, taken by themselves. For it is in proportion as we search our hearts and understand our own nature, that we understand what is meant by an Infinite Governor and Judge; in proportion as we comprehend the nature of disobedience and our actual sinfulness, that we feel what is the blessing of the removal of sin, redemption, pardon, sanctification, which otherwise are mere words. God speaks to us primarily in our hearts. Self-knowledge is the key to the precepts and doctrines of Scripture. The very utmost any outward notices of religion can do, is to startle us and make us turn inward and search our hearts; and then, when we have experienced what it is to read ourselves, we shall profit by the doctrines of the Church and the Bible.

P.S., i, 42-3.

4

How can we feel our need of His help, or our dependence on Him, or our debt to Him, or the nature of His gift to us, unless we know ourselves? How can we in any sense be said to have that "mind of Christ," to which the Apostle exhorts us, if we cannot follow Him to the height above, or the depth beneath; if we do not in some measure discern the cause and meaning of His sorrows, but regard the world, and man, and the system of Providence, in a light different from that which His words and acts supply? . . . .

Without self-knowledge you have no root in yourselves personally; you may endure for a time, but under affliction or persecution your faith will not last. This is why many in this age (and in every age) become infidels, heretics, schismatics, disloyal despisers of the Church. . . . They endure not, because they never have tasted that the Lord is gracious; and they never have had experience of His power and love, because they have never known their own weakness and need.

P.S., i, 54-5.

5

When a man's spirits are high, he is pleased with every thing; and with himself especially. He can act with vigour and promptness, and he mistakes this mere constitutional energy for strength of faith. He is cheerful and contented; and he mistakes this for Christian peace. And, if happy in his family, he mistakes mere natural affection for Christian benevolence, and the confirmed temper of Christian love. In short, he is in a dream, from which nothing could have saved him except deep humility, and nothing will ordinarily rescue him except sharp affliction.

Other accidental circumstances are frequently causes of a similar self-deceit. While we remain in retirement from the world, we do not know ourselves; or after any great mercy or trial, which has affected us much, and given a temporary strong impulse to our obedience; or when we are in keen pursuit of some good object, which excites the mind, and for a time deadens it to temptation. Under such circumstances we are ready to think far too well of ourselves. The world is away; or, at least, we are insensible to its seductions; and we mistake our merely temporary tranquillity, or our over-wrought fervour of mind, on the one hand for Christian peace, on the other for Christian zeal.

P.S., i, 50-51.

6

The office of self-examination lies rather in detecting what is bad in us than in ascertaining what is good. No harm can follow from contemplating our sins, so that we keep Christ before us, and attempt to overcome them; such a review of self will but lead to repentance and faith. And, while it does this, it will undoubtedly be moulding our hearts into a higher and more heavenly state;—but still indirectly;—just as the mean is attained in action or art, not by directly contemplating and aiming at it, but negatively, by avoiding extremes.

P.S., ii, 161.

II. THE ALL-HOLY

7

Not indeed that the notion of transgression and of forgiveness was introduced by Christianity, and is unknown beyond its pale . . . . but what is peculiar to our divine faith, as to Judaism before it, is this, that confession of sin enters into the idea of its highest saintliness, and that its pattern worshippers and the very heroes of its history are only, and can only be, and cherish in their hearts the everlasting memory that they are, and carry with them into heaven the rapturous avowal of their being redeemed, restored transgressors. . . . Whatever be their advance in the spiritual life, they never rise from their knees, they never cease to beat their breasts, as if sin could possibly be strange to them while they were in the flesh. . . . Others may look up to them, but they ever look up to God; others may speak of their merits, but they only speak of their defects. The young and unspotted, the aged and most mature, he who has sinned least, he who has repented most, the fresh innocent brow, and the hoary head, they unite in this one litany, "O God, be merciful to me, a sinner." So it was with St. Aloysius; so, on the other hand, was it with St. Ignatius; so was it with St. Rose, the youngest of the saints, who, as a child, submitted her tender frame to the most amazing penances; so was it with St. Philip Neri, one of the most aged, who, when some one praised him, cried out, "Begone! I am a devil, and not a saint"; and when going to communicate, would protest before his Lord, that he "was good for nothing, but to do evil." Such utter self-prostration, I say, is the very badge and token of the servant of Christ;—and this indeed is conveyed in His own words, when He says, "I am not come to call the just, but sinners."

O.S., 15-17.

8

Surely to obey in simple tranquillity and unsolicitous confidence, is the noblest conceivable state of the creature, and the most acceptable worship he can pay to the Creator. Doubtless it is the noblest and most acceptable worship; such has ever been the worship of the angels; such is the worship now of the spirits of the just made perfect; such will be the worship of the whole company of the glorified after the general resurrection. But we are engaged in considering the actual state of man, as found in this world; and I say, considering what he is, any standard of duty, which does not convict him of real and multiplied sins, and of incapacity to please God of his own strength, is untrue; and any rule of life which leaves him contented with himself, without fear, without anxiety, without humiliation, is deceptive; it is the blind leading the blind. . . .

Yet such in one shape or other is the way with the multitude of men everywhere and at all times; they do not see the Image of Almighty God before them, and ask themselves what He wishes: if once they did this they would begin to see how much He requires, and they would earnestly come to Him, both to be pardoned for what they do wrong, and for the power to do better. And, for the same reason that they do not please Him, they succeed in pleasing themselves. For that contracted, defective range of duties, which falls so short of God's law, is just what they can fulfil; or rather they choose it, and keep to it, *because* they can fulfil it. Hence, they become both self-satisfied and self-sufficient; —they think they know just what they ought to do, and that they do it all; and in consequence they are very well content with themselves, and rate their merit very high, and have no fear at all of any future scrutiny into their conduct, which may befall them. . . .

There is no apprehension of Almighty God, no insight into His claims on us, no sense of the creature's shortcomings, no self-condemnation, confession, and deprecation, nothing of those deep and sacred feelings which ever characterize the religion of a Christian, and more and more, not less and less, as he mounts up from mere ordinary obedience to the perfection of a saint.

O.S., 20-21, 25.

9

And such, I say, is the religion of the natural man in every age and place;—often very beautiful on the surface, but worthless in God's sight; good, as far as it goes, but worthless and hopeless, because it does not go further, because it is based on self-sufficiency, and results in self-satisfaction. I grant, it may be beautiful to look at, as in the instance of the young ruler whom our Lord looked at and loved, yet sent away sad; it may have all the delicacy, the amiableness, the tenderness, the religious sentiment, the kindness, which is actually seen in many a father of a family, many a mother, many a daughter, in the length and breadth of these kingdoms, in a refined and polished age like this; but still it is rejected by the heart-searching God, because all such persons walk by their own light, not by the True Light of men, because self is their supreme teacher, and because they pace round and round in the small circle of their own thoughts and of their own judgments, careless to know what God says to them, and fearless of being condemned by Him, if only they stand approved in their own sight. . . .

Yes, it is the ignorance of our understanding, it is our spiritual blindness, it is our banishment from the presence of Him, who is the source and the standard of all Truth, which is the cause of this meagre, heartless religion of which men are commonly so proud. Had we any proper insight into things as they are, had we any real apprehension of God as He is, of ourselves as we are, we should never dare to serve Him without fear, or to rejoice unto Him without trembling. And it is the removal of this veil which is spread between our eyes and heaven, it is the pouring in upon the soul of the illuminating grace of the New Covenant, which makes the religion of the Christian so different from that of the various human rites and philosophies, which are spread over the earth. The Catholic saints alone confess sin, because the Catholic saints alone see God. That awful Creator Spirit. . . . it is who brings into religion the true devotion, the true worship, and changes the self-satisfied Pharisee into the broken-hearted, self-abased Publican. It is the sight of God, revealed to the eye of faith, that makes us hideous to ourselves, from the contrast which we find ourselves to present to that great God at whom we look. It is the vision of Him in His infinite gloriousness, the All-holy, the All-beautiful, the All-perfect, which makes us sink into the earth with self-contempt and self-abhorrence. We are contented with ourselves till we contemplate Him. Why is it, I say, that the moral code of the world is so precise and well-defined? Why is the worship of reason so calm? Why was the religion of classic heathenism so joyous? Why is the framework of civilized society all so graceful and so correct? Why, on the other hand, is there so much of emotion, so much of conflicting and alternating feeling, so much that is high, so much that is abased, in the devotion of Christianity? It is because the Christian, and the Christian alone, has a revelation of God; it is because he has upon his mind, in his heart, on his conscience, the idea of one who is Self-dependent, who is from Everlasting, who is Incommunicable. He knows that One alone is holy, and that His own creatures are so frail in comparison of Him, that they would dwindle and melt away

193

in His presence, did He not uphold them by His power. He knows that there is One whose greatness and whose blessedness are not affected, the centre of whose stability is not moved, by the presence or the absence of the whole creation with its innumerable beings and portions; whom nothing can touch, nothing can increase or diminish; who was as mighty before He made the worlds as since, and as serene and blissful since He made them as before. He knows that there is just One Being, in whose hand lies his own happiness, his own sanctity, his own life, and hope, and salvation. He knows that there is One to whom he owes every thing, and against whom he can have no plea or remedy. All things are nothing before Him; the highest beings do but worship Him the more; the holiest beings are such, only because they have a greater portion of Him. . . . This then, my Brethren, is the reason why every son of man, whatever be his degree of holiness, whether a returning prodigal or a matured saint, says with the Publican, "O God, be merciful to me"; it is because created natures, high and low, are all on a level in the sight and in comparison of the Creator, and so all of them have one speech, and one only, whether it be the thief on the cross, Magdalen at the feast, or St. Paul before his martyrdom:—not that one of them may not have, what another has not, but that one and all have nothing but what comes from Him, and are as nothing before Him, who is all in all.

O.S., 25-9.

10

We are apt to deceive ourselves, and to consider heaven a place like this earth; I mean, a place where every one may choose and take his *own* pleasure. We see that in this world, active men have their own enjoyments, and domestic men have theirs; men of literature, of science, of political talent, have their respective pursuits and pleasures. Hence we are led to act as if it will be the same in another world. The only difference we put between this world and the next, is that *here* (as we know well) men are *not always sure*, but *there*, we suppose they *will be always sure*, of obtaining what they seek after. And accordingly we conclude,

194

that *any man*, whatever his habits, tastes, or manner of life, if *once admitted* into heaven, would be happy there. Not that we altogether deny that some preparation is necessary for the next world; but we do not estimate its real extent and importance. We think we can reconcile ourselves to God when we will; as if nothing were required in the case of men in general, but some temporary attention, more than ordinary, to our religious duties, —some strictness, during our last sickness, in the services of the Church, as men of business arrange their letters and papers on taking a journey or balancing an account. But an opinion like this, though commonly acted on, is refuted as soon as put into words. For heaven, it is plain from Scripture, is not a place where many different and discordant pursuits can be carried on at once, as is the case in this world. Here every man can do his *own* pleasure, but there he must do *God's* pleasure. It would be presumption to attempt to determine the employments of that eternal life which good men are to pass in God's presence, or to deny that that state which eye hath not seen, nor ear heard, nor mind conceived, may comprise an infinite variety of pursuits and occupations. Still so far we are distinctly told, that that future life will be spent in God's *presence*, in a sense which does not apply to our present life; so that it may be best described as an endless and uninterrupted worship of the Eternal Father, Son, and Spirit.

P.S., *i*, 3-5.

II

It is fearful, but it is right to say it;—that if we wished to imagine a punishment for an unholy, reprobate soul, we perhaps could not fancy a greater than to *summon it to heaven*. Heaven would be hell to an irreligious man. We know how unhappy we are apt to feel at present, when alone in the midst of strangers, or of men of different tastes and habits from ourselves. How miserable, for example, would it be to have to live in a foreign land, among a people whose faces we never saw before, and whose language we could not learn. And this is but a faint illustration of the loneliness of a man of earthly dispositions and tastes, thrust into the society of saints and angels. How forlorn

195

would he wander through the courts of heaven! He would find no one like himself . . . . he would find no discourse but that which he had shunned on earth, no pursuits but those he had disliked or despised, nothing which bound him to aught *else* in the universe, and made him feel at home, nothing which he could enter into and rest upon. He would perceive himself to be an isolated being, cut away by Supreme Power from those objects which were still entwined around his heart. Nay, he would be in the presence of that Supreme Power, whom he never on earth could bring himself steadily to think upon, and whom now he regarded only as the destroyer of all that was precious and dear to him. Ah! he could not *bear* the face of the Living God; the Holy God would be no object of joy to him. "Let us alone! What have we to do with thee?" is the sole thought and desire of unclean souls, even while they acknowledge His majesty. . . .

[Further] he would see in every direction the marks of God's holiness, and these would make him shudder. He would feel himself always in His presence. He could no longer turn his thoughts another way, as he does now, when conscience reproaches him. He would know that the Eternal Eye was ever upon him; and that Eye of holiness, which is joy and life to holy creatures, would seem to him an Eye of wrath and punishment. God cannot change His nature. Holy He must ever be. But while He is holy, no unholy soul can be happy in heaven. Fire does not inflame iron, but it inflames straw. It would cease to be fire if it did not. And so heaven itself would be fire to those who would fain escape across the great gulf from the torments of hell. The finger of Lazarus would but increase their thirst. The very "heaven that is over their head" will be brass to them.

P.S., i, 6-8.

III. BE MERCIFUL TO ME A SINNER

12

We are ever in a degree lame in this world, even in our best estate. All Christians are such; but when in consequence of their lameness they proceed to turn aside, or, as the text says, to "draw back," then they differ from those who are merely lame, as widely as those who halt along a road differ from those who fall out of it. Those who have turned aside, have to return; they have fallen into a different state: those who are lame must be "healed" *in* the state of grace in which they are, and while they are in it; and that, *lest* they "turn out" of it. Thus lameness is at once distinct from backsliding, yet leads to it. . . .

On the whole, then, this may be considered a Christian's state, ever about to fall, yet by God's mercy never falling; ever dying, yet always alive; full of infirmities, yet free from transgressions: and, as time goes on, more and more free from infirmities also, as tending to that perfect righteousness which is the fulfilling of the Law;—on the other hand, should he fall, recoverable, but not without much pain, with fear and trembling.

P.S., *v*, 205-206.

13

The continual results, as I may call them, of [the Christian's] faith, are righteous and holy, but the process through which they are obtained is one of imperfection; so that could we see his soul as Angels see it, he would, when seen at a distance, appear youthful in countenance, and bright in apparel; but approach him, and his face has lines of care upon it, and his dress is tattered. His righteousness then seems, I do not mean superficial, this would be to give a very wrong idea of it, but though reaching deep within him, yet not whole and entire in the depth of it; but, as it were, wrought out of sin, the result of a continual struggle,— not spontaneous nature, but habitual self-command.

True faith is not shown here below in peace, but rather in conflict; and it is no proof that a man is not in a state of grace that he continually sins, provided such sins do not remain on him as what I may call ultimate results, but are ever passing on into something beyond and unlike themselves, into truth and righteousness. As we gain happiness through suffering, so do we arrive at holiness through infirmity, because man's very condition is a fallen one, and in passing out of the country of sin he necessarily passes through it. And hence it is that holy men are kept from regarding themselves with satisfaction, or resting in any thing short of our Lord's death, as their ground of confidence; for, though that death has already in a measure wrought life in them, and effected the purpose for which it took place, yet to themselves they seem but sinners, their renewal being hidden from them by the circumstances attending it. The utmost they can say of themselves is, that they are not in the commission of any such sins as would plainly exclude them from grace; but how little of firm hope can be placed on such negative evidence is plain from St. Paul's own words on the subject, who speaking of the censures passed upon him by the Corinthians, says, "I know nothing by myself," that is, I am conscious of nothing, "yet am I not hereby justified; but He that judgeth me is the Lord." As men in a battle cannot see how it is going, so Christians have no certain signs of God's presence in their hearts, and can but look up towards their Lord and Saviour, and timidly hope. . . .

We have much to be forgiven; nay, we have the more to be forgiven the more we attempt. The higher our aims, the greater our risks. They who venture much with their talents, gain much, and in the end they hear the words, "Well done, good and faithful servant"; but they have so many losses in trading by the way, that to themselves they seem to do nothing but fail. They cannot believe that they are making any progress; and though they do, yet surely they have much to be forgiven in all their services. They are like David, men of blood; they fight the good fight of faith, but they are polluted with the contest.

P.S., *v*, 210-211, 214.

14

This is the highest excellence to which we ordinarily attain; to understand our own hypocrisy, insincerity, and shallowness of mind,—to own, while we pray, that we cannot pray aright,— to repent of our repentings,—and to submit ourselves wholly to His judgment, who could indeed be extreme with us, but has already shown His loving-kindness in bidding us to pray. And, while we thus conduct ourselves, we must learn to feel that God knows all this before we say it, and far better than we do. He does not need to be informed of our extreme worthlessness. We must pray in the spirit and the temper of the extremest abasement, but we need not search for adequate words to express this, for in truth no words are bad enough for our case.

P.S., *i*, 147.

IV. DO UNTO ME ACCORDING TO THY WILL

15

You say well that you are unclean. But in what time do you propose to become otherwise? Do you expect in this life ever to be clean? Yes, in one sense, by the presence of the Holy Ghost within you; but that presence we trust you have now. But if by "clean," you mean free from that infection of nature, the least drop of which is sufficient to dishonour all your services, clean you never will be till you have paid the debt of sin, and lose that body which Adam has begotten. Be sure that the longer you live, and holier you become, you will only perceive that misery more clearly. The less of it you have, the more it will oppress you; its full draught does but confuse and stupify you; as you come to yourself, your misery begins. The more your soul becomes one with Him who deigns to dwell within it, the more it sees with His eyes. . . . To the end of the longest life you are still a beginner. What Christ asks of you is not sinlessness, but diligence. Had you lived ten times your present age, ten times more service would be required of you. Every day you live longer, more will be required. If He were to come to-day, you would be judged up to to-day. Did He come to-morrow, you would be judged up to to-morrow. Were the time put off a year, you would have a year more to answer for. You cannot elude your destiny, you cannot get rid of your talent; you are to answer for your opportunities, whatever they may be, not more nor less. You cannot be profitable to Him even with the longest life; you can show faith and love in an hour.

P.S., *v*, 52-3.

A true Christian, or one who is in a state of acceptance with God, is he, who, in such sense, has faith in Him, as to live in the thought that He is present with him,—present not externally, not in nature merely, or in providence, but in his innermost heart, or in his *conscience*. A man is justified whose conscience is illuminated by God, so that he habitually realizes that all his thoughts, all the first springs of his moral life, all his motives and his wishes, are open to Almighty God. Not as if he was not aware that there is very much in him impure and corrupt, but he wishes that all that is in him should be bare to God. He believes that it is so, and he even joys to think that it is so, in spite of his fear and shame at its being so. He alone admits Christ into the shrine of his heart; whereas others wish in some way or other, to be by themselves, to have a home, a chamber, a tribunal, a throne, a self where God is not,—a home within them which is not a temple, a chamber which is not a confessional, a tribunal without a judge, a throne without a king;—that self may be king and judge; and that the Creator may rather be dealt with and approached as though a second party, instead of His being that true and better self, of which self itself should be but an instrument and minister. . . . The true Christian . . . enthrones the Son of God in his conscience, refers to Him as a sovereign authority, and uses no reasoning with Him. He does not reason, but he says, "Thou, God, seest me." He feels that God is too near him to allow of argument, self-defence, excuse, or objection. He appeals in matters of duty, not to his own reason, but to God Himself, whom with the eyes of faith he sees, and whom he makes the Judge.

P.S., *v*, 225-7.

17
I am in myself nothing but a sinner, a man of unclean lips and earthly heart. I am not worthy to enter into His presence. I am not worthy of the least of all His mercies. I know He is All-holy, yet I come before Him; I place myself under His pure and piercing eyes, which look

me through and through, and discern every trace and every motion of evil within me. Why do I do so? First of all, for this reason. To whom should I go? What can I do better? Who is there in the whole world that can help me? Who that will care for me, or pity me, or have any kind thought of me, if I cannot obtain it of Him? I know He is of purer eyes than to behold iniquity; but I know again that He is All-merciful, and that He so sincerely desires my salvation that He has died for me. Therefore, though I am in a great strait, I will rather fall into His hands than into those of any creature. . . . I have an instinct within me which leads me to rise and go to my Father, to name the Name of His well-beloved Son, and having named it, to place myself unre-reservedly in His hands, saying, "If Thou, Lord, wilt be extreme to mark what is done amiss, O Lord, who may abide it? But there is forgiveness with Thee."

P.S., *v*, 54, 55.

18
The most noble repentance (if a fallen being can be noble in his fall), the most decorous conduct in a conscious sinner, is an *unconditional surrender* of himself to God—not a bargaining about terms, not a scheming (so to call it) to be received back again, but an instant *surrender* of himself in the first instance. Without knowing what will become of him, whether God will spare or not, merely with so much hope in his heart as not utterly to despair of pardon, still not looking merely to *pardon* as an *end*, but rather looking to the claims of the Benefactor whom he has offended, and smitten with shame, and the sense of his ingratitude, he must *surrender himself* to his lawful Sovereign. He is a runaway offender; he must come back, as a very first step, before anything can be determined about him, bad or good; he is a rebel, and must lay down his arms. Self-devised offerings might do in a less serious matter; as an atonement for sin, they imply a defective view of the evil and extent of sin in his own case. Such is that perfect way which nature shrinks from, but which our Lord enjoins in the parable*—a surrender. . . . We must put

*The prodigal son.

aside the idea of finding a remedy for our sin; then, though we feel the guilt of it, yet we must set out firmly towards God, not knowing for certain that we shall be forgiven. He, indeed, meets us on our way with the tokens of His favour, and so He bears up human faith, which else would sink under the apprehension of meeting the Most High God; still, for our repentance to be Christian, there must be in it that generous temper of self-surrender, the acknowledgment that we are unworthy to be called any more His sons, the abstinence from all ambitious hopes of sitting on His right hand or His left, and the willingness to bear the heavy yoke of bond-servants, if He should put it upon us.

P.S., iii, 96-7.

19

The truest kind of repentance as little comes at first, as perfect conformity to any other part of God's Law. It is gained by long practice—it will come at length. The dying Christian will fulfil the part of the returning prodigal more exactly than he ever did in his former years. When first we turn to God in the actual history of our lives, our repentance is mixed with all kinds of imperfect views and feelings. Doubtless there is in it something of the true temper of simple submission; but the wish of appeasing God on the one hand, or a hard-hearted insensibility about our sins on the other, mere selfish dread of punishment, or the expectation of a sudden easy pardon, these, and such-like principles, influence us, whatever we may say or may think we feel. It is, indeed, easy enough to have good words put into our mouths, and our feelings roused, and to profess the union of utter self-abandonment and enlightened sense of sin; but to claim is not really to possess these excellent tempers. Really to gain these is a work of time. . . . When the Christian has long fought the good fight of faith, and by experience knows how few and how imperfect are his best services, ... He can but *surrender* himself to God, as after all, a worse than unprofitable servant, resigned to God's will, whatever it is, with more or less hope of pardon, as the case may be . . . His true stay is, that Christ came "to call sinners to repentance," that "He died for the ungodly." He

202

acknowledges and adopts, as far as he can, St. Paul's words, and nothing beyond them, "This is a faithful saying, and worthy of all acceptation, that Christ Jesus came into the world to save *sinners*, of whom I am chief."

P.S., iii, 98-100.

20

In the mixture of humbling and cheerful thoughts thus wrought in her,* she recognized the presence of her Maker and Lord, who ever comes to His servants in a two-fold aspect, severe because He is holy, yet soothing as abounding in mercy. In consequence, she called the name of the Lord that spoke unto her, "Thou God seest me."

P.S., iii, 114.

*Hagar.

XI: GOD, OUR GUIDE

ANALYTICAL SUMMARY

Thus surrendered unconditionally and unreservedly into the Hands of God, the Christian's sole knowledge henceforward is to listen for God's voice, "to look upon the pillar of cloud as it moves before him."

He has learned that in himself there is nothing but darkness and impotence, and he therefore no longer places his heart in the power of his own will, but surrenders it to the gentle guidance of God.

(Nos. 1-7.)

He has learned that in himself there is nothing but instability and endless change, he therefore commits the changes of his life to the guidance of Immutability, that it may become in Him a process of change which brings him ever nearer to God.

(Nos. 8-19.)

But because our guide is the God who dwells in light inaccessible His guidance is the twilight of faith;

(Nos. 20-22.)

and because He is a God who is Himself the ground of His own Will, it is a guidance which demands an obedience, unconditional, unquestioning and blind to everything that is not God;

(Nos. 23-30.)

but also—because it is the Divine Majesty that condescends to guide us— the conduct of our life must consist in being led by His Hand in profound awe;

(Nos. 31-32.)

in such wise that we are gently guided on—that everything is His work, that it may be our work also;

(Nos. 33-35.)

that He leads us on the path of trial that our work may be gradually accomplished in quietness of spirit;

(Nos. 36-41.)

and the goal of His entire guidance is rest in Him, the Everlasting Rest.

(Nos. 42-43.)

I. OUR ONLY GUIDE

1

We are in the dark about ourselves. When we act, we are groping in the dark, and may meet with a fall any moment. Here and there, perhaps, we see a little; or, in our attempts to influence and move our minds, we are making experiments (as it were) with some delicate and dangerous instrument, which works we do not know how, and may produce unexpected and disastrous effects. The management of our hearts is quite above us. Under these circumstances it becomes our comfort to look up to God. "Thou, God, seest me!" Such was the consolation of the forlorn Hagar in the wilderness. He knoweth whereof we are made, and He alone can uphold us. He sees with most appalling distinctness all our sins, all the windings and recesses of evil within us; yet it is our only comfort to know this, and to trust Him for help against ourselves. To those who have a right notion of their weakness, the thought of their Almighty Sanctifier and Guide is continually present. They believe in the necessity of a spiritual influence to change and strengthen them, not as a mere abstract doctrine, but as a practical and most consolatory truth, daily to be fulfilled in their warfare with sin and Satan.

P.S., i, 173-4.

2

We can never answer how we shall act under new circumstances. A very little knowledge of life and of our own hearts will teach us this. Men whom we meet in the world turn out, in the course of their trial, so differently from what their former conduct promised, they view things so differently *before* they were tempted and *after*, that we, who see and wonder at it, have abundant cause to look to ourselves, not to be "high-minded," but

207

to "fear." Even the most matured saints, those who imbibed in largest measure the power and fulness of Christ's Spirit, and worked righteousness most diligently in their day, could they have been thoroughly scanned even by man, would (I am persuaded) have exhibited inconsistencies such as to surprise and shock their most ardent disciples. After all, one good deed is scarcely the pledge of another, though I just now said it was. The best men are uncertain; they are great, and they are little again; they stand firm, and then fall. Such is human virtue; reminding us to call no one Master on earth, but to look up to our sinless and perfect Lord; reminding us to humble ourselves, each within himself, and to reflect what we must appear to God, if even to ourselves and each other we seem so base and worthless.

P.S., *i*, 169-70.

3

My God, Thou seest me; I cannot see myself. Were I ever so good a judge about myself, ever so unbiassed, and with ever so correct a rule of judging, still, from my very nature, I cannot look at myself and view myself truly and wholly. But Thou, as Thou comest to me, contemplates me.

M.D., 564-5.

4

Be our mind as heavenly as it may be, most loving, most holy, most zealous, most energetic, most peaceful, yet if we look off from Him for a moment, and look towards ourselves, at once these excellent tempers fall into some extreme or mistake. Charity becomes over-easiness, holiness is tainted with spiritual pride, zeal degenerates into fierceness, activity eats up the spirit of prayer, hope is heightened into presumption. We cannot guide ourselves. God's revealed word is our sovereign rule of conduct; and therefore, among other reasons, is faith so principal a grace, for it is the directing power which receives the commands of Christ, and applies them to the heart.

P.S., *ii*, 278-9.

5

Ah, Lord, we know not what is good for us, and what is bad. We cannot foretell the future, nor do we know, when Thou comest to visit us, in what form Thou wilt come. And therefore, we leave it all to Thee. Do Thou Thy good pleasure to us and in us. Let us ever look at Thee, and do Thou look upon us, and give us the grace of Thy bitter Cross and Passion, and console us in Thy own way and at Thy own time.

M.D., 233-4.

6

God knows what is my greatest happiness, but I do not. There is no rule about what is happy and good; what suits one would not suit another. And the ways by which perfection is reached vary very much; the medicines necessary for our souls are very different from each other. Thus God leads us by strange ways; we know He wills our happiness, but we neither know what our happiness is, nor the way. We are blind; left to ourselves we should take the wrong way; we must leave it to Him. . . . O my God, I will put myself without reserve into Thy hands. Wealth or woe, joy or sorrow, friends or bereavement, honour or humiliation, good report or ill report, comfort or discomfort, Thy presence or the hiding of Thy countenance, all is good if it comes from Thee. Thou art Wisdom and Thou art love—what can I desire more?

M.D., 397-9.

7

I believe, O my Saviour, that Thou knowest just what is best for me. I believe that Thou lovest me better than I love myself, that Thou art all-wise in Thy Providence, and all-powerful in Thy protection. I am as ignorant as Peter was as to what is to happen to me in time to come; but I resign myself entirely to my ignorance, and thank Thee with all my heart that Thou hast taken me out of my own keeping, and, instead of putting such a serious charge upon me, hast bidden me put myself into Thy hands. I can ask nothing better than this, to be Thy care, not my own.

M.D., 522-3.

II. EVER OUR GUIDE

8

For in truth we are not called once only, but many times; all through our life Christ is calling us. He called us first in Baptism; but afterwards also; whether we obey His voice or not, He graciously calls us still. . . . He calls us on from grace to grace, and from holiness to holiness, while life is given us. Abraham was called from his home, Peter from his nets, Matthew from his office, Elisha from his farm, Nathanael from his retreat; we are all in course of calling, on and on, from one thing to another, having no resting-place, but mounting towards our eternal rest, and obeying one command only to have another put upon us. He calls us again and again, in order to justify us again and again,—and again and again, and more and more, to sanctify and glorify us.

It were well if we understood this; but we are slow to master the great truth, that Christ is, as it were, walking among us, and by His hand, or eye, or voice, bidding us follow Him. We do not understand that His call is a thing which takes place now. We think it took place in the Apostles' days; but we do not believe in it, we do not look out for it in our own case. We have not eyes to see the Lord; far different from the beloved Apostle, who knew Christ even when the rest of the disciples knew Him not. When He stood on the shore after His resurrection, and bade them cast the net into the sea, "that disciple whom Jesus loved saith unto Peter, It is the Lord."

P.S., *viii*, 23-4.

9

Thou didst know that what man stands most of all in need of, and in the first place, is not an outward guide, though that he needs too, but an inward, intimate, invisible aid. Thou didst

210

intend to heal him thoroughly, not slightly; not merely to reform the surface, but to remove and destroy the heart and root of all his ills. Thou then didst purpose to visit his soul, and Thou didst depart in body, that Thou mightest come again to him in Spirit. Thou didst not stay with Thy Apostles therefore, as in the days of Thy flesh, but Thou didst come to Them and abide with them for ever, with a much more immediate and true communion in the power of the Paraclete.

M.D., 527-30.

10

Give me, O my Lord, that purity of conscience which alone can receive, which alone can improve Thy inspirations. My ears are dull, so that I cannot hear Thy voice. My eyes are dim, so that I cannot see Thy tokens. Thou alone canst quicken my hearing, and purge my sight, and cleanse and renew my heart. Teach me, like Mary, to sit at Thy feet, and to hear Thy word. Give me that true wisdom which seeks Thy will by prayer and meditation, by direct intercourse with Thee, more than by reading and reasoning. Give me the discernment to know Thy voice from the voice of strangers, and to rest upon it and to seek it in the first place, as something external to myself; and answer me through my own mind, if I worship and rely on Thee as above and beyond it.

M.D., 521-2.

11

What happens to us in providence is in all essential respects what His voice was to those whom He addressed when on earth: whether He commands us by a visible presence, or by a voice, or by our consciences, it matters not, so that we feel it to be a command. If it is a command, it may be obeyed or disobeyed; it may be accepted as Samuel or St. Paul accepted it, or put aside after the manner of the young man who had great possessions.

And these Divine calls are commonly, from the nature of the

case, sudden now, and as indefinite and obscure in their consequences as in former times. The accidents and events of life are,
as is obvious, one special way in which the calls I speak of come
to us; and they, as we all know, are in their very nature, and as
the word accident implies, sudden and unexpected. A man is
going on as usual; he comes home one day, and finds a letter, or
a message, or a person, whereby a sudden trial comes on him,
which, if met religiously, will be the means of advancing him to a
higher state of religious excellence, which at present he as little
comprehends as the unspeakable words heard by St. Paul in
paradise. . . . Many persons will find it very striking on looking
back on their past lives, to observe what different notions they
entertained at different periods, of what Divine truth was, what
was the way of pleasing God, and what things were allowable or
not, what excellence was, and what happiness. I do not scruple
to say, that these differences may be as great as that which may
be supposed to have existed between St. Peter's state of mind
when quietly fishing on the lake, or Elisha's when driving his
oxen, and that new state of mind of each of them when called to
be Apostle or Prophet. . . . He may be able to see that there is a
connexion between the two; that his former has led to his latter;
and yet he may feel that after all they differ in kind; that he has
got into a new world of thought, and measures things and persons by a different rule.

P.S., viii, 24-26.

12

Only one is the truth and the perfect truth; and which that is,
none know but those who are in possession of it, if even they.
But God knows which it is; and towards that one and only Truth
He is leading us forward. . . .

Perhaps it may be the loss of some dear friend or relative
through which the call comes to us; which shows us the vanity of
things below, and prompts us to make God our sole stay. We
through grace do so in a way we never did before; and in the
course of years, when we look back on our life, we find that that
sad event has brought us into a new state of faith and judgment,

and that we are as though other men from what we were. We thought, before it took place, that we were serving God, and so we were in a measure; but we find that, whatever our present infirmities may be, and however far we be still from the highest state of illumination, then at least we were serving the world under the show and the belief of serving God.

Or again, perhaps something occurs to force us to take a part for God or against Him. The world requires of us some sacrifice which we see we ought not to grant to it. Some tempting offer is made us; or some reproach or discredit threatened us; or we have to determine and avow what is truth and what is error. We are enabled to act as God would have us act; and we do so in much fear and perplexity. We do not see our way clearly; we do not see what is to follow from what we have done, and how it bears upon our general conduct and opinions: yet perhaps it has the most important bearings. That little deed, suddenly exacted of us, almost suddenly resolved on and executed, may be as though a gate into the second or third heaven—an entrance into a higher state of holiness, and into a truer view of things than we have hitherto taken.

Or again, we get acquainted with some one whom God employs to bring before us a number of truths which were closed on us before; and we but half understand them, and but half approve of them; and yet God seems to speak in them, and Scripture to confirm them. This is a case which not unfrequently occurs, and it involves a call "to follow on to know the Lord."

Or again, we may be in the practice of reading Scripture carefully, and trying to serve God, and its sense may, as if suddenly, break upon us, in a way it never did before. Some thought may suggest itself to us which is a key to a great deal in Scripture, or which suggests a great many other thoughts. A new light may be thrown on the precepts of our Lord and His Apostles. We may be able to enter into the manner of life of the early Christians, as recorded in Scripture, which before was hidden from us, and into the simple maxims on which Scripture bases it. We may be led to understand that it is very different from the life which men live now. Now knowledge is a call to action: an insight into the way of perfection is a call to perfection.

Once more, it may so happen, that we find ourselves, how or why we cannot tell, much more able to obey God in certain respects than heretofore. Our minds are so strangely constituted, it is impossible to say whether it is from the growth of habit suddenly showing itself, or from an unusual gift of Divine grace poured into our hearts, but so it is; let our temptation be to sloth, or irresolution, or worldly anxiety, or pride, or to other more base and miserable sins, we may suddenly find ourselves possessed of a power of self-command which we had not before. Or again, we may have a resolution grow on us to serve God more strictly in His house and in private than heretofore. This is a call to higher things; let us beware lest we receive the grace of God in vain. Let us beware of lapsing back; let us avoid temptation. Let us strive by quietness and caution to cherish the feeble flame, and shelter it from the storms of this world. God may be bringing us into a higher world of religious truth; let us work with Him.

P.S., viii, 27-30.

13

It is useless, surely, attempting to inquire or judge, unless a Divine command enjoin the work upon us, and a Divine promise sustain us through it. Supposing, indeed, such a command and promise be given, then, of course, there is no difficulty in the matter. Whatever be our personal infirmities, He whom we serve can overrule or supersede them. An act of duty must always be right; and will be accepted, whatever be its success, because done in obedience to His will. And He can bless the most unpromising circumstances; He can even lead us forward by means of our mistakes; He can turn our mistakes into a revelation; He can convert us, if He will, through the very obstinacy, or self-will, or superstition which mixes itself up with our better feelings, and defiles, yet is sanctified by our sincerity. . . .

He continually leads us forward in the midst of darkness; and we live, not by bread only, but by His word converting the hard rock or salt sea into nourishment. . . . Our business is to ask with St. Paul, when arrested in the midst of his frenzy, "Lord, what wilt Thou have me to do?"

Ess., ii, 342-3.

14

I know, O my God, I must change, if I am to see Thy face! . . . . Body and soul must die to this world. My real self, my soul, must change by a true regeneration. None but the holy can see Thee. . . . Oh, support me, as I proceed in this great, awful, happy change, with the grace of Thy unchangeableness. My unchangeableness here below is perseverance in changing. Let me day by day be moulded upon Thee, and be changed from glory to glory, by ever looking towards Thee, and ever leaning on Thy arm. I know, O Lord, I must go through trial, temptation, and much conflict, if I am to come to Thee. I know not what lies before me, but I know as much as this. I know, too, that if Thou art not with me, my change will be for the worse, not for the better. Whatever fortune I have, be I rich or poor, healthy or sick, with friends or without, all will turn to evil if I am not sustained by the Unchangeable; all will turn to good if I have Jesus with me, yesterday and to-day the same, and for ever.

M.D., 508-9.

15

God has created me to do Him some definite service; He has committed some work to me which He has not committed to another. I have my mission—I never may know it in this life, but I shall be told it in the next. . . . I have a part in a great work; I am a link in a chain, a bond of connexion between persons. He has not created me for naught. I shall do good, I shall do His work; I shall be an angel of peace, a preacher of truth in my own place, while not intending it, if I do but keep His commandments and serve Him in my calling.

Therefore I will trust Him. Whatever, wherever I am, I can never be thrown away. If I am in sickness, my sickness may serve Him; in perplexity, my perplexity may serve Him; if I am in sorrow, my sorrow may serve Him. My sickness, or perplexity,

or sorrow may be necessary causes of some great end, which is
quite beyond us. He does nothing in vain; He may prolong my
life, He may shorten it; He knows what He is about. He may
take away my friends, He may throw me among strangers, He
may make me feel desolate, make my spirits sink, hide the future
from me—still He knows what He is about.

M.D., 400-1.

16

Nothing is more certain in matter of fact, than that some men
do feel themselves called to high duties and works, to which
others are not called. Why this is we do not know; whether it be
that those who are not called, forfeit the call from having failed in
former trials, or have been called and have not followed; or that
though God gives baptismal grace to all, yet He really does call
some men by His free grace to higher things than others; but so
it is; this man sees sights which that man does not see, has a larger
faith, a more ardent love, and a more spiritual understanding.
No one has any leave to take another's lower standard of holiness
for his own. It is nothing to us what others are. If God calls us
to greater renunciation of the world, and exacts a sacrifice of our
hopes and fears, this is our gain, this is a mark of His love for us,
this is a thing to be rejoiced in. Such thoughts, when properly
entertained, have no tendency to puff us up; for if the prospect is
noble, yet the risk is more fearful. While we pursue high excellence, we walk among precipices, and a fall is easy. Hence the
Apostle says, "Work out your own salvation with fear and
trembling, for it is God that worketh in you." Again, the more
men aim at high things, the more sensitive perception they have
of their own shortcomings; and this again is adapted to humble
them especially. We need not fear spiritual pride then, in
following Christ's call, if we follow it as men in earnest. Earnestness has no time to compare itself with the state of other men;
earnestness has too vivid a feeling of its own infirmities to be
elated at itself. Earnestness is simply set on doing God's will.
It simply says, "Speak, Lord, for Thy servant heareth," "Lord,
what wilt Thou have me to do?" Oh that we had more of this

spirit! Oh that we could take that simple view of things, as to feel that the one thing which lies before us is to please God! What gain is it to please the world, to please the great, nay, even to please those whom we love, compared with this? What gain is it to be applauded, admired, courted, followed, compared with this one aim, of not being disobedient to a heavenly vision? What can this world offer comparable with that insight into spiritual things, that keen faith, that heavenly peace, that high sanctity, that everlasting righteousness, that hope of glory, which they have who in sincerity love and follow our Lord Jesus Christ?

P.S., viii, 30-2.

17

Act up to your light, though in the midst of difficulties, and you will be carried on, you do not know how far. Abraham obeyed the call and journeyed, not knowing whither he went; so we, if we follow the voice of God, shall be brought on step by step into a new world, of which before we had no idea. This is His gracious way with us: He gives, not all at once, but by measure and season, wisely. To him that hath, more shall be given. But we must begin at the beginning. Each truth has its own order; we cannot join the way of life at any point of the course we please; we cannot learn advanced truths before we have learned primary ones.

P.S., viii, 195-6.

18

May it be our blessedness, as years go on, to add one grace to another, and advance upward, step by step, neither neglecting the lower after attaining the higher, nor aiming at the higher before attaining the lower. The first grace is faith, the last is love; first comes zeal, afterwards comes loving-kindness; first comes humiliation, then comes peace; first comes diligence, then comes resignation. May we learn to mature all graces in us;—fearing and trembling, watching and repenting, because Christ is coming; joyful, thankful, and careless of the future, because He is come.

P.S., v, 71.

In a higher world it is otherwise, but here below to live is to change, and to be perfect is to have changed often.

Dev., 40.

III. IN THE DARKNESS OF FAITH

20

God's presence is not discerned at the time when it is upon us, but afterwards, when we look back upon what is gone and over. . . Thus the presence of God is like His glory as it appeared to Moses; He said, "Thou canst not see my face . . . . and live"; but He passed by, and Moses saw that glory, as it retired, which he might not see in front, or in passing; he saw it, and he acknowledged it, and "made haste and bowed his head toward the earth and worshipped. . . ."

So, again, in a number of other occurrences, not striking, not grievous, not pleasant, but ordinary, we are able afterwards to discern that He has been with us, and, like Moses, to worship Him. Let a person who trusts he is on the whole serving God acceptably, look back upon his past life, and he will find how critical were moments and acts, which at the time seemed the most indifferent: as for instance, the school he was sent to as a child, the occasion of his falling in with those persons who have most benefited him, the accidents which determined his calling or prospects whatever they were. God's hand is ever over His own, and He leads them forward by a way they know not of. The utmost they can do is to believe, what they cannot see now, what they shall see hereafter; and as believing, to act together with God towards it. . . .

[Like this] is the sweetness and softness with which days long passed away fall upon the memory, and strike us. The most ordinary years, when we seemed to be living for nothing, these shine forth to us in their very regularity and orderly course. What was sameness at the time, is now stability; what was dullness, is now a soothing calm; what seemed unprofitable, has now its treasure in itself; what was but monotony, is now harmony; all is pleasing and comfortable, and we regard it all with affection. Nay, even sorrowful times (which at first sight is wonderful) are thus softened and illuminated afterwards: yet why should they not be so, since then, more than at other times, our Lord is present, when He seems leaving His own to desolateness and orphanhood? The planting of Christ's Cross in the heart is sharp and trying; but the stately tree rears itself aloft, and has fair branches and rich fruit, and is good to look upon. . . .

We come, like Jacob, in the dark, and lie down with a stone for our pillow; but when we rise again, and call to mind what has passed, we recollect we have seen a vision of Angels, and the Lord manifested through them, and we are led to cry out, "How dreadful is this place! This is *none other* than the house of God, and this is the gate of heaven. . . ."

The world seems to go on as usual. There is nothing of heaven in the face of society; in the news of the day there is nothing of heaven; in the faces of the many, or of the great, or of the rich, or of the busy, there is nothing of heaven; in the words of the eloquent, or the deeds of the powerful, or the counsels of the wise, or the resolves of the lordly, or the pomps of the wealthy, there is nothing of heaven. And yet the Ever-blessed Spirit of God is here; the Presence of the Eternal Son, ten times more glorious, more powerful than when He trod the earth in our flesh, is with us. Let us ever bear in mind this divine truth,—the more secret God's hand is, the more powerful—the more silent, the more awful.

P.S., *iv*, 256, 258, 261-2, 264-5.

21

Well were it for us, if we had . . . the temper of dependence upon God's providence, and thankfulness under it, and careful memory of all He has done for us. It would be well if we were in the habit of looking at all we have as God's gift, undeservedly given, and day by day continued to us solely by His mercy. He gave; He may take away. He gave us all we have, life, health, strength, reason, enjoyment, the light of conscience; whatever we have good and holy within us; whatever faith we have;

219

whatever of a renewed will; whatever love towards Him; whatever power over ourselves; whatever prospect of heaven. He gave us relatives, friends, education, training, knowledge, the Bible, the Church. All comes from Him. He gave; He may take away. Did He take away, we should be called on to follow Job's pattern, and be resigned: "The Lord gave, and the Lord hath taken away. Blessed be the Name of the Lord." While He continues His blessings, we should follow David and Jacob, by living in constant praise and thanksgiving, and in offering up to Him of His own.

P.S., *v*, 82-3.

22

We are not our own, any more than what we possess is our own. We did not make ourselves; we cannot be supreme over ourselves. We cannot be our own masters. We are God's property by creation, by redemption, by regeneration. He has a triple claim upon us. Is it not our happiness thus to view the matter? Is it any happiness, or any comfort, to consider that we *are* our own? It may be thought so by the young and prosperous. These may think it a great thing to have everything, as they suppose, their own way,—to depend on no one,—to have to think of nothing out of sight, to be without the irksomeness of continual acknowledgment, continual prayer, continual reference of what they do to the will of another. But as time goes on, they, as all men, will find that independence was not made for man—that it is an unnatural state—may do for a while, but will not carry us on safely to the end. No, we are creatures; and as being such, we have two duties, to be resigned and to be thankful.

P.S., *v*, 83, 84.

IV. IN THE BLINDNESS OF OBEDIENCE

23

It was a lesson continually set before the Israelites, that they were never to presume to act of themselves, but to wait till God wrought for them, to look on reverently, and then follow His guidance. God was their All-wise King: it was their duty to have no will of their own, distinct from His will, to form no plan of their own, to attempt no work of their own. *"Be still,* and know that I am God." Move not, speak not—look to the pillar of the cloud, see how *it* moves—then follow. Such was the command.

P.S., iii, 16.

24

We cannot change ourselves; this we know full well, or, at least, a very little experience will teach us. God alone can change us; God alone can give us the desires, affections, principles, views, and tastes which a change implies: this, too, we know. . . What then is it that we who profess religion lack? I repeat it, this: a willingness to *be* changed, a willingness to suffer (if I may use such a word), to suffer Almighty God to change us. . .But when a man comes to God to be saved, then, I say, the essence of true conversion is a *surrender* of himself, an unreserved, unconditional surrender; and this is a saying which most men who come to God cannot receive. They wish to be saved, but in their own way; they wish (as it were) to capitulate upon terms, to carry off their goods with them; whereas the true spirit of faith leads a man to look off from self to God, to think nothing of his own wishes, his present habits, his importance or dignity, his rights, his opinions, but to say, "I put myself into Thy hands, O Lord; make Thou me what Thou wilt; I forget myself; I divorce myself from myself; I am dead to myself; I will follow Thee." . . . . Here is the very voice of self-surrender, "What wilt thou have me to do? Take Thy own way with me; whatever it be, pleasant or painful, I will do it."

P.S., v, 241-2.

25

He may have made resolves before, he may have argued himself into a belief of his own sincerity, he may have (as it were) convinced himself that nothing can be required of him more than he has done, he may have asked himself what more *is* there to do, and yet have felt a something in him still which *needed* quieting, which was ever rising up and troubling him, and had to be put down again. But when he really gives himself up to God, when he gets himself honestly to say, "I sacrifice to Thee this cherished wish, this lust, this weakness, this scheme, this opinion: make me what *Thou* wouldest have me; I bargain for nothing; I make no terms; I seek for no previous information whither Thou art taking me; I will be what Thou wilt make me, and all that Thou wilt make me. I say not, I will follow Thee whithersoever Thou goest, for I am weak; but I give myself to Thee, to lead me anywhither. I will follow Thee in the dark, only begging Thee to give me strength according to my day. Try me, O Lord, and seek the ground of my heart; prove me, and examine my thoughts; look well if there be any way of wickedness in me"; search each dark recess with Thy own bright light, "and lead me in the way everlasting,"—what a difference is this! what a plain perceptible change, which cannot be mistaken! what a feeling of satisfaction is poured over the mind! what a sense that at length we are doing what we should do, and approving ourselves to God our Saviour!

P.S., v, 248-9.

26

What is meant by faith? It is to feel in good earnest that we are creatures of God; it is a practical perception of the unseen world; it is to understand that this world is not enough for our happiness, to look beyond it on towards God, to realize His presence, to wait upon Him, to endeavour to learn and to do His will, and to seek our good from Him. It is not a mere temporary strong act or impetuous feeling of the mind, an impression or a view coming upon it, but it is a *habit*, a state of mind, lasting and consistent. To have faith in God is to surrender one's self to God, humbly to put one's interests, or to wish to be allowed to put them, into His hands who is the Sovereign Giver of all good.

Now, again, let me ask, what is obedience? it is the obvious mode, suggested by nature, of a creature's conducting himself in God's sight, who fears Him as his Maker, and knows that, as a sinner, he has especial cause for fearing Him. Under such circumstances he "will do what he can" to please Him, as the woman

222

whom our Lord commended. He will look every way to see how it is possible to approve himself to Him, and will rejoice to find any service which may stand as a sort of proof that He is in earnest. And he will find nothing better as an offering, or as an evidence, than obedience to that Holy Law, which conscience tells him has been given us by God Himself; that is, he will be diligent in doing all his duty as far as he knows it and can do it. Thus, as is evident, the two states of mind are altogether one and the same: it is quite indifferent whether we say a man seeks God in faith, or say he seeks Him by obedience. . . .

But, in very truth, from the beginning to the end of Scripture, the one voice of inspiration consistently maintains not a uniform contrast between faith and obedience but this *one* doctrine, that the only way of salvation open to us is the *surrender* of ourselves to our Maker in all things—supreme devotion, resignation of our will, the turning with all our heart to God.

P.S., iii, 79-80, 82-83.

27

Doubtless, peace of mind, a quiet conscience, and a cheerful countenance are the gift of the Gospel, and the sign of a Christian; but the same effects (or, rather, what appear to be the same) may arise from very different causes. Jonah slept in the storm,—so did our Blessed Lord. The one slept in an evil security: the Other in the "peace of God which passeth all understanding." The two states cannot be confounded together, they are perfectly distinct; and as distinct is the calm of the man of the world from that of the Christian. . . . Now take the case of the sailors on board the vessel; they cried to Jonah, "What meanest thou, O sleeper?"—so the Apostles said to Christ; "Lord we perish." This is the case of the superstitious; they stand between the false peace of Jonah and the true peace of Christ; they are better than the one, though far below the Other. Applying this to the present religion of the educated world, full as it is of security and cheerfulness, and decorum and benevolence, I observe that these appearances may arise either from a great deal of religion, or from the absence of it; they may be the fruits of shallowness of mind

223

and a blinded conscience, or of that faith which has peace with God through our Lord Jesus Christ. . . .

You never can be sure of salvation, while you are here; and therefore you must always fear while you hope. Your knowledge of your sins increases with your view of God's mercy in Christ. And this is the true Christian state, and the nearest approach to Christ's calm and placid sleep in the tempest;—not perfect joy and certainty in heaven, but a deep resignation to God's will, surrender of ourselves, soul and body, to Him; hoping indeed that we shall be saved, but fixing our eyes more earnestly on Him than on ourselves; that is, acting for His glory, seeking to please Him, devoting ourselves to Him in all manly obedience and strenuous good works; and, when we do look within, thinking of ourselves with a certain abhorrence and contempt as being sinners, mortifying our flesh, scourging our appetites, and composedly awaiting that time when, if we be worthy, we shall be stripped of our present selves, and new made in the kingdom of Christ.

P.S., *i*, 321, 323-324.

28

Let us feel what we really are,—sinners attempting great things, and succeeding at best only so far as to show that we do attempt them. Let us simply obey God's will, whatever may befall; whether it tend to elate us or to depress us, what is that to us? He can turn all things to our eternal good. He can bless and sanctify even our infirmities. He can lovingly chastise us, if we be puffed up, and He can cheer us when we despond. He can and will exalt us the more we afflict ourselves; and we shall afflict ourselves the more, in true humbleness of mind, the more we really obey Him.

P.S., *iv*, 78.

29

Absolute certainty about our state cannot be attained at all in this life; but the nearest approach to such certainty which is possible, would seem to be afforded by this consciousness of openness and singleness of mind . . . . Those who have this integrity will more or less be conscious of it, therefore, after all exceptions duly made on the score of depression of spirits, perplexity of mind, horror at past sins, and the like, still, on the whole, really religious persons will commonly enjoy a subdued but comfortable hope and trust that they are in a state of justification. They may have this hope more or less; they may deserve to have it more or less; at times they may even be unconscious of it, and yet it may secretly support them; they may fancy themselves in perfect darkness, yet it may be a light cheering them forward; they may vary in their feelings about their state from day to day, and yet, whether or not they can collect evidence to satisfy their reason, still if they be really perfect in heart, there will be this secret sense of their sincerity, with their reason or against reason, to whisper to them peace. And on the other hand, it never will rise above a sober trust, even in the most calm, peaceful, and holy minds. They to the end will still but say, "Lord, I believe; help Thou mine unbelief." They still will say, in St. Paul's words, "I am conscious to myself of nothing, yet am I not hereby justified, but he that judgeth me is the Lord." "Judge me, O Lord; examine me; search the ground of my heart; judge *Thou* me, who art the sole Judge; I judge not myself. I do but say, *Thou* knowest me: I say not, I know."

P.S., v, 250-1.

30

O my Lord and Saviour, in Thy arms I am safe; keep me and I have nothing to fear; give me up and I have nothing to hope for. I know not what will come upon me before I die. I know nothing about the future, but I rely upon Thee. I pray Thee to give me what is good for me; I pray Thee to take from me whatever may imperil my salvation; I pray Thee not to make me rich, I pray Thee not to make me very poor; but I leave it all to Thee, because Thou knowest and I do not. If Thou bringest pain or sorrow on me, give me grace to bear it well—keep me from fretfulness, and selfishness. If Thou givest me health and strength

225

and success in this world, keep me ever on my guard lest these great gifts carry me away from Thee.

O Thou who didst die on the Cross for me, even for me, sinner as I am, give me to know Thee, to believe on Thee, to love Thee, to serve Thee; ever to aim at setting forth Thy glory; to live to and for Thee; to set a good example to all around me; give me to die just at that time and in that way which is most for Thy glory, and best for my salvation.

M.D., 285-6.

V. IN AWE

31

In a Christian's course, *fear and love must go together.* . . . In heaven, love will absorb fear; but in this world, *fear and love must go together.* No one can love God aright without fearing Him; though many fear Him, and yet do not love Him. Self-confident men who do not know their own hearts, or the reasons they have for being dissatisfied with themselves, do not fear God, and they think this bold freedom is to love Him. Deliberate sinners fear but cannot love Him. But devotion to Him consists in love and fear. . . . The bitter and the sweet, strangely tempered, thus leave upon the mind the lasting taste of Divine truth, and satisfy it; not so harsh as to be loathed; nor of that insipid sweetness which attends enthusiastic feelings, and is wearisome when it becomes familiar. Such is the feeling of conscience, too, God's original gift; how painful! yet who would lose it?

P.S., i, 303-5.

32

Were we pure as the Angels, yet in His sight, one should think, we could not but fear, before whom the heavens are not clean, nor the Angels free from folly. The Seraphim themselves veiled their faces while they cried, Glory! Even then were it true that sin was not a great evil, or was no great evil in us, nevertheless the mere circumstance that God is infinite and all-perfect is an overwhelming thought to creatures and mortal men, and ought to lead all persons who profess religion to profess also religious fear, however natural it is for irreligious men to disclaim the feeling. . . .

[This religious fear belongs to] the class of feelings we *should* have,—yes, have in an intense degree—if we literally had the sight of Almighty God; therefore they are the class of feelings which we shall have, *if* we realize His presence. In proportion as we believe that He is present we shall have them; and not to have them is not to realize, not to believe that He is present. . . .

If a man believes Him present, he will shrink from addressing Him familiarly, or using before Him unreal words, or peremptorily and on his own judgment deciding what God's will is, or claiming His confidence, or addressing Him in a familiar posture of body. I say, take the man who is most confident that he has nothing to fear from the presence of God, and that Almighty God is at peace with him, and place him actually before the throne of God; and would he have no misgivings? and will he dare to say that those misgivings are a weakness, a mere irrational perturbation, which he ought not to feel?

This will be seen more clearly, by considering how differently we feel towards and speak of our friends as present or absent. Their presence is a check upon us; it acts as an external law, compelling us to do or not do what we should not do or do otherwise, or should do but for it. This is just what most men lack in their religion at present,—such an external restraint arising from the consciousness of God's presence. Consider, I say, how differently we speak of a friend, however intimate, when present or absent; consider how we feel, should it so happen that we have begun to speak of him as if he were not present, on finding suddenly that he is; and that, though we are conscious of nothing but what is loving and open towards him. There is a tone of voice and a manner of speaking about persons absent, which we should consider disrespectful, or at least inconsiderate, if they were present. When that is the case, we are ever thinking more or less, even though we don't say, how it will affect them, what they will say to us or think of us in turn. When a person is absent, we are tempted perhaps confidently to say what his opinion is on certain points;—but should he be present, we qualify our words; we hardly like to speak at all, from the vivid consciousness that we may be wrong, and that he is present to tell us so. We are very cautious of pronouncing what his feelings are on the matter in hand, or how he is disposed towards ourselves; and in all things we observe a deference and delicacy in our conduct towards him. Now, if we feel this towards our fellows, what shall we feel in the presence of an Angel? and if so, what in the presence of the All-knowing, All-searching Judge of men? What is respect and consideration in the case of our fellows becomes godly fear as regards Almighty God; and they who do not fear Him, in one word, do not believe that He sees and hears them. If they did, they would cease to boast so confidently of His favourable thoughts of them, to foretell His dealings, to pronounce upon His revelations, to make free with His Name, and to address Him familiarly. . .

We shall in time, in our mode of talking and acting, in our religious services, and our daily conduct, manifest, not with constraint and effort, but spontaneously and naturally, that we fear Him while we love Him.

P.S., *v*, 16; 21-24; 28.

VI. OF OUR OWN WORK

33

There are two opposite errors: one, the holding that salvation is not of God; the other, that it is not in ourselves. Now it is remarkable that the maintainers of both the one and the other error, whatever their differences in other respects, agree in this,— in depriving a Christian life of its mysteriousness. He who believes that he can please God of himself, or that obedience can be performed by his own powers, of course has nothing more of awe, reverence, and wonder in his personal religion than when he moves his limbs and uses his reason, though he might well feel awe then also. And in like manner he also who considers that Christ's passion once undergone on the Cross absolutely secured his own personal salvation, may see mystery indeed in that Cross (as he ought), but he will see no mystery, and feel little solemnity, in prayer, in ordinances, or in his attempts at obedience. He will be free, familiar, and presuming, in God's presence. Neither will "work out their salvation with fear and trembling"; for neither will realize, though they use the words, that God is in them "to will and to do." Both the one and the other will be content with a low standard of duty: the one, because he does not believe that God requires much; the other, because he thinks that Christ in His own person has done all. Neither will honour and make much of God's Law: the one, because he brings down the Law to his own power of obeying it; the other, because he thinks that Christ has taken away the Law by obeying it in his stead. They only feel awe and true seriousness who think that the Law remains; that it claims to be fulfilled by them; and that it can be fulfilled in them through the power of God's grace. Not that any man alive arises up to that perfect fulfilment, but that such fulfilment is not impossible; that it is begun in all true Christians; that they all are tending to it; are growing into it; and are pleasing to God because they are becoming, and in proportion as they are becoming like Him who, when He came on earth in our flesh, fulfilled the Law perfectly.

P.S., v, 140-142.

34

"Work out" or accomplish "your own salvation with fear and trembling, *for* it is God which worketh" or acts "in you." So far was he from thinking man's distinct working inconsistent with God's continual aiding, that he assigns the knowledge of the latter as an encouragement to the former. Let me challenge then a Predestinarian to paraphrase this text. We, on the contrary, find no insuperable difficulty in it, considering it to enjoin upon us a deep awe and reverence, while we engage in those acts and efforts which are to secure our salvation from the belief that God is in us and with us, inspecting and succouring our every thought and deed. Would not the Jewish High Priest, on the Great Day of Atonement, when going through his several acts of propitiation in God's presence, without and within the Veil, "exceedingly fear and quake," lest he should fail in aught

229

put upon him? and shall not we, in our more blessed Covenant, knowing that God himself is within us, and in all we do, fear the more from the thought that, after all, we have our own part in the work, and must do it well, if we are to be saved?

P.S., ii, 327.

35

Those whom Christ saves are they who at once attempt to save themselves, yet despair of saving themselves; who aim to do all, and confess they do nought; who are all love, and all fear; who are the most holy, and yet confess themselves the most sinful; who ever seek to please Him, yet feel they never can; who are full of good works, yet of works of penance. All this seems a contradiction to the natural man, but it is not so to those whom Christ enlightens. They understand in porportion to their illumination, that it is possible to work out their salvation, yet to have it wrought out for them, to fear and tremble at the thought of judgment, yet to rejoice always in the Lord, and hope and pray for His coming.

P.S., vii, 12.

VII.   THROUGH TRIAL
36

There will ever be persons who take a favourable view of human nature, as it actually is found in the world, and of the spiritual condition and the prospects of mankind. And certainly the face of things is so fair, and contains so much that is interesting and lofty, that the spectator may be pardoned if, on the first sight, he is disposed to believe them to be as cheerful and as happy as they appear,—the evils of life as light and transitory, and its issue as satisfactory. Such easy confidence is natural in youth; nay, it is even commendable at a time of life in which suspicion and incredulity are unbecoming; that is, it *would* be commendable did not Scripture acquaint us from the very first (by way of warning, previous to our actual experience) with the deceitfulness of the world's promises and teaching; telling us of the opposition between Sight and Faith, of that strait gate and that narrow way, the thought of which is to calm us in youth, that it may enliven and invigorate us in old age.

Yet, on the other hand, it cannot be denied that even the information of Scripture results in a cheerful view of human affairs, and condemns gloom and sadness as a sin, as well as a mistake; and thus, in fact, altogether sanctions the conclusions gathered from the first sight of the course of the world. . . .

The Gospel is in its very name a message of peace, but it must never be separated from the bad tidings of our fallen nature, which it reverses; and he who speaks of the state of the world in a sanguine way, may indeed be an advanced Christian, but he may also be much less even than a proselyte of the gate; and if his security and peace of mind be merely the calm of ignorance, surely the men whom he looks down upon as narrow-minded and superstitious, whose religion consists in fear not in love, shall go into the kingdom of heaven before him.

Easter Day, our Chief Festival, is preceded by the forty days of Lent, to show us that they, and they only, who sow in tears, shall reap in joy.

U.S., 99-102.

37

Sometimes we speak (at least the poor often so speak) as though present hardship and suffering were in some sense a ground of confidence in themselves as to our future prospects, whether as expiating our sins or bringing our hearts nearer to God. Nay, even the more religious among us may be misled to think that pain makes them better than it really does; for the effect of it at length, on any but very proud or ungovernable tempers, is to cause a languor and composure of mind, which looks like resignation, while it necessarily throws our reason upon the especial *thought* of God, our only stay in such times of trial. . . . Pain does not commonly improve us, but without care it has a strong tendency to do our souls harm, viz., by making us selfish; an effect produced even when it does us good in other ways. . . .

231

Men find an excuse in their infirmities for some extraordinary attention to their comforts; they consider they may fairly consult, on all occasions, their own convenience rather than that of another. They indulge their wayward wishes, allow themselves in indolence when they really might exert themselves, and think they may be fretful because they are weak. . . .

Doubtless suffering does really benefit the Christian, and in no scanty measure; and he may thank God who thus blesses it; only let him be cautious of *measuring* his spiritual state by the particular exercise of faith and love in his heart at the time, especially if that exercise be limited to the affections themselves, and have no opportunity of showing itself in works.

P.S., iii, 144-5.

38

All afflictions of the flesh, such as the Gospel enjoins, and St. Paul practised, watchings and fastings, and subjecting of the body, have no tendency whatever in themselves to make men better; they often have made men worse; they often (to appearance) have left them just as they were before. They are no sure test of holiness and true faith, taken by themselves. A man may be most austere in his life, and, by that very austerity, learn to be cruel to others, not tender. And, on the other hand (what seems strange), he may be austere in his personal habits, and yet be a waverer and a coward in his conduct. Such things have been,—I do not say they are likely in this state of society,—but I mean, it should ever be borne in mind, that the severest and most mortified life is as little a passport to heaven, or a criterion of saintliness, as benevolence is, or usefulness, or amiableness. Self-discipline is a necessary condition, but not a sure sign of holiness. It may leave a man worldly, or it may make him a tyrant. It is only in the hands of God that it is God's instrument. It only ministers to God's purposes when God uses it. It is only when grace is in the heart, when power from above dwells in a man, that anything outward or inward turns to his salvation. Whether persecution, or famine, or the sword, they as little

232

bring the soul to Christ as they separate it from Him. He alone can work, and He can work through all things.

P.S., *v*, 304-5.

39

On such a day [Easter day], then, from the very intensity of joy which Christians ought to feel, and the trial which they have gone through, they will often be disposed to say little. Rather, like sick people convalescent, when the crisis is past, the illness over, but strength not yet come, they will go forth to the light of day and the freshness of the air, and silently sit down with great delight under the shadow of that Tree, whose fruit is sweet to their taste. They are disposed rather to muse and be at peace, than to use many words; for their joy has been so much the child of sorrow, is of so transmuted and complex a nature, so bound up with painful memories and sad associations, that though it is a joy only the greater from the contrast, it is not, cannot be, as if it had never been sorrow.

For in this does Christian mirth differ from worldly, that it is subdued; and how shall it be subdued except that the past keeps its hold upon us, and while it warns and sobers us, actually indisposes and tames our flesh against indulgence? In the world feasting comes first and fasting afterwards; men first glut themselves, and then loathe their excesses; they take their fill of good, and then suffer; they are rich that they may be poor; they laugh that they may weep; they rise that they may fall. But in the Church of God it is reversed; the poor *shall* be rich, the lowly shall be exalted, those that sow in tears shall reap in joy, those that mourn shall be comforted, those that suffer with Christ shall reign with Him. . . . Our Festivals are preceded by humiliation, that we may keep them duly; not boisterously or fanatically, but in a refined, subdued, chastised spirit, which is the true rejoicing in the Lord. . . .

A holy, tender, reverent, manly joy, not *so* manly as to be rude, not *so* tender as to be effeminate, but (as if) an Angel's mood, the mingled offering of all that is best and highest in man's and woman's nature brought together,—St. Mary Magdalen and St. Peter blended into St. John.

P.S., *iv*, 339-41.

40

Easter is a Day which has made us greater than we know. It is our Day of rest, the true Sabbath. Christ entered into His rest, and so do we. It brings us, in figure, through the grave and gate of death to our season of refreshment in Abraham's bosom. We have had enough of weariness, and dreariness, and listlessness, and sorrow, and remorse. We have had enough of this troublesome world. We have had enough of its noise and din. Noise is its best music. But now there is stillness; and it is a stillness that speaks. We know how strange the feeling is of perfect silence after continued sound. Such is our blessedness now. Calm and serene days have begun; and Christ is heard in them, and His still small voice, because the world speaks not. Let us only put off the world, and we put on Christ. The receding from one is an approach to the other.

P.S., *vi*, 103.

41

If we had been told merely to fear, we should have mistaken a slavish dread, or the gloom of despair, for godly fear; and if we had been told merely to rejoice, we should perhaps have mistaken a rude freedom and familiarity for joy; but when we are told both to fear and to rejoice, we gain thus much at first sight, that our joy is not to be irreverent, nor our fear to be desponding; that though both feelings are to remain, neither is to be what it would be by itself. . .

The duty of fearing does but perfect our joy; that joy alone is true Christian joy which is informed and quickened by fear, and made thereby sober and reverent.

P.S., *v*, 65-6.

42

All God's providences, all God's dealings with us, all His judgments, mercies, warnings, deliverances, tend to peace and repose as their ultimate issue.   All our troubles and pleasures here, all our anxieties, fears, doubts, difficulties, hopes, encouragements, afflictions, losses, attainments, tend this one way.   After Christmas, Easter, Whitsuntide, comes Trinity Sunday, and the weeks that follow; and in like manner, after our soul's anxious travail; after the birth of the Spirit; after trial and temptation; after sorrow and pain; after daily dyings to the world; after daily risings unto holiness; at length comes that "rest which remaineth unto the people of God."   After the fever of life; after weariness and sicknesses; fightings and despondings; languor and fretfulness; struggling and failing; struggling and succeeding; after all the changes and chances of this troubled unhealthy state, at length comes death, at length the White Throne of God, at length the Beatific Vision.

P.S., vi, 369-70.

43

It is our blessedness to be made like the all-holy, all-gracious, long-suffering, and merciful God; who made and who redeemed us; in whose presence is perfect rest, and perfect peace; whom the Seraphim are harmoniously praising, and the Cherubim tranquilly contemplating, and Angels silently serving, and the Church thankfully worshipping.

P.S., vi, 326.

XII: THE BODY OF CHRIST

ANALYTICAL SUMMARY

It is no doubt true that God must be "all in all," and therefore in the last resort the soul must stand alone face to face with God.

But Christ, in whom alone God shines upon fallen man, has willed a society as "His Body," and therefore this ultimate solitude with God is first given to us, restored in this society: a solitude through society, solitude in society; Love to God in Love to my neighbour, God in God's children. "He that loveth not his brother whom he hath seen—how can he love God whom he hath not seen?"

(Nos. 1-2.)

Thus is the law of responsibility for oneself bound up with the law of responsibility for our fellows; Personal Guilt with Social Guilt, penance with vicarious atonement; "I fill up in my flesh that which is lacking of the suffering of Christ for His body's sake which is the Church."

(No. 3.)

And prayer, the most intimate intercourse between God and the soul, is expanded into an intercourse between souls in God; mediation, intercession becomes the distinctive characteristic of the Christian life of prayer, the prayer of "Christ's body."

(Nos. 4-5.)

237

BUT *cui bono* is a visible kingdom, when the great end of our Lord's
ministry is moral advancement and preparation for a future
state? It is easy to understand, for instance, how a sermon may
benefit, or personal example, or religious friends, or household
piety. We can learn to imitate a saint or martyr . . . we can obey a
rule; but what is the definite advantage to a preacher or a
moralist of an external organization or a visible kingdom? Yet
Christ says, "Seek ye *first* the Kingdom of God," as well as "His
justice." Socrates wished to improve man, but he laid no stress on
their acting in concert in order to secure that improvement; on
the contrary, the Christian law is political, as certainly as it is
moral.

Why is this? It arises out of the intimate relation between Him
and His subjects, which, in bringing them all to Him as their
common Father, necessarily brings them to each other. Our
Lord says, "where two or three are gathered together in My
name, I am in the midst of them." Fellowship between His
followers is made a distinct object and duty, because it is a means,
according to the provisions of His system, by which in some special
way they are brought near to Him. This is declared, still more
strikingly than in the text we have just quoted, in the parable of
the Vine and its Branches, and in that (if it is to be called a
parable) of the Bread of Life. The almighty King of Israel was
ever, indeed, invisibly present in the glory above the Ark, but He
did not manifest Himself there or anywhere else as a present
cause of spiritual strength to His people; but the new King is not
only ever present, but to every one of His subjects individually is
He a first element and perennial source of life. He is not only the

Head of His Kingdom, but also its animating principle and its centre of power.

D.A., 378-9.

2

Christ finds us in the double tabernacle, of a house of flesh and a house of brethren, and He sanctifies both, not pulls them down. Our first life is in ourselves; our second in our friends. They whom God forces to part with their near of kin, for His sake, find brethren in the spirit at their side. They who remain solitary, for His sake, have children in the spirit raised up to them. How should we thank God for this great benefit! Now especially, when we are soon to retire, more or less, into ourselves, and to refrain from our ordinary intercourse with one another, let us acknowledge the blessing, whether of the holy marriage bond, or of family affection, or of the love of friends, which He so bounteously bestows. He gives, He takes away; blessed be His Name. But He takes away to give again, and He withdraws one blessing, to restore fourfold. Abraham offered his only son, and received Him back again at the Angel's voice. Isaac "took Rebekah, and she became his wife, and he loved her; and Isaac was comforted after his mother's death." Jacob lost Joseph, and found him governor of Egypt. Job lost all his children, yet his end was more blessed than his beginning. We, too, through God's mercy, whether we be young or old, whether we have many friends or few, if we be Christ's, shall all along our pilgrimage find those in whom we may live, who will love us and whom we may love, who will aid us and help us forward, and comfort us, and close our eyes. For His love is a secret gift, which, unseen by the world, binds together those in whom it lives, and makes them live and sympathise in one another.

P.S., *v*, 279-280.

3

It is the law, or the permission, given to our whole race, to use the Apostle's words, to "bear one another's burdens"; and this, as I said when on the subject of Atonement, is quite consistent with his antithesis that "every one must bear his own burden." The final burden of responsibility when we are called to judgment is our own; but among the media by which we are prepared for that judgment are the exertions and pains taken in our behalf by others. On this vicarious principle, by which we appropriate to ourselves what others do for us, the whole structure of society is raised. Parents work and endure pain, that their children may prosper; children suffer for the sin of their parents, who have died before it bore fruit. "Delirant reges, plectuntur Achivi." Sometimes it is a compulsory, sometimes a willing mediation. The punishment which is earned by the husband falls upon the wife; the benefits in which all classes partake are wrought out by the unhealthy or dangerous toil of the few. Soldiers endure wounds and death for those who sit at home; and ministers of state fall victims to their zeal for their countrymen, who do little else than criticize their actions. And so in some measure or way this law embraces all of us. We all suffer for each other, and gain by each other's sufferings; for man never stands alone here, though he will stand by himself one day hereafter; but here he is a social being, and goes forward to his long home as one of a large company.

When the time comes, which conscience forebodes, of our being called to judgment, then, at least, we shall have to stand in and by ourselves, whatever we shall have by that time become, and must bear our own burden. But it is plain that in this final account, as it lies between us and our Master, He alone can decide how the past and the present will stand together who is our Creator and our Judge.

G. A., 394-5.

4

Intercession. . . . is the Christian's especial prerogative; and if he does not exercise it, certainly he has not risen to the conception of his real place among created beings. Say not he is a son of Adam and has to undergo a future judgment; I know it; but he is something besides. How far he is advanced into that higher state of being, how far he still languishes in his first condition, is, in the case of individuals, a secret with God. Still every Christian is in a certain sense both in the one and in the other; viewed in himself he ever prays for pardon, and confesses sin; but viewed in Christ, he "has access into this grace wherein we stand, and rejoices in hope of the glory of God." Viewed in his place in "the Church of the First-born enrolled in heaven," with his original debt cancelled in Baptism, and all subsequent penalties put aside by Absolution, standing in God's presence upright and irreprovable, accepted in the Beloved, clad in the garments of righteousness, anointed with oil, and with a crown upon his head, in royal and priestly garb, as an heir of eternity, full of grace and good works, as walking in all the commandments of the Lord blameless—such a one, I repeat it, is plainly in his fitting place when he intercedes. He is made after the pattern and in the fulness of Christ—he is what Christ is. Christ intercedes above, and he intercedes below.

P.S., iii, 362-3.

5

Prayer indeed is the very essence of all religion; but in the heathen religions it was either public or personal; it was a state ordinance, or a selfish expedient for the attainment of certain tangible, temporal goods. Very different from this was its exercise among Christians, who were thereby knit together in one body, different, as they were in races, ranks, and habits, distant from each other in country, and helpless amid hostile populations...

Christians could not correspond; they could not combine; but they could pray one for another. Even their public prayers partook of this character of intercession; for to pray for the welfare of the whole Church was in fact prayer for all the classes of men and all the individuals of which it was composed. . . . Intercession thus being a first principle of the Church's life, next it is certain again that the vital force of that intercession, as an availing power, is, (according to the will of God), sanctity.

Diff., ii, 68, 69, 71.

XIII: THE BOND OF LOVE

ANALYTICAL SUMMARY

Love (Charity) is thus the fundamental characteristic distinctive of the Christian, the life of the one body—"if I have not charity, I am nothing:"

But the love of which Christ spoke—"Love one another as I have loved you": love in the spirit and imitation of Christ.

As Christ first called two disciples, and by their means gradually called the others, first of all the twelve, then the seventy and through the work of this "little flock" the large flock, the many by means of the few; so the life of the one Body continues to maintain and renew itself and to develop by the selection of a "few" for a blameless following and imitation of Christ, that they may be a leaven for the "Many."

(Nos. 1-3.)

Thus wise Christian love begins its work with those individual souls which God's providence has specially entrusted to it, to spread thence in quiet growth to the many; a heartfelt personal love to every man individually, but a love which does not remain tied to earth; which includes a holy detachment and is always prepared for separation when God calls.

(Nos. 4-11.)

243

I. THE FEW FOR THE MANY

I

Our Saviour says, "Narrow is the way." This, of course, must not be interpreted without great caution; yet surely the whole tenor of the Inspired Volume leads us to believe that His Truth will not be heartily received by the many, that it is against the current of human feeling and opinion, and the course of the world, and so far forth as it *is* received by a man, will be opposed by himself, i.e., by his old nature which remains about him, next by all others, so far forth as they have not received it. "The light shining in darkness" is the token of true religion; and, though doubtless there are seasons when a sudden enthusiasm arises in favour of the Truth, . . . yet such a popularity of the Truth is *but* sudden, comes at once and goes at once, has no regular growth, no abiding stay. It is error alone which grows and is received heartily on a large scale . . . Truth, indeed, has that power in it, that it forces man to profess it in words; but when they go on to act, instead of obeying *it*, they substitute some idol in the place of it. On these accounts, when there is much talk of religion in a country, and much congratulation that there is a general concern for it, a cautious mind will feel anxious lest some counterfeit be, in fact, honoured instead of it: lest it be the dream of man rather than the verities of God's word which has become popular, and lest the received form have no more of truth in it than is just necessary to recommend it to the reason and conscience:—lest, in short, it be Satan transformed into an angel of light, rather than the Light itself, which is attracting followers.

P.S., *i*, 61, 62.

Unless it be maintained that the Church has never done her duty towards the nations where she has sojourned, it must be granted that success in the hearts of the many is not promised her. Christianity has raised the tone of morals, has restrained the passions, and enforced external decency and good conduct in the world at large; it has advanced certain persons in virtuous or religious habits, who otherwise might have been imbued with the mere rudiments of truth and holiness; it has given a firmness and consistency to religious profession in numbers, and perhaps has extended the range of really religious practice. Still on the whole the great multitude of men have to all appearance remained, in a spiritual point of view, no better than before. The state of great cities now is not so very different from what it was of old; or at least not so different as to make it appear that the main work of Christianity has lain with the face of society, or what is called the world. Again, the highest class in the community and the lowest, are not so different from what they would be respectively without the knowledge of the Gospel, as to allow it to be said that Christianity has succeeded with the world, *as* the world, in its several ranks and classes. And so of its pursuits and professions; they are in character what they were, softened or restrained in their worst consequences, but still with the same substantial fruits. Trade is still avaricious, not in tendency only but in fact, though it has heard the Gospel; physical science is still sceptical as it was when heathen. Lawyers, soldiers, farmers, politicians, courtiers, nay, shame to say, the priesthood, still savour of the old Adam. Christian states move forward upon the same laws as before, and rise and fall as time goes on upon the same internal principles. Human nature remains what it was, though it has been baptized; the proverbs, the satires, the pictures, of which it was the subject in heathen times, have their point still. In a word, taking religion to mean, as it well may, the being bound by God's law, the acting under God's will instead of our own, how few are there in a country called Christian who even profess religion in this sense! how few there are who live by any other rule than that of their own ease: habit, inclination, as the case may be, on the one hand, and of external circumstances on the other! with how few is the will of God an habitual object of thought, or search, or love, or obedience!. . . . There are in every age a certain number of souls in the world, known to God, unknown to us, who will obey the Truth when offered to them, whatever be the mysterious reason that they do and others do not. These we must contemplate, for these we must labour, these are God's special care, for these are all things; of these and among these we must pray to be, and our friends with us, at the Last Day. They are the true Church, ever increasing in number, ever gathering in, as time goes on; with them lies the Communion of Saints; they have power with God; they are His armies who follow the Lamb, who overcome princes of the earth, and who shall hereafter judge Angels. . . .

In like manner St. Paul says that Christ came, not to convert the world, but "to purify unto Himself a *peculiar people* zealous of good works"; not to sanctify this evil world, but to "deliver us *out of* this present evil world according to the will of God and our Father." Not to turn the whole world into a heaven, but to bring down a heaven upon earth. This has been the real triumph of the Gospel, to raise those beyond themselves and beyond human nature, in whatever rank and condition of life, whose wills mysteriously co-operate with God's grace, who while God visits them really fear and really obey God, whatever be the unknown reason why one man obeys Him, and another not. It has made men saints, and brought into existence specimens of faith and holiness, which without it are unknown and impossible. It has laboured for the elect, and it has succeeded with them. This is, as it were, its token. An ordinary kind of religion, praiseworthy and respectable in its way, may exist under many systems; but saints are creations of the Gospel and the Church. Not that such a one need in his lifetime seem to be more than other well-living men, for his graces lie deep, and are not known and understood till after his death, even if then. But then, it may be, he "shines forth as the sun in the kingdom of his Father," figuring in his memory on earth what will be fulfilled in soul and body in heaven.

P.S., iv, 153, 154-5, 156-7.

It is indeed, a *general* characteristic of the course of His providence to make the few the channels of His blessings to the many. .

It is plain that every great change is effected by the few, not by the many; by the resolute, undaunted zealous few. . . .

One or two men, of small outward pretensions, but with their hearts in their work, these do great things. These are prepared, not by sudden excitement, or by vague general belief in the truth of their cause, but by deeply impressed, often repeated instruction; and since it stands to reason that it is easier to teach a few than a great number, it is plain such men always will be few. . . .

He that believeth on the Son of God hath the witness in himself. Truth bears witness by itself to its Divine Author. He who obeys God conscientiously, and lives holily, forces all about him to believe and tremble before the unseen power of Christ. To the world indeed at large he witnesses not; for few can see him near enough to be moved by his manner of living. But to his neighbours he manifests the Truth in proportion to their knowledge of him; and some of them, through God's blessing, catch the holy flame, cherish it, and in their turn transmit it. And thus in a dark world Truth still makes way in spite of the darkness, passing from hand to hand. And thus it keeps its station in high places, acknowledged as the creed of nations, the multitude of which are ignorant, the while, on what it rests, how it came there, how it keeps its ground; and despising it, think it easy to dislodge it. But "the Lord reigneth."

P.S., 286-8, 292-3.

II.   GROWTH IN LOVE

4

It is obviously impossible to love all men in any strict and true sense. What is meant by loving all men, is, to feel well-disposed to all men, to be ready to assist them, and to act towards those who come in our way, as if we loved them. We cannot love those about whom we know nothing; except indeed we view them in

Christ, as the objects of His Atonement, that is, rather in faith than in love. And love, besides, is a habit, and cannot be obtained without actual *practice*, which on so large a scale is impossible. We see then how absurd it is when writers (as is the manner of some who slight the Gospel) talk magnificently about loving the whole human race with a comprehensive affection, of being the friends of all mankind, and the like. Such vaunting professions, what do they come to? that such men have certain benevolent *feelings* towards the world,—feelings and nothing more;—nothing more than unstable feelings, the mere offspring of an indulged imagination, which exist only when their minds are wrought upon, and are sure to fail them in the hour of need. This is not to love men, it is but to talk about love.—The real love of man *must* depend on practice, and therefore, must begin by exercising itself on our friends around us, otherwise it will have no existence. By trying to love our relations and friends, by submitting to their wishes, though contrary to our own, by bearing with their infirmities, by overcoming their occasional waywardness by kindness, by dwelling on their excellences, and trying to copy them, thus it is that we form in our hearts that root of charity, which, though small at first, may, like the mustard seed, at last even overshadow the earth.

P.S., ii, 54, 55.

5

A man, who would fain begin by a general love of all men, necessarily puts them all on a level, and, instead of being cautious, prudent, and sympathising in his benevolence, is hasty and rude; does harm, perhaps, when he means to do good, discourages the virtuous and well-meaning, and wounds the feelings of the gentle. Men of ambitious and ardent minds, for example, desirous of doing good on a large scale, are especially exposed to the temptation of sacrificing individual to general good in their plans of charity. Ill-instructed men, who have strong abstract notions about the necessity of showing generosity and candour towards opponents, often forget to take any thought of those who are associated with themselves; and commence their (so-called) liberal treatment of their enemies by an unkind desertion of their friends. This can hardly be the case, when men cultivate the private charities as an introduction to more enlarged ones. By laying a foundation of social amiableness, we insensibly learn to observe a due harmony and order in our charity; we learn that all men are not on a level; that the interests of truth and holiness must be religiously observed; and that the Church has claims upon us before the world. We can easily afford to be liberal on a large scale, when we have no affections to stand in the way. Those who have not accustomed themselves to love their neighbours whom they have seen, will have nothing to lose or gain, nothing to grieve at or rejoice in, in their larger plans of benevolence. They will take no interest in them for their own sake; rather they will engage in them, because expedience demands, or credit is gained, or an excuse found for being busy.

P.S., *ii*, 56-7.

6

Nothing is more likely to engender selfish habits (which is the direct opposite and negation of charity), than *independence* in our worldly circumstances. Men who have no tie on them, who have no calls on their daily sympathy and tenderness, who have no one's comfort to consult, who can move about as they please, and indulge the love of variety and the restless humours which are so congenial to the minds of most men, are very unfavourably situated for obtaining that heavenly gift which is described in our Liturgy as being "the very bond of peace and of all virtues." On the other hand, I cannot fancy any state of life more favourable for the exercise of high Christian principle, and the matured and refined Christian spirit (that is, where the parties really seek to do their duty), than that of persons who differ in tastes and general character, being obliged by circumstances to live together, and mutually to accommodate to each other their respective wishes and pursuits. And this is one among the many providential benefits (to those who will receive them) arising out of the Holy Estate of Matrimony; which not only calls out the tenderest and gentlest feelings of our nature, but, where persons do their duty, must be in various ways more or less a state of self-denial.

P.S., ii, 58.

7

Supposing a monastic life were nothing else than seclusion in the cloister, would it in consequence have no trials and duties? Is there not trial, duty, self-denial of many kinds in a family? Is it not as difficult as it is "good and joyful for brethren to dwell together in unity?" Is there not much exercise of temper, much call on a placable, unselfish patient, forbearing cheerful disposition, much occasion for self-control in word and in deed, in family life. . . . Nor is even the eremitical life itself, nor (surely) much less are associations for the main purpose of prayer and intercession incapable of justification. . . . To be shut out from the world is their very duty to the world; to be in leisure is their business; and as well might we call a schoolmaster inactive, or a private circle anti-social, as an institution which devotes itself to repentance, intercession, and giving of thanks for the benefit of seculars,—as a propitiation in the sight of heaven, and a witness and warning before men,—as the home of the helpless, and the refuge of the downcast,—as a common mould of character, and a bond of mutual love, and a principle of united worship to all, because it is successively the school and confessional of each.

Ess., 413, 418, 419.

8

Young people, indeed, readily love each other, for they are cheerful and innocent; more easily yield to each other, and are full of hope;—types, as Christ says, of His true converts. But this happiness does not last; their tastes change. Again, grown persons go on for years as friends; but these do not live together; and, if any accident throws them into familiarity for a while, they find it difficult to restrain their tempers and keep on terms, and discover that they are best friends at a distance. But what is it that can bind two friends together in intimate converse for a course of years, but the participation in something that is Unchangeable and essentially Good, and what is this but religion? Religious tastes alone are unalterable. The Saints of God continue in one way, while the fashions of the world change; and a faithful indestructible friendship may thus be a test of the parties, so loving each other, having the love of God seated deep in their hearts. Not an infallible test certainly; for they may have dispositions remarkably the same, or some engrossing object of this world, literary or other; they may be removed from the temptation to change, or they may have a natural sobriety of temper, which remains contented wherever it finds itself. However, under certain circumstances, it is a lively token of the presence of divine grace in them; and it is always a sort of symbol of it, for there is at first sight something of the nature of virtue in the very notion of constancy, dislike of change being not only the characteristic of a virtuous mind, but in some sense a virtue itself.

P.S., ii, 59-60.

9

Christ has sanctioned and enjoined love and care for our relations and friends. Such love is a great duty; but should at any time His guidance lead us by a strange way, and the light of His providence pass on, and cast these objects of our earthly affection into the shade, then they must be at once in the shade to *us,*—they must, for the time, disappear from our hearts. "He that loveth father or mother more than Me, is not worthy of Me." So He says; and at such times, though still loving them, we shall seem to hate them; for we shall put aside the thought of them, and act as if they did not exist. And in this sense an ancient and harsh proverb is true: we must always so love our friends as feeling that one day or other we may perchance be called upon to hate them,—that is, forget them in the pursuit of higher duties. . . .

If a person says it is painful thus to feel, and that it checks the spontaneous and continual flow of love towards our friends to have this memento sounding in our ears, we must boldly acknowledge that it *is* painful. It is a sad thought, not that we can ever be called upon actually to put away the love of them, but to have to act as if we did not love them,—as Abraham when called

252

on to slay his son. And this thought of the uncertainty of the future, doubtless, does tinge all our brightest affections (as far as this world is concerned) with a grave and melancholy hue. We need not shrink from this confession, remembering that this life is not our rest or happiness: "*that* remaineth" to come.

P.S., *vii*, 96-7.

10

No one really loves another who does not feel a certain reverence towards him. When friends transgress this sobriety of affection, they may indeed continue associates for a time, but they have broken the bond of union. It is mutual respect which makes friendship lasting.

P.S., *i*, 304.

11

Thus it is a dangerous thing, it is too high a privilege, for sinners like ourselves, to know the best and innermost thoughts of God's servants. We cannot bear to see such men in their own place, in the retirement of private life, and the calmness of hope and joy. The higher their gifts, the less fitted they are for being seen. Even St. John the Apostle was twice tempted to fall down in worship before an Angel who showed him the things to come. And, if he who had seen the Son of God was thus overcome by the creature, how is it possible we could bear to gaze upon the creature's holiness in its fulness, especially as we should be more able to enter into it, and estimate it, than to comprehend the infinite perfections of the Eternal Godhead?

P.S., *ii*, 134.

XIV: THE OPERATION OF LOVE

ANALYTICAL SUMMARY

Thus a love ripens which is so thoroughly impregnated with the Spirit of God that, as He "knows my sitting down and rising up," it is able to attain the distinctive individuality of all its objects;

a love which can combine burning zeal with careful respect for the personality of the individual, a holy awe of the "secret of the king" in my neighbour's heart—and a tender reverence for God Himself, to whose providential guidance it humbly submits, and whose words and graces are far too sacred in its eyes—for it to dare attempt to force His Hand;

(Nos. 1-8.)

and finally a love which on no account will water the streets with the precious liquid of the interior life; whose favourite method is the silent example of a holy life and which is scrupulously on its guard lest its words and acts should display calculation, still less hypocrisy, and works in such a way that its left hand does not know what its right hand doeth.

(Nos. 9-16.)

255

I. REVERENT ZEAL

I

Nothing is so difficult as to enter into the characters and feelings of men who have been brought up under a system of religion different from our own; and to discern how they may be most forcibly and profitably addressed, in order to win them over to the reception of Divine truths, of which they are at present ignorant. Now St. Paul had had experience in his own case of a state of mind very different from that which belonged to him as an Apostle. . . .

His awful rashness and blindness, his self-confident, headstrong, cruel rage against the worshippers of the true Messiah, then his strange conversion, then the length of time that elapsed before his solemn ordination, during which he was left to meditate in private on all that had happened, and to anticipate the future,—all this constituted a peculiar preparation for the office of preaching to a lost world, dead in sin. It gave him an extended insight, on the one hand, into the ways and designs of Providence, and, on the other hand, into the workings of sin in the human heart, and the various modes of thinking in which the mind is actually trained. It taught him not to despair of the worst sinners, to be sharp-sighted in detecting the sparks of faith amid corrupt habits of life, and to enter into the various temptations to which human nature is exposed. It wrought in him a profound humility, which disposed him (if we may say so) to bear meekly the abundance of the revelations given him; and it imparted to him a practical wisdom how to apply them to the conversion of others, so as to be weak with the weak, and strong with the strong, to bear their burdens, to instruct and encourage them, to "strengthen his brethren," to rejoice and weep with them; in a word, to be an earthly *Paraclete*, the comforter, help and guide

257

of his brethren. It gave him to know in some good measure the *hearts of men;* an attribute (in its fulness) belonging to God alone, and possessed by Him in union with perfect purity from all sin; but which in us can scarcely exist without our own melancholy experience, in some degree of moral evil in ourselves, since the innocent (it is their privilege) have not eaten of the tree of the knowledge of good and evil.

P.S., ii, 100-102.

2

A heathen poet has said, *Homo sum, humani nihil a me alienum puto.* "I am a man; nothing human is without interest to me"; and the sentiment has been widely and deservedly praised. Now this, in a fulness of meaning which a heathen could not understand, is, I conceive, the characteristic of this great Apostle. He is ever speaking, to use his own words, "human things," and "as a man," and "according to man," and "foolishly": —that is, human nature, the common nature of the whole race of Adam, spoke in him, acted in him, with an energetical presence, with a sort of bodily fulness, always under the sovereign command of divine grace, but losing none of its real freedom and power because of its subordination. And the consequence is, that, having the nature of man so strong within him, he is able to enter into human nature, and to sympathize with it, with a gift peculiarly his own. . . .

I spoke of St. Paul's characteristic gift as being a special apprehension of human nature as a fact, and an intimate familiarity with it as an object of continual contemplation and affection. He made it his own to the very full, instead of annihilating it; he sympathized with it, while he mortified it by penance, while he sanctified it by the grace given him. Though he had never been a heathen, though he was no longer a Jew, yet he was a heathen in capability, as I may say, and a Jew in the history of the past. His vivid imagination enabled him to throw himself into the state of heathenism, with all those tendencies which lay dormant in his human nature carried out, and its infirmities developed into sin. His wakeful memory enabled him to recall those past feelings and ideas of a Jew, which in the case of others a miraculous conversion might have obliterated; and thus, while he was a Saint inferior to none, he was emphaitcally still a man, and to his own apprehension still a sinner. . .

It is the habit of this great Apostle to have such full consciousness that he is a man, and such love of others as his kinsmen, that in his own inward conception, and in the tenor of his daily thoughts, he almost loses sight of his gifts and privileges, his station and dignity, except he is called by duty to remember them, and he is to himself merely a frail man speaking to frail men, and he is tender towards the weak from a sense of his own weakness; nay, that his very office and functions in the Church of God do but suggest to him that he has the imperfections and the temptations of other men. . . .

A man who thus divests himself of his own greatness, and puts himself on the level of his brethren, and throws himself upon the sympathies of human nature, and speaks with such simplicity and such spontaneous outpouring of heart, is forthwith in a condition both to conceive great love of them, and to inspire great love towards himself. . . .

He who had the constant contemplation of his Lord and Saviour, and if he saw Him with his bodily eyes, was nevertheless as susceptible of the affections of human nature and the influences of the external world, as if he were a stranger to that contemplation. Wonderful to say, he who had rest and peace in the love of Christ, was not satisfied without the love of man; he whose supreme reward was the approbation of God, looked out for the approval of his brethren. He who depended solely on the Creator, yet made himself dependent on the creature. Though he had That which was Infinite, he would not dispense with the finite. He loved his brethren, not only "for Jesus' sake," to use his own expression, but for their own sake also. He lived in them; he felt with them and for them; he was anxious about them; he gave them help, and in turn he looked for comfort from them. His mind was like some instrument of music, harp or viol, the strings of which vibrate, though untouched, by the notes which other instruments give forth. . . .

He who reveals to us the mystery of God's Sovereign Decrees manifests at the same time the tenderest interest in the souls of individuals. . . .

Putting aside forms as far as it was right to do so, and letting influence take the place of rule, and charity stand instead of authority, they* drew souls to them by their interior beauty, and held them captive by the regenerate affections of human nature.

O.S., 95, 102, 103, 112, 114, 116, 119.

3

Many holy men have died in exile, many holy men have been successful preachers; and what more can we write upon St. Chrysostom's monument than this, that he was eloquent and that he suffered persecution? He is not an Athanasius, expounding a sacred dogma with a luminousness which is almost an inspiration; nor is he Athanasius, again, in his romantic long-life adventures, in his sublime solitariness, in his ascendency over all classes of men, in his series of triumphs over material force and civil tyranny. Nor, except by the contrast, does he remind us of that Ambrose who kept his ground obstinately in an imperial city, and fortified himself against the heresy of a court by the living rampart of a devoted population. Nor is he Gregory or Basil, rich in the literature and philosophy of Greece, and embellishing the Church with the spoils of heathenism. Again, he is not an Augustine, devoting long years to one masterpeice of thought, and laying, in successive controversies, the foundations of theology. Nor is he a Jerome, so dead to the world that he can imitate the point and wit of its writers without danger to himself or scandal to his brethren. He has not trampled upon heresy, nor smitten emperors, nor beautified the house or the service of God, nor knit together the portions of Christendom, nor founded a religious order, nor built up the framework of doctrine, nor expounded the science of the Saints; yet I love him, as I love David or St. Paul. . . .

It is not force of words, nor cogency of argument, nor harmony

* St. Paul and St. Philip Neri. The preacher had been comparing the two.

of composition, nor depth or richness of thought, which constitutes his power,—whence, then, has he this influence, so mysterious, yet so strong?

I consider St. Chrysostom's charm to lie in his intimate sympathy and compassionateness for the whole world, not only in its strength, but in its weakness; in the lively regard with which he views everything that comes before him, taken in the concrete, whether as made after its own kind or as gifted with a nature higher than its own. . . . [It is] the interest which he takes in all things, not so far as God has made them alike, but as He has made them different from each other. I speak of the discriminating affectionateness with which he accepts everyone for what is personal in him and unlike others. I speak of his versatile recognition of men, one by one, for the sake of that portion of good, be it more or less, of a lower order or a higher, which has severally been lodged in them; his eager contemplation of the many things they do, effect, or produce, all of their great works as nations or as state; nay, even as they are corrupted or disguised by evil, so far as that evil may in imagination be disjoined from their proper nature, or may be regarded as a mere material disorder apart from its formal character of guilt. I speak of the kindly spirit and the genial temper with which he looks round at all things which this wonderful world contains; of the graphic fidelity with which he notes them down upon the tablets of his mind, and of the promptitude and propriety with which he calls them up as arguments or illustrations in the course of his teaching as the occasion requires. Possessed though he be by the fire of divine charity, he has not lost one fibre, he does not miss one vibration, of the complicated whole of human sentiment and affection; like the miraculous bush in the desert, which for all the flame that wrapt it round, was not thereby consumed.

H.S., *ii*, 284-7.

4

Some men have two natures with contrary tendencies, and have an inward conflict, and an external inconsistency in consequence. They are happy in retirement and happy in society;

they are fit for both, and would, if they could, be both men of
action and recluses at once. Thus we find Basil and Gregory
drawn to each of these vocations, and attempting to combine
them, though in the event Basil was forced to give up his loved
retirement for public life, and Gregory fell back from his arch-
bishopric into solitude, prayer, and literary work. So was it with
Theodoret. He dearly loved the monastic state; but he had large
sympathies, keen sensibilities, an indignation at the sight of
tyranny, an impatience at wrong, a will of his own, a zeal for the
triumph of the truth. He loved solitude, but he loved preaching,
controversy, ecclesiastical politics, also; he thought he could do
things which others could not do, nay, could do them well; and
he would feel that, much as he might labour, and with success,
in the direct duties of his episcopal charge, in his provincial
town and among his rude superstitious peasantry, still he was
able to exert an influence higher and wider than Cyrrhestica
gave him room for.

H.S., ii, 328-9.

5

Zeal is as essentially a duty of all God's rational creatures,
as prayer and praise, faith and submission; and, surely, if so,
especially of sinners whom He has redeemed; that zeal consist-
in a strict attention to His commands—a scrupulousness, vigilance, heartiness, and punctuality, which bears with no reasoning or questioning about them—an intense thirst for the advancement of His glory—a shrinking from the pollution of sin and sinners—an indignation, nay impatience, at witnessing His honour
insulted—a quickness of feeling when His name is mentioned, and
a jealousy how it is mentioned—a fulness of purpose, an heroic
determination to yield Him service at whatever sacrifice of
personal feeling—an energetic resolve to push through all
difficulties, were they as mountains, when His eye or hand but
gives the sign—a carelessness of obloquy, or reproach, or persecution, a forgetfulness of friend and relative, nay, a hatred (so to
say) of all that is naturally dear to us, when He says, "Follow
me. . . ."

Thus a certain fire of zeal, showing itself, not by force and blood, but as really and certainly as if it did—cutting through natural feelings, neglecting self, preferring God's glory to all things, firmly resisting sin, protesting against sinners, and steadily contemplating their punishment, is a duty belonging to all creatures of God, a duty of Christians, in the midst of all that excellent overflowing charity which is the highest Gospel grace and the fulfilling of the second table of the Law. . . .

Who unites them? We think we cannot be kind without ceasing to be severe. Who is there that walks through the world, wounding according to the rule of zeal, and scattering balm freely in the fulness of love; smiting as a duty, and healing as a privilege; loving most when he seems sternest, and embracing them most tenderly whom in semblance he treats roughly?

P.S., iii, 175, 183, 188.

6

Here we have the pattern of reformers; singleness of heart, gentleness of temper, in the midst of zeal, resoluteness, and decision in action. All God's Saints have this union of opposite graces; Joseph, Moses, Samuel, David, Nehemiah, St. Paul. . . . "Out of the strong came forth sweetness."

P.S., viii, 99-100.

7

Christian Zeal, therefore, ever bears in mind that the Mystery of Iniquity is to continue on till the Avenger solves it once for all; it renounces all hope of hastening His coming, all desire of intruding upon His work. It has no vain imaginings about the world's real conversion to Him, however men may acknowledge Him outwardly, knowing that "the world lies in wickedness." It has recourse to no officious modes of propagating or strengthening His truth. It does not flatter and ally itself with Samaria, in order to repress Syria. It does not exalt an Idumæan as its king, though he be willing to beautify the Temple, or has influence with the Emperors of the World. It plans no intrigues; it recognises no parties; it relies on no arm of flesh. It looks for no essential improvements or permanent reformations, in the dispensation of those precious gifts, which are ever pure in their origin, ever corrupted in man's use of them. It acts according to God's will, this time or that, as it comes, boldly and promptly; yet letting each act stand by itself, as a sufficient service to Him, not connecting them in one, or working them into system, further than He commands.

P.S., ii, 389.

8

He manifested His love towards us, "in deed and in truth," and we, His Ministers, declare it in word; yet for the very reason that it is so abundant, we must in very gratitude learn reverence towards Him. We must not take advantage (so to say) of His goodness; or misuse the powers committed to us. Never must we solicitously press the truth upon those who do not profit by what they already possess. It dishonours Christ, while it does the scorner harm, not good. It is casting pearls before swine. We must wait for all opportunities of being useful to men, but beware of attempting too much at once. We must impart the Scripture doctrines, in measure and season, as they can bear them; not being eager to recount them all, rather, hiding them from the world. Seldom must we engage in controversy or dispute; for it lowers the sacred truths to make them a subject for ordinary debate. Common propriety suggests rules like these at once. Who would speak freely about some revered friend in the presence of those who did not value him? or who would think he could with a few words overcome their indifference towards him? or who would hastily dispute about him when his hearers had no desire to be made to love him?

Rather, shunning all intemperate words, let us show our light before men by our *works*. Here we must be safe. In doing justice, showing mercy, speaking the truth, resisting sins, obeying the Church,—in thus glorifying God, there can be no irreverence.

P.S., i, 307-8.

9

God requires of us a modest silence in our religion; but we cannot be religious in the eyes of men without displaying religion. . . . God sees our thoughts without our help, and praises *them;* but we cannot be praised by men without being seen by men: whereas often the very excellence of a religious action, according to our Saviour's precept, consists in the not being seen by others. This is a frequent cause of hypocrisy in religion. Men begin by feeling as they should feel, then they think it a very hard thing that men should not know how well they feel, and in course of time they learn to speak without feeling. Thus they have learned to "love the praise of men more than the praise of God."

P.S., vii, 51, 52.

10

[True Christians] look just the same to the world as . . . . the great mass of what are called respectable men . . . . who in their hearts are very different; they make no great show, they go on in the same quiet ordinary way as the others, but really they are training to be saints in Heaven. They do all they can to change themselves, to become like God, to obey God, to discipline themselves, to renounce the world; but they do it in secret, both because God tells them so to do, and because they do not like it to be known. Moreover, there are a number of others between these two with more or less of worldliness and more or less of faith. Yet they all look about the same to common eyes, because true religion is a hidden life in the heart; and though it cannot exist without deeds, yet these are for the most part secret deeds, secret charities, secret prayers, secret self-denials, secret struggles, secret victories. . . .

And yet, though we have no right to judge others, but must leave this to God, it is very certain that a really holy man, a true saint, though he looks like other men, still has a sort of secret power in him to attract others to him who are like-minded, and to influence all who have any thing in them like him. And thus it often becomes a test, whether we are like-minded with the Saints of God, whether they have influence over us. And though we have seldom means of knowing at the time who are God's own Saints, yet after all is over we have; and then on looking back at what is past, perhaps after they are dead and gone, if we knew them, we may ask ourselves what power they had over us, whether they attracted us, influenced us, humbled us, whether they made our hearts burn within us. Alas! too often we shall find that we were close to them for a long time, had means of knowing them and knew them not, and that is a heavy condemnation on us indeed. . . . The holier a man is, the less he is understood by men of the world. All who have any spark of living faith will understand him in a measure, and the holier he is, they will, for the most part, be attracted the more; but those who serve the world will be blind to him, or scorn and dislike him, the holier he is.

P.S., *iv*, 243-5.

11

"Behold, I send you forth as sheep in the midst of wolves"; what our Lord addressed to His Apostles is fulfilled to this day in all those who obey Him. They are sprinkled up and down the world; they are separated the one from the other, they are bid quit each other's dear society, and sent afar off to those who are differently minded. Their choice of profession and employment is not their own. Outward circumstances, over which they have no control, determine their line of life; accidents bring them to this place or that place, not knowing whither they go; not knowing the persons to whom they unite themselves, they find, almost blindly, their home and their company. . . .

They do not know each other; they do not know themselves; they do not dare take to themselves the future titles of God's elect, though they be really reserved for them; and the nearer they are towards heaven, so much the more lowly do they think of themselves. "Lord, I am not worthy that Thou shouldest come under my roof," was the language of him who had greater faith than any in Israel. Doubtless, they do not know their own

266

blessedness, nor can they single out those who are their fellows in blessedness. God alone sees the heart; now and then, as they walk their way, they see glimpses of God's work in others; they take hold of them awhile in the dark, but soon lose them; they hear their voices, but cannot find them. Some few, indeed, are revealed to them in a measure. Among those with whom their lot is cast, whom they see continually, one or two, perhaps, are given them to rejoice in, but not many even of these. For so it has pleased the Dresser of the Vineyard, who seems to have purposed that His own should not grow too thick together; and if they seem to do so, He prunes His vine, that, seeming to bear less, it may bear better. He plucks off some of the promise of the vintage; and they who are left, mourn over their brethren whom God has taken to Himself, not understanding that it is no strange providence, but the very rule of His government, to leave His servants few and solitary. . . .

They are scattered about amid the leaves of that Mystical Vine which is seen, and receive their nurture from its trunk and branches. They live on its Sacraments and its Ministry; they gain light and salvation from its rites and ordinances; they communicate with each other through it; they obey its rulers; they walk together with its members; they do not dare to judge of this man or that man, on their right hand or their left, whether or not he is absolutely of the number of those who shall be saved; they accept all as their brethren in Christ, as partakers of the same general promises, who have not openly cast off Christ—as really brethren, till death comes, as those are who fulfil their calling most strictly.

Yet, at the same time, while in faith they love those, all around them, who are called by Christ's name, and forbear to judge about their real state in God's sight, they cannot but see much in many of them to hurt and offend them; they cannot but feel, most painfully, the presence of that worldly atmosphere which, however originating, encircles them; they feel the suffocation of those vapours in which the many are content to remain; and while they cannot trace the evil to its real authors individually, they are sure that it is an evil to be avoided and pointed out, and originating somewhere or other in the Church. Hence, in their spheres, whether high or low, the faithful few are witnesses; they are witnesses for God and Christ, in their lives, and by their protestations, without judging others, or exalting themselves. They are witnesses in various degrees, to various persons, more or less, as each needs it—differing from the multitude variously, as each of that multitude, before whom they witness, is better or worse, and as they themselves are more or less advanced in the truth; still, on the whole, they are witnesses, as light witnesses against darkness by the contrast;—giving good and receiving back evil; receiving back on themselves the contempt, the ridicule, and the opposition of the world, mixed, indeed, with some praise and reverence, reverence which does not last long, but soon becomes fear and hatred.

P.S., iii, 239-42.

12

Now, the truest obedience is indisputably that which is done from love of God, without narrowly measuring the magnitude or nature of the sacrifice involved in it. He who has learned to give names to his thoughts and deeds, to appraise them as if for the market, to attach to each its due measure of commendation or usefulness, will soon involuntarily corrupt his motives by pride or selfishness. A sort of self-approbation will insinuate itself into his mind: so subtle as not at once to be recognised by himself,—an habitual quiet self-esteem, leading him to prefer his own views to those of others, and a secret, if not avowed persuasion, that he is in a different state from the generality of those around him. This is an incidental, though, of course, not a necessary evil of religious journals; nay, of such compositions as Ministerial duties involve. They lead those who write them, in some respect or other, to a contemplation of self. Moreover, as to religious journals, useful as they often are, at the same time I believe persons find great difficulty, while recording their feelings, in banishing the thought that one day these good feelings will be known to the world, and are thus insensibly led to modify and prepare their language as if for a representation. Seldom indeed is any one in the *practice* of contemplating his better thoughts or doings without proceeding to display them to others; and hence it is that it is so easy to discover a conceited man. When this is encouraged in the sacred province of religion, it produces a certain unnatural solemnity of manner, arising from a wish to be, nay, to appear spiritual, which is at once very painful to beholders, and surely quite at variance with our Saviour's rule of anointing our head and washing our face, even when we are most self-abased in heart.

P.S., ii, 171-2.

13

We shall aim at doing right, and so glorifying our Father, and shall exhort and constrain others to do so also; but as for talking on the appropriate subjects of religious meditation, and *trying* to show piety, and to excite corresponding feelings in another, even though our nearest friend, far from doing this, we shall account it a snare and a mischief. Yet this is what many persons consider the highest part of religion, and call it spiritual conversation, the test of a spiritual mind; whereas, putting aside the incipient and occasional hypocrisy, and again the immodesty of it, I call all formal and intentional expression of religious emotions, all studied passionate discourse, *dissipation,*—dissipation the same in nature, though different in subject, as what is commonly so called; for it is a drain and a waste of our religious and moral strength, a general weakening of our spiritual powers (as I have already shown); and all for what?—for the pleasure of the immediate excitement. Who can deny that this religious disorder is a parallel case to that of the sensualist? Nay, precisely the same as theirs, from whom the religionists in question think themselves very far removed, of the fashionable world I mean, who read works of fiction, frequent the public shows, are ever on the watch for novelties, and affect a pride of manners and a "mincing" deportment, and are ready with all kinds of good thoughts and keen emotions on all occasions.

P.S., ii, 377.

14

If a man stands forth *on his own ground*, declaring himself as an individual a witness for Christ, then indeed he *is* grieving and disturbing the calm spirit given us by God. But God's merciful providence has saved us this temptation, and forbidden us to admit it. He bids us unite together in one, and to shelter our personal profession under the authority of the general body. Thus, while we show ourselves as lights to the world far more effectively than if we glimmered separately in the lone wilderness without communication with others, at the same time we do do so with far greater secrecy and humility. . . .

How great a profession, and yet a profession how unconscious and modest, arises from the mere ordinary manner in which any strict Christian lives! . . .

Your *life* displays Christ without your intending it. You cannot help it. Your *words and deeds* will show on the long run (as it is said), where your treasure is, and your heart. Out of the abundance of your heart your mouth speaketh words "seasoned with salt." We sometimes find men who aim at doing their duty in the common course of life *surprised* to hear that they are ridiculed, and called hard names by careless or worldly persons. This is as it should be; it is as it should be that they are *surprised* at it. If a private Christian sets out with *expecting* to make a disturbance in the world, the fear is lest he be not so humble-minded as he should be. But those who go on quietly in the way of obedience, and yet are detected by the keen eye of the jealous, self-condemning, yet proud, world, and who, on discovering their situation, first shrink from it and are distressed, then look to see if they have done aught wrongly, and after all are sorry for it, and but slowly and very timidly (if at all) learn to rejoice in it—these are Christ's flock. . . .

"Wait on God and be doing good," and you must, you cannot but be showing your light before men as a city on a hill. . . .

We must witness and glorify God, as lights on a hill, through evil report and good report; but the evil and the good report is not so much of our own making as the natural consequence of our Christian profession.

P.S., 153-5, 157, 163.

The men commonly held in popular estimation are greatest at a distance; they become small as they are approached; but the attraction, exerted by unconscious holiness, is of an urgent and irresistible nature; it persuades the weak, the timid, the wavering, and the inquiring; it draws forth the affection and loyalty of all who are in a measure like-minded; and over the thoughtless or perverse multitude it exercises a sovereign compulsory sway, bidding them fear and keep silence, on the ground of its own right divine to rule them,—its hereditary claim on their obedience, though they understand not the principles or counsels of that spirit, which is "born, not of blood, nor of the will of the flesh, nor of the will of man, but of God."

U.S., 95.

16

Stay with me, and then I shall begin to shine as Thou shinest: so to shine as to be a light to others. The light, O Jesus, will be all from Thee. None of it will be mine. No merit to me. It will be Thou who shinest through me upon others. O let me thus praise Thee, in the way which Thou dost love best, by shining on all those around me. Give light to them as well as to me; light them with me, through me. Teach me to show forth Thy praise, Thy truth, Thy will. Make me preach Thee without preaching— not by words, but by my example and by the catching force, the sympathetic influence, of what I do—by my visible resemblance to Thy saints, and the evident fulness of the love which my heart bears to Thee.

M.D., 500-1.

XV: THE LIFE OF THE ONE BODY

ANALYTICAL SUMMARY

Thus the Body of Christ is built up in the "sincere love" which "seeketh not its own, but what is Jesus Christ's," and therefore is "magnanimous, and kind, envieth not, imputeth no evil; seeketh not its own advantage, is not provoked to anger, is not suspicious, rejoiceth not in doing hurt— but rejoiceth always in the truth, beareth all things, believeth all things, hopeth all things, overcometh all things," and in a peaceful imitation of "the mind of Christ" "subjects" itself to all and "lays down life itself for the brethren";

inasmuch as all live, offer themselves and die for each other; fall that others may rise;

(Nos. 1-2.)

in the sacred intimacy in which the man of prayer, the offerer, the dying, the completely mortified, the penitent and the perfected Christian touch each other, so to speak, in Christ and grace pours from vessel into vessel:

in the mystery of the Communion of Saints.

(Nos. 3-5.)

I. LIFE FROM DEATH

I

It is notorious that those who first suggest the most happy inventions, and open a way to the secret stores of nature,—those who weary themselves in the search after Truth, who strike out momentous principles of action, who painfully force upon their contemporaries the adoption of beneficial measures, or, again, who are the original cause of the chief events in national history, are commonly supplanted, as regards celebrity and reward, by inferior men. Their works are not called after them; nor the arts and systems which they have given the world. Their schools are usurped by strangers; and their maxims of wisdom circulate among the children of their people, forming, perhaps, a nation's character, but not embalming in their own immortality the names of their original authors.

Such is the history of the social and political world; and the rule discernible in it is still more clearly established in the world of morals and religion.

Now I know that reflections of this kind are apt to sadden and vex us; and such of us particularly as are gifted with ardent and enthusiastic minds, with a generous love of what is great and good and a noble hatred of injustice. These men find it difficult to reconcile themselves to the notion that the triumph of the Truth, in all its forms, is postponed to the next world. They would fain anticipate the coming of the righteous Judge: nay, perhaps they are somewhat too favourably disposed towards the present world, to acquiesce without resistance in a doctrine which testifies to the corruption of its decisions, and the worthlessness of its honours. But that it is a truth has already been shown almost as matter of fact, putting the evidence of Scripture out of consideration; and if it be such, it is our wisdom, as it will become our

275

privilege, to accustom our minds to it, and to receive it, not in word merely, but in seriousness.

Why, indeed, should we shrink from this gracious law of God's present providence in our own case, or in the case of those we love, when our subjection to it does but associate us with the best and noblest of our race, and with beings of nature and condition superior to our own? Andrew is scarcely known except by name; while Peter has ever held the place of honour all over the Church; yet Andrew brought Peter to Christ. And are not the blessed Angels unknown to the world? and is not God Himself, the Author of all good, hid from mankind at large, partially manifested and poorly glorified in a few scattered servants here and there? and His Spirit, do we know whence It cometh, and whither It goeth? and though He has taught men whatever there has been of wisdom among them from the beginning, yet when He came on earth in visible form, even then it was said of Him, "The world knew Him not." His marvellous providence works beneath a veil, which speaks but an untrue language; and to see Him who is the Truth and the Life, we must stoop underneath it, and so in our turn hide ourselves from the world. They who present themselves at kings' courts pass on to the inner chambers, where the gaze of the rude multitude cannot pierce; and we, if we would see the King of kings in His glory, must be content to disappear from the things that are seen.

P.S., *ii*, 5-6, 8-9.

2

This is a thought which is particularly soothing as regards the loss of friends; or of especially gifted men, who seem in their day the earthly support of the Church. For what we know, their removal hence is as necessary for the furtherance of the very objects we have at heart as was the departure of our Saviour.

Doubtless, "it is expedient" they should be taken away; otherwise some great mercy will not come to us. They are taken away perchance to other duties in God's service, equally ministrative to the salvation of the elect as earthly service. Christ went to intercede with the Father: we do not know, we may not boldly speculate,—yet, it may be, that Saints departed intercede, unknown to us, for the victory of the Truth upon earth; and their prayers above may be as really indispensable conditions of that victory as the labours of those who remain among us. They are taken away for some purpose surely: their gifts are not lost to us; their soaring minds, the fire of their contemplations, the sanctity of their desires, the vigour of their faith, the sweetness and gentleness of their affections, were not given without an object.

P.S., ii, 213-4.

II. THE COMMUNION OF SAINTS

3

See what a noble principle faith is. Faith alone lengthens a man's existence, and makes him, in his own feelings, live in the future and in the past. Men of this world are full of plans of the day. Even in religion they are ever coveting immediate results, and will do nothing at all, unless they can do every thing,—can have their own way, choose their methods, and see the end. But the Christian throws himself fearlessly upon the future, because he believes in Him which is, and which was, and which is to come. He can endure to be one of an everlasting company while in this world, as well as in the next. He is content to begin and break off; to do his part, and no more; to set about what others must accomplish; to sow where others must reap. None has finished his work, and cut it short in righteousness, but He who is One. We, His members, who have but a portion of His fulness, execute but a part of His purpose. One lays the foundation, and another builds thereupon; one levels the mountain, and another "brings forth the headstone with shoutings. . . ."

Does it not seem a very strange thing that *we* should be fed, and lodged, and clothed in spiritual things by persons we never saw or heard of, and who never saw us, or could think of us, hundreds of years ago? Does it not seem strange that men should be able, not merely by acting on others, not by a continued influence carried on through many minds in a long succession, but by one simple and direct act, to come into contact with us, and as if with their own hand to benefit us, who live centuries later? . . . .

By little and little the work of grace went forward; and they could afford to take time about it, and be at pains to do it best, who had a promise that the gates of hell should not prevail against it.

P.S., vi, 274-5.

4

It is one great peculiarity of the Christian character to be dependent. Men of the world, indeed, in proportion as they are active and enterprising, boast of their independence, and are proud of having obligations to no one. But it is the Christian's excellence to be diligent and watchful, to work and persevere, and yet to be in spirit *dependent;* to be willing to serve, and to rejoice in the permission to do so; to be content to view himself in a subordinate place; to love to sit in the dust. Though in the Church a son of God, he takes pleasure in considering himself Christ's "servant" and "slave"; he feels glad whenever he can put himself to shame. So it is the natural bent of his mind freely and affectionately to visit and trace the footsteps of the saints, to sound the praises of the great men of old who have wrought wonders in the Church and whose words still live; being jealous of their honour, and feeling it to be even too great a privilege for such as he is to be put in trust with the faith once delivered to them, and following them strictly in the narrow way, even as they have followed Christ. To the ears of such persons the words of the text are as sweet music: "Thus saith the Lord, stand ye in the ways, and see, and ask for the old paths, where is the good way, and walk therein, and ye shall find rest for your souls."

P.S., vii, 251-2.

5

It is a Christian's characteristic to look back on former times. The man of this world lives in the present, or speculates about the future; but faith rests upon the past and is content. It makes the past the mirror of the future. It recounts the list of faithful servants of God, to whom St. Paul refers in the text, and no longer feels sad as if it were alone. Abraham and the Patriarchs, Moses Samuel, and the Prophets, David and the kings who walked in his steps, these are the Christian's forefathers. By degrees he learns to have them as familiar images before his mind, to unite his cause with theirs, and, since their history comforts him, to defend them in his own day. . . .

In seasons of unusual distress or alarm, when men's minds faint for fear, then he will have a natural power over the world, and will seem to speak, not as an individual, but as if in him was concentrated all the virtue and the grace of those many Saints who have been his life-long companions. He has lived with those who are dead, and he will seem to the world as one coming from the dead, speaking in the name of the dead, using the language of souls dead to things that are seen, revealing the mysteries of the heavenly world, and aweing and controlling those who are wedded to this.

P.S., iii, 244-5, 252.

XVI: THE NEXT WORLD

ANALYTICAL SUMMARY

The Christian's God is essentially a God of the hereafter, who calls upon him to believe that his true life lies beyond this and to look for it there, where every seed yields its harvest, all seemingly broken threads are interwoven in one pattern and our hopelessly divergent paths meet in one goal;

(Nos. 1-4.)

and therefore bids him surrender, sacrifice and venture everything visible for the unseen, earthly sight for the darkness of faith, a pilgrim led by the hand of the unseen God into the dim light of a dawning future;

(Nos. 5-6.)

by mortification and abstinence to loosen and sever the all too strong bands which tie this earthly body to its native soil, that the eyes of our soul may be opened to the light beyond and its ears may catch the soft voice of Him who is drawing near;

(Nos. 7-14.)

and in conclusion make his entire life on earth an anxious and eager watch and expectation, loins girt, sandals on the feet and a lamp in the hand, the faithful waiting of the servant for his Master, the maiden's expectation of her bridegroom—"Come, Lord Jesus."

(Nos. 15-20.)

I. PRESENTIMENT AND FULFILMENT

I

When we contemplate human life in itself, in however small a portion of it, we see implied in it the presence of a soul, the energy of a spiritual existence, of an accountable being; consciousness tells us this concerning it every moment. But when we look back on·it in memory, we view it but externally, as a mere lapse of time, as a mere earthly history. And the longest duration of this external world is as dust and weighs nothing, against one moment's life of the world within. Thus we are ever expecting great things from life, from our internal consciousness every moment of our having souls; and we are ever being disappointed, on considering what we have gained from time past, or can hope from time to come. And life is ever promising and never fulfilling; and hence, however long it be, our days are few and evil. . .

Our earthly life then gives promise of what it does not accomplish. It promises immortality, yet it is mortal; it contains life in death and eternity in time; and it attracts us by beginnings which faith alone brings to an end. . .

The very greatness of our powers makes this life look pitiful; the very pitifulness of this life forces on our thoughts to another; and the prospect of another gives a dignity and value to this life which promises it; and thus this life is at once great and little, and we rightly contemn it while we exalt its importance.

P.S., iv, 215-18.

2

Men there are, who, in a single moment of their lives, have shown a superhuman height and majesty of mind which it would take ages for them to employ on its proper objects, and, as it were, to exhaust; and who by such passing flashes, like rays

283

of the sun, and the darting of lightning, give token of their immortality, give token to us that they are but Angels in disguise, the elect of God sealed for eternal life, and destined to judge the world and to reign with Christ for ever. Yet they are suddenly taken away, and we have hardly recognized them when we lose them. Can we believe that they are not removed for higher things elsewhere? This is sometimes said with reference to our intellectual powers; but it is still more true of our moral nature. There is something in moral truth and goodness, in faith, in firmness, in heavenly-mindedness, in meekness, in courage, in loving-kindness, to which this world's circumstances are quite unequal, for which the longest life is insufficient, which makes the highest opportunities of this world disappointing, which must burst the prison of this world to have its appropriate range. So that when a good man dies one is led to say, "He has not half showed himself, he has had nothing to exercise him; his days are gone like a shadow, and he is withered like grass."

I say the word "disappointing" is the only word to express our feelings on the death of God's saints. Unless our faith be very active, so as to pierce beyond the grave, and realize the future, we feel depressed at what seems like a failure of great things. And from this very feeling surely, by a sort of contradiction, we may fairly take hope; for if this life be so disappointing, so unfinished, surely it is not the whole. This feeling of disappointment will often come upon us in an especial way, on happening to hear of or to witness the deathbeds of holy men. The hour of death seems to be a season, of which, in the hands of Providence, much might be *made*, if I may use the term; much might be done for the glory of God, the good of man, and the manifestation of the person dying. And beforehand friends will perhaps look forward, and expect that great things are then to take place, which they shall never forget. Yet, "how dieth the wise man? as the fool." Such is the preacher's experience, and our own bears witness to it. King Josiah, the zealous servant of the Living God, died the death of wicked Ahab, the worshipper of Baal. True Christians die as other men. One dies by a sudden accident, another in battle, another without friends to see how

284

he dies, a fourth is insensible or not himself. Thus the opportunity seems thrown away, and we are forcibly reminded that "the manifestation of the sons of God" is hereafter; that "the earnest expectation of the creature" is but waiting for it; that this life is unequal to the burden of so great an office as the due exhibition of those secret ones who shall one day "shine forth as the sun in the kingdom of their Father."

P.S., iv, 218-220

3

We should remember that this life is scarcely more than an accident of our being—that it is no part of ourselves, who are immortal; that we are immortal spirits, independent of time and space, and that this life is but a sort of outward stage, on which we act for a time, and which is only sufficient and only intended to answer the purpose of trying whether we will serve God or no. We should consider ourselves to be in this world in no fuller sense than players in any game are in the game; and life to be a sort of dream, as detached and as different from our real eternal existence, as a dream differs from waking; a serious dream, indeed, as affording a means of judging us, yet in itself a kind of shadow without substance, a scene set before us, in which we seem to be, and in which it is our duty to act just as if all we saw had a truth and reality, because all that meets us influences us and our destiny. The regenerate soul is taken into communion with Saints and Angels, and its "life is hid with Christ in God;" it has a place in God's court, and is not of this world,—looking into this world as a spectator might look at some show or pageant except when called from time to time to take a part. And while it obeys the instinct of the senses, it does so for God's sake, and it submits itself to things of time so far as to be brought to perfection by them, that, when the veil is withdrawn and it sees itself to be, where it ever has been, in God's kingdom, it may be found worthy to enjoy it. It is this view of life, which removes from us all surprise and disappointment that it is so incomplete: as well might we expect any chance event which happens in the course of it to be complete, any casual conversation with a stranger, or the toil and amusement of an hour.

P.S., iv, 221·2.

4

These are suitable feelings towards this attractive but deceitful world. What have we to do with the gifts and honours of this attractive but deceitful world, who, having been already baptized into the world to come, are no longer citizens of this? Why should we be anxious for a long life, or wealth, or credit, or comfort, who know that the next world will be everything which our hearts can wish, and that not in appearance only, but truly and everlastingly? Why should we rest in this world, when it is the token and promise of another? Why should we be content with its surface, instead of appropriating what is stored beneath it? To those who live by faith, everything they see speaks of that future world; the very glories of nature, the sun, moon, and stars, and the richness and the beauty of the earth, are as types and figures witnessing and teaching the invisible things of God. All that we see is destined one day to burst forth into a heavenly bloom, and to be transfigured into immortal glory. Heaven at present is out of sight, but in due time, as snow melts and discovers what it lay upon, so will this visible creation fade away before those greater splendours which are behind it, and on which at present it depends.

P.S., iv, 223.

II. STAKE AND PRIZE

5

Our duty as Christians lies in making ventures for eternal life without the absolute certainty of success. . . . This, indeed, is the very meaning of the word "venture"; for that is a strange venture which has nothing in it of fear, risk, danger, anxiety uncertainty. Yes; so it certainly is; and in this consists the excellence and nobleness of *faith*; this is the very reason why *faith* is singled out from other graces, and honoured as the especial means of our justification, because its presence implies that we have the heart to make a venture.

286

If, then, faith be the essence of a Christian life, and if it be what I have now described, it follows that our duty lies in risking upon Christ's word what we have for what we have not ; and doing so in a noble, generous way, not indeed rashly or lightly, still without knowing accurately what we are doing, not knowing either what we give up, nor again what we shall gain ; uncertain about our reward, uncertain about our extent of sacrifice, in all respects leaning, waiting upon Him, trusting in Him to fulfil His promise, trusting in Him to enable us to fulfil our own vows, and so in all respects proceeding without carefulness or anxiety about the future.

P.S., iv, 295-6, 299.

6

Consider for an instant. Let every one who hears me ask himself the question, what stake has *he* in the truth of Christ's promise? How would he be a whit the worse off, supposing (which is impossible), but, supposing it to fail? What have we ventured for Christ? What have we given to Him on a belief of His promise? The Apostle said, that he and his brethren would be of all men most miserable, if the dead were not raised. Can we in any degree apply this to ourselves? We think, perhaps, at present, we have some hope of heaven; well, *this* we should lose of course; but after all, how should we be worse off as to our *present* condition? A trader, who has embarked some property in a speculation which fails, not only loses his prospect of gain, but somewhat of his own, which he ventured with the *hope* of the gain. This is the question, What have *we* ventured? I really fear, when we come to examine, it will be found that there is nothing we resolve, nothing we do, nothing we do not do, nothing we avoid, nothing we choose, nothing we give up, nothing we pursue, which we should not resolve, and do, and not do, and avoid, and choose, and give up, and pursue, if Christ had not died, and heaven were not promised us. I really fear that most men called Christians, whatever they may profess, whatever they may think they feel, whatever warmth and illumination and love they may claim as their own, yet would go on

287

almost as they do, neither much better nor much worse, if they believed Christianity to be a fable. When young, they indulge their lusts, or at least pursue the world's vanities; as time goes on, they get into a fair way of business, or other mode of making money; then they marry and settle; and their interest coinciding with their duty, they seem to be, and think themselves, respectable and religious men; they grow attached to things as they are; they begin to have a zeal against vice and error; and they follow after peace with all men. Such conduct, indeed, as far as it goes, is right and praiseworthy. Only I say, it has not necessarily anything to do with religion at all; there is nothing in it which is any proof of the presence of religious principle in those who adopt it; there is nothing they would not do still, though they had nothing to gain from it, except what they gain from it now: they do gain something now, they do gratify their present wishes, they are quiet and orderly, because it is their interest and taste to be so; but they *venture* nothing; they risk, they sacrifice, they abandon nothing on the faith of Christ's word.

P.S., iv, 299, 301.

III. SHELL AND KERNEL

7

When with their fleshly eyes and ears the Apostles saw Him no more, when He had ascended whither flesh and blood cannot enter, and the barrier of the flesh was interposed between Him and them, how should they any longer see and hear Him? "Lord, whither goest Thou?" they said; and He answered to Peter, "Whither I go thou canst not follow Me now, but thou shalt follow Me afterwards." They were to follow Him through the veil, and to break the barrier of the flesh after His pattern. They must, as far as they could, weaken and attenuate what stood between them and Him; they must anticipate that world where flesh and blood are not; they must discern truths which flesh and blood could not reveal; they must live a life, not of sense, but of spirit; they must practise those mortifications which former religions had enjoined, which the Pharisees and John's disciples observed, with better fruit, for a higher end, in a more heavenly way, in order to see Him who is invisible. By fasting, Moses saw God's glory; by fasting, Elijah heard the "still small voice;" by fasting, Christ's disciples were to express their mourning over the Crucified and Dead, over the Bridegroom taken away: but that mourning would bring Him back, that mourning would be turned to joy; in that mourning they would see Him, they would hear of Him, again; they would see Him, as they mourned and wept. And while they mourned, so long would they see Him and rejoice—for "blessed are they that mourn, for they shall be comforted;" they are "sorrowful, yet always rejoicing;" hungering and thirsting after and unto righteousness,—fasting in body, that their soul may hunger and thirst after its true good; fasting in body, that they may be satisfied in spirit; in a "barren and dry land, where no water is," that they may look for Him in holiness, and behold His power and glory.

P.S., vi, 31-2.

8

Till we, in a certain sense, detach ourselves from our bodies, our minds will not be in a state to receive divine impressions, and to exert heavenly aspirations. A smooth and easy life, an uninterrupted enjoyment of the goods of Providence, full meals, soft raiment, well-furnished homes, the pleasures of sense, the feeling of security, the consciousness of wealth,—these, and the like, if we are not careful, choke up all the avenues of the soul, through which the light and breath of heaven might come to us. A hard life is, alas! no certain method of becoming spiritually minded, but it is one out of the means by which Almighty God makes us so. We must, at least at seasons, defraud ourselves of nature, if we would not be defrauded of grace. If we attempt to force our minds into a loving and devotional temper, without this preparation, it is too plain what will follow,—the grossness and coarseness, the affectation, the effeminacy, the unreality, the presumption, the hollowness (suffer me, my brethren, while I say plainly, but seriously, what I mean), in a word, what Scripture calls the Hypocrisy, which we see around us; that state of mind in which the reason, seeing what we should be, and the conscience enjoining it, and the heart being unequal to it, some or other pretence is set up, by way of compromise, that men may say, "Peace, peace, when there is no peace."

P.S., v, 337-8.

9

Temporal advantages, as they are considered, have a strong tendency to render us self-confident. When a man has been advanced in the world by means of his own industry and skill, when he began poor and ends rich, how apt will he be to pride himself, and confide, in his own contrivances and his own resources! Or when a man feels himself possessed of good abilities; of quickness in entering into a subject, or of powers of argument to discourse readily upon it, or of acuteness to detect fallacies in dispute with little effort, or of a delicate and cultivated taste, so as to separate with precision the correct and beautiful in thought and feeling from the faulty and irregular, how will such an one be tempted to self-complacency and self-approbation! how apt will he be to rely upon himself, to rest contented with himself; to be harsh and impetuous; or supercilious; or to be fastidious, indolent, unpractical; and to despise the pure, self-denying, humble temper of religion, as something irrational, dull, enthusiastic, or needlessly rigorous!

P.S., vii, 65.

10

In truth, so has it been ordered by Divine Providence, that in the Gospel kingdom is instanced a remarkable law of ethics, which is well known to all who have given their minds to the subject. All virtue and goodness tend to make men powerful in this world; but they who aim at the power have not the virtue. Again: virtue is its own reward, and brings with it the truest and highest pleasures; but they who cultivate it for the pleasure-sake are selfish, not religious, and will never gain the pleasure, because they never can have the virtue. So is it with the Church of Christ. If she were to *seek* power, wealth, and honour, this were to fall from grace; but it is not less true that she *will* have them, though she seeks them not, or, rather, *if* she seeks them not. For when men see disinterested goodness, and holiness which has no selfish aims, and conscientiousness which is strictly bound by a sense of duty, and faith which sacrifices this world for the next, they cannot help giving to those who display these excellences that which such persons are content to lose, and for which they ask not,—credit and influence. He who withdraws himself, is courted; he who solicits favour, is disdained.

Such, then, is the law of Christ's kingdom, such the paradox which is seen in its history. It belongs to the poor in spirit; it belongs to the persecuted; it is possessed by the meek; it is sustained by the patient. It conquers by suffering; it advances by retiring; it is made wise through foolishness.

Such is the rule of our warfare. We advance by yielding; we rise by falling; we conquer by suffering; we persuade by silence; we become rich by bountifulness; we inherit the earth through meekness; we gain comfort through mourning; we earn glory by penitence and prayer. Heaven and earth shall sooner fall than this rule be reversed; it is the law of Christ's kingdom, and nothing can reverse it but sin.

S.D., 162, 245, 249.

II

Do you desire to be great? make yourselves little. There is a mysterious connexion between real advancement and self-abasement. If you minister to the humble and despised, if you feed the hungry, tend the sick, succour the distressed; if you bear with the froward, submit to insult, endure ingratitude, render good for evil, you are, as by a divine charm, getting power over the world and rising among the creatures. God has established this law. Thus He does His wonderful works. His instruments are poor and despised; the world hardly knows their names, or not at all. They are busied about what the world thinks petty actions, and no one minds them. They are apparently set on no great works; nothing is seen to come of what they do: they seem to fail. Nay, even as regards religious objects which they themselves profess to desire, there is no natural and visible connexion between their doings and sufferings and these desirable ends; but there is an unseen connexion in the kingdom of God. They rise by falling. Plainly so, for no condescension *can* be so great as that of our Lord *Himself.* Now the more they abase themselves the more *like* they are to Him; and the more like they are to Him, the greater must be their power with Him. . . . When a man discerns in himself most sin and humbles himself most, when his comeliness seems to him to vanish away and all his graces to wither, when he feels disgust at himself, and revolts at the thought of himself,—seems to himself all dust and ashes, all foulness and odiousness, then it is that he is really rising in the kingdom of God.

P.S., vi, 319-20, 324-5.

12

Jesus when He was nearest to His everlasting triumph, seemed to be farthest from triumphing. When He was nearest upon entering upon His Kingdom, and exercising all power in heaven and earth, He was lying dead in a cave of the rock. . . . Make us to trust in Thee, O Jesus, that Thou wilt display in us a similar providence. Make us sure, O Lord, that the greater is our distress, the nearer we are to Thee. The more men scorn us, the more Thou dost honour us. The more men insult over us, the higher Thou wilt exalt us. The more they forget us, the more Thou dost keep us in mind. The more they abandon us, the closer Thou wilt bring us to Thyself.

M.D., 245-7.

13

Earth must fade away from our eyes, and we must anticipate that great and solemn truth, which we shall not fully understand until we stand before God in judgment, that to us there are but two beings in the whole world, God and ourselves. The sympathy of others, the pleasant voice, the glad eye, the smiling countenance, the thrilling heart, which at present are our very life, all will be away from us when Christ comes in judgment.

Every one will have to think of himself. Every eye shall see *Him;* every heart will be full of *Him.* He will speak to every one; and every one will be rendering to Him his own account. By self-restraint, by abstinence, by prayer, by meditation, by recollection, by penance, we now anticipate in our measure that dreadful season. By thinking of it beforehand, we hope to mitigate its terrors when it comes. By humbling ourselves now, we hope to escape humiliation then. By owning our faults now, we hope to avert the disclosures of that day. By judging ourselves now, we hope to be spared that judgment which mercy tempers not. We prepare now to meet our God; we retire, as it were, to our sick room, and put our house in order. . . . We leave the goods of earth before they leave us.

S.D., 38-9.

14

God has graciously willed to bring us to heaven; to practise a heavenly life on earth, certainly, is a thing above earth. It is like trying to execute some high and refined harmony on an insignificant instrument. In attempting it, that instrument would be taxed beyond its powers, and would be sacrificed to great ideas beyond itself. And so, in a certain sense, this life, and our present nature, is sacrificed for heaven and the new creature; that while our outward man perishes, our inward man may be renewed day by day.

S.D., 87.

IV. WAIT AND WATCH

15

This is the very definition of a Christian—one who looks for Christ; not who looks for gain, or distinction, or power, or pleasure, or comfort, but who looks "for the Saviour, the Lord Jesus Christ." This, according to Scripture, is the essential mark, this is the foundation of a Christian, from which every thing else follows; whether he is rich or poor, high or low, is a further matter, which may be considered apart; but he surely is a primitive Christian, and he only, who has no aim of this world, who has no wish to be other in this world than he is; whose thoughts and aims have relation to the unseen, the future world; who has lost his taste for this world, sweet and bitter being the same to him. . . .

There was no barrier, no cloud, no earthly object, interposed between the soul of the primitive Christian and its Saviour and Redeemer. Christ was in his heart, and therefore all that came from his heart, his thoughts, words, and actions, savoured of Christ. The Lord was his light, and therefore he shone with the illumination of the refined joy, peaceful, serene, thankful, gentle, affectionate, sweet-tempered, pleasant, hopeful; graceful, tender, touching, winning. All this were the Christians of the New Testament, for they had obtained what they desired. They had desired to sacrifice the kingdom of the world and all its pomps for the love of Christ, whom they had seen, whom they loved, in whom they believed, in whom they delighted; and when their wish was granted, they could but "rejoice in that day, and leap for joy, for, behold, their reward was great in heaven:" blessed were they, thrice blessed, because they in their lifetime had evil things, and their consolation was to come hereafter. . . .

We often hear it said, that the true way of serving God is to serve man, as if religion consisted merely in acting well our part in life, not in direct faith, obedience, and worship: how different is the spirit of this prayer!* Evil round about him, enemies and persecutors in his path, temptation in prospect, help for the day, sin to be expiated, God's will in his heart, God's Name on his lips, God's kingdom in his hopes: this is the view it gives us of a Christian.

S.D., 278-9, 281, 286-7, 289.

16

The thought of our Saviour absent yet present is like that of a friend taken from us, but, as it were in a dream, returned to us, though in this case not in dream but in reality and truth. When

* The Lord's Prayer.

He was going away He said to His disciples, "I will see you again, and your heart shall rejoice." Yet He had at another time said, "The days will come when the Bridegroom shall be taken from them, and then shall they fast in those days." See what an apparent contradiction, such as attends the putting any high feeling into human language! They were to joy because Christ was come, and yet weep because He was away; that is, to have a feeling so refined, so strange and new, that nothing could be said of it, but that it combined in one all that was sweet and soothing in contrary human feelings, as commonly experienced. As some precious fruits of the earth are said to taste like all others at once, not as not being really distinct from all others, but as being thus best described, when we would come as near the truth as we can, so the state of mind which they are in who believe that the Son of God is here, yet away,—is at the right hand of God, yet in His very flesh and blood among us,—is present, though invisible,—is one of both joy and pain, or rather one far above either; a feeling of awe, wonder, and praise, which cannot be more suitably expressed than by the Scripture word *fear*; or by holy Job's words, though he spoke in grief, and not as being possessed of a blessing : "Behold, I go forward, but He is not there; and backward, but I cannot perceive Him: on the left hand, where He doth work, but I cannot behold Him: He hideth Himself on the right hand, that I cannot see Him. Therefore am I troubled at His presence; when I consider, I am afraid of Him."

P.S., *v*, 25-6.

17

And this I conceive is one of the main points which, in a practical way, will be found to separate the true and perfect servants of God from the multitude called Christians—true Christians, whoever they are, watch, and inconsistent Christians do not. Now what is watching?

I conceive it may be explained as follows:—Do you know the feeling in matters of this life, of expecting a friend, expecting him to come, and he delays? Do you know what it is to be in unpleasant company and to wish for the time to pass away and the hour strike when you may be at liberty? Do you know what it is to be in anxiety lest something should happen which may happen or may not, or to be in suspense about some important event which makes your heart beat when you are reminded of it, and of which you think the first thing in the morning? Do you know what it is to have a friend in a distant country, to expect news of him, and to wonder from day to day what he is now doing, and whether he is well? Do you know what it is so to live upon a person who is present with you, that your eyes follow his, that you read his soul, that you see all its changes in his countenance, that you anticipate his wishes, that you smile in his smile, and are sad in his sadness, and are downcast when he is vexed, and rejoice in his successes? To watch for Christ is a feeling such as all these; as far as feelings of this world are fit to shadow out those of another.

He watches for Christ who has a sensitive, eager, apprehensive mind; who is awake, alive, quick-sighted, zealous in seeking and honouring Him; who looks out for Him in all that happens, and who would not be surprised, who would not be over-agitated or overwhelmed, if he found that He was coming at once.

And he watches *with* Christ, who, while he looks on to the future, looks back on the past, and does not so contemplate what his Saviour has purchased for him, as to forget what He has suffered for him. He watches with Christ, who ever commemorates and renews in his own person Christ's Cross and Agony, and gladly takes up the mantle of affliction which Christ wore here, and left behind Him when he ascended. . . .

This then is to watch; to be detached from what is present, and to live in what is unseen; to live in the thought of Christ as He came once, and as He will come again; to desire His second coming, from our affectionate and grateful remembrance of His first.

P.S., iv, 322-5.

18

We must not only have faith in Him, but must wait on Him; not only must hope, but must watch for Him; not only love Him, but must long for Him; not only obey Him, but must look out, look up earnestly for our reward, which is Himself. We must not only make Him the Object of our faith, hope, and charity, but we must make it our duty not to believe the world, not to hope in the world, not to love the world. . . .

They, then, watch and wait for their Lord, who are tender and sensitive in their devotion towards Him; who feed on the thought of Him, hang on His words ; live in His smile, and thrive and grow under His hand. They are eager for His approval, quick in catching His meaning, jealous of His honour. They see Him in all things, expect Him in all events, and amid all the cares, the interests, and the pursuits of this life, still would feel an awful joy, not a disappointment, did they hear that He was on the point of coming. . . .

You know there are subtle instincts in the inferior animals, by which they apprehend the presence of things which man cannot discern, as atmospheric changes or convulsions of the earth or their natural enemies, whom yet they do not actually see; and we consider the uneasiness or the terror which they exhibit to be a proof that there is something near them which is the object of the feeling, and is the evidence of its own reality. Well, in some such way the continuous watching and waiting for Christ, which Prophets, Apostles, and the Church built upon them, have manifested age after age, is a demonstration that the Object of it is not a dream or a fancy, but really exists; in other words, that He lives still, that He has ever lived, who was once upon earth, who died, who disappeared, who said He would come again.

O.S., 34-7.

19

Let us pray God to give us *all* graces; and while, in the first place, we pray that He would make us holy, really holy, let us also pray Him to give us the *beauty* of holiness, which consists in tender and eager affection towards our Lord and Saviour; which is, in the case of the Christian, what beauty of person is to the outward man, so that through God's mercy our souls may

297

have, not strength and health only, but a sort of bloom and comeliness; and that as we grow older in body, we may, year by year, grow more youthful in spirit.

P.S., vii, 134.

20

To have a virgin soul, is, to love nothing on earth in comparison of God, or except for His sake. That soul is virginal which is ever looking for its Beloved who is in heaven, and which sees Him in whatever is lovely upon earth, loving earthly friends very dearly, but in their proper place as His gifts and His representatives . . . loving Jesus alone with sovereign affection, and bearing to lose all . . . [to] keep Him.

M.D., 311-2.

XVII: THIS WORLD

ANALYTICAL SUMMARY

But God is also a God of this world, whose purpose in requiring from the Christian such detachment from it is that without worldliness or self-seeking, in love of His Master and in His Master's Spirit, he may labour and struggle in God's Creation till, refashioned by his handiwork, it reflects in its splendour the divine Beauty;

(Nos. 1-9.)

and that man himself by this unselfish task, which spares no labour, but becomes ever more intense may ripen and grow purer in the love of his inmost heart for God, so that the world and his work in the world brings him ever closer to God and reveals more of His Glory;

(Nos. 10-14.)

that, nevertheless, as in this death-sentenced world it cannot be otherwise, the goal of all work, toil, success and failure—shall be the untroubled Peace of complete resignation, the Christian's deepest and ultimate disposition.

(Nos. 15-20.)

I. THE WORLD TRANSFORMED

I

The Jews had a grant of this world; they entered the vineyard in the morning; they had time before them; they might reckon on the future. They were bid "go their way, eat their bread with joy, and drink their wine with a merry heart, and let their garments be always white, and let their head lack no ointment, and live joyfully with the wife whom they loved all the days of the life of their vanity: . . . for that was their portion in this life, and in their labour which they took under the sun." But it is otherwise with us. Earth and sky are ever failing; Christ is ever coming; Christians are ever lifting up their heads and looking out, and therefore it is the evening. We may not set our hearts on things present; we may not say to our soul, "Thou hast much goods laid up for many years, take thine ease, eat, drink, and be merry": and therefore it is the evening. We may not think of home, or brethren, or sister, or father, or mother, or wife, or children, or land; and therefore it is the evening. The evening is long and the day was short; for the first shall be last, and the last first. What seems vigorous perishes; what seems ever expiring is carried on; and this last age, though ever-failing, has lasted longer than the ages before it, and Christians have more time for a greater work than if they had been hired in the morning.

S.D., 10.

2

When persons are convinced that life is short, that it is unequal to any great purpose, that it does not display adequately, or bring to perfection the true Christian, when they feel that the next life is all in all, and that eternity is the only subject that really can claim or can fill their thoughts, then they are apt to undervalue this life altogether, and to forget its real importance. They are apt to wish to spend the time of their sojourning here in a positive separation from active and social duties. . . . It is difficult to realize both truths at once, and to connect both truths together; steadily to contemplate the life to come, yet to act in this. Those who meditate are likely to neglect those active duties which are, in fact, incumbent on them, and to dwell upon the thought of God's glory till they forget to act to His glory. . . . But it is possible to do *all things* whatever we are about to God's glory; we may do all things *heartily*, as to the Lord, and not to man, being both active yet meditative . . . . The true Christian will feel that the true contemplation of that Saviour lies *in* his worldly business; that as Christ is seen in the poor, and in the persecuted, and in children, so is He seen in the employments which He puts upon His chosen, whatever they be; that in attending to his own calling he will be meeting Christ; that if he neglect it he will not on that account enjoy His presence at all the more, but that while performing it he will see Christ revealed to his soul amid the ordinary actions of the day, as by a sort of sacrament. Thus he will take his worldly business as a gift from Him, and will love it as such. . . . The highest Christian of all is he . . . . whose heart is so set on things above, that things below as little excite, agitate, unsettle, distress, and seduce him as they stop the course of nature, as they stop the sun and moon, or change summer and winter. Such were the Apostles, who, as the heavenly bodies, went out "to all lands," full of business, and yet full too of sweet harmony, even to the ends of the earth. Their calling was heavenly, but their work was earthly; they were in labour and trouble till the last; yet consider how calmly St. Paul and St. Peter write in their last days.

P.S., viii, 154-5, 161, 165, 169.

3

The Creator of this world is none other than the Father of our Lord Jesus Christ; there are not two Gods, one of matter, one of spirit; one of the Law, and one of the Gospel. There is one God, and He is Lord of all we are, and all we have; and, therefore, all we do must be stamped with His seal and signature. We must begin, indeed, with the heart; for out of the heart proceed all good and evil ; but while we begin with the heart we must not end with the heart. We must not give up this visible world as if it came of the evil one. It is our duty to change it into the kingdom of heaven. We must manifest the kingdom of heaven upon earth. The light of Divine truth must proceed *from* our hearts, and shine out *upon* every thing we are, and every thing we do.

P.S., vi, 304-5.

4

A great object of Christ's coming was to subdue this world, to claim it as His own, to assert His rights as its Master, to destroy the usurped dominion of the enemy, to show Himself to all men, and to take possession. He is that Mustard-tree which was destined silently to spread and over-shadow all lands; He is that Leaven which was secretly to make its way through the mass of human opinions and institutions till the whole was leavened. Heaven and earth had hitherto been separate. His gracious purpose was to make them one, and that by making earth like heaven. He was in the world from the beginning, and man worshipped other gods; he came into the world in the flesh, and the world knew Him not; He came unto His own, and His own received Him not. But He came in order to *make* them receive Him, know Him, worship Him. He came to absorb this world into Himself; that, as He was light, so it might be light also. When He came, He had not a place to lay his Head; but He came to make Himself a place, to make Himself a home, to make Himself houses, to fashion for Himself a glorious dwelling out of this whole world, which the powers of evil had taken captive. He came in the dark, in the dark night was He born, in a cave underground; in a cave where cattle were stabled, there was He housed; in a rude manger was He laid. There first He laid His head; but He meant not, blessed be His Name! He meant not there to remain for ever. He did not resign Himself

303

to that obscurity; He came into that cave to leave it. . . . He purposed to change the earth, and He began "in the lowest pit, in a place of darkness, and in the deep." All was to be by Him renewed, and He availed Himself of nothing that was, that out of nothing He might make all things. He was not born in the Temple of Jerusalem; He abhorred the palace of David; He laid Himself on the damp earth in the cold night, a light shining in a dark place, till by the virtue that went out of Him He should create a Temple worthy of His Name. . . .The Invisible Temple has become visible. As on a misty day, the gloom gradually melts and the sun brightens, so have the glories of the spiritual world lit up this world below. The dull and cold earth is penetrated by the rays. All around we see glimpses or reflections of those heavenly things, which the elect of God shall one day see face to face.

P.S., vi, 283-6.

5

To be out of conceit with our lot in life, is no high feeling,—it is discontent or ambition; but to be out of conceit with the ordinary way of *viewing* our lot, with the ordinary thoughts and feelings of mankind, is nothing but to be a Christian. This is the difference between worldly ambition and heavenly. It is a heavenly ambition which prompts us to soar above the vulgar and ordinary *motives* and *tastes* of the world, the while we abide *in* our calling; like our Saviour who, though the Son of God and partaking of His Father's fulness, yet all His youth long was obedient to His earthly parents, and learned a humble trade. But it is a sordid, narrow, miserable ambition to attempt to *leave* our earthly lot; to be wearied or ashamed of what we are, to hanker after greatness of station, or novelty of life.

P.S., iv, 162-3.

6

Gloom is no Christian temper ; that repentance is not real which has not love in it; that self-chastisement is not acceptable which is not sweetened by faith and cheerfulness. We must live in sunshine, even when we sorrow ; we must live in God's presence, we must not shut ourselves up in our own hearts, even when we are reckoning up our past sins. . . .We must look abroad into this fair world, which God made "very good," while we mourn over the evil which Adam brought into it. We must hold communion with what we see there while we seek Him who is invisible; we must admire it while we abstain from it; acknowledge God's love while we deprecate His wrath; confess that, many as are our sins, His grace is greater. Our sins are more in number than the hairs of our head; yet even the hairs of our head are all numbered by Him. He counts our sins, and, as He counts, so can He forgive; for that reckoning, great though it be, comes to an end; but His mercies fail not, and His Son's merits are infinite.

P.S., v, 271-2.

7

To put off idle hopes of earthly good, to be sick of flattery and the world's praise, to see the emptiness of temporal greatness, and to be watchful against self-indulgence,—these are but the beginnings of religion; these are but the preparation of heart, which religious earnestness implies; without a good share of them, how can a Christian move a step?

But to love our brethren with a resolution which no obstacles can overcome, so as almost to consent to an anathema on ourselves, if so be we may save those who hate us,—to labour in God's cause against hope, and in the midst of sufferings,—to read the events of life, as they occur, by the interpretation which Scripture gives them, and that, not as if the language were strange to us, but to do it promptly,—to perform all our relative daily duties most watchfully,—to check every evil thought, and bring the whole mind into captivity to the law of Christ,— to be patient, cheerful, forgiving, meek, honest, and true,— to persevere in this good work till death, making fresh and fresh advances towards perfection—and after all, even to the end, to confess ourselves unprofitable servants, nay, to feel ourselves corrupt and sinful creatures, who (with all our proficiency) would still be lost unless God bestowed on us His mercy in Christ : these are some of the difficult realities of religious obedience which we must pursue, and which the Apostles in high measure attained, and which we may well bless God's holy name, if He enables us to make our own.

P.S., i, 343-4.

8

As it is possible to watch for Christ in spite of earthly reasonings to the contrary, so is it possible to engage in earthly duties, in spite of our watching. Christ has told us, that when He comes two men shall be in the field, two women at the mill: "the one shall be taken, and the other left." You see that good and bad are engaged in the same way; nor need it hinder any one from having his heart firmly fixed on God, that he is engaged in worldly business with those whose hearts are upon the world. Nay, we may form large plans, we may busy ourselves in new undertakings, we may begin great works which we cannot do more than begin; we may make provision for the future, and anticipate in our acts the certainty of centuries to come, yet be looking out for Christ. Thus indeed we are bound to proceed, and to leave "times and seasons in His Father's power." Whenever He comes, He will cut things short; and, for what we know, our efforts and beginnings, though they be nothing more, are just as necessary in the course of His Providence, as could be the most successful accomplishment. Surely, He will end the world abruptly, whenever He comes; He will break off the designs and labours of His elect, whatever they are, and give them what their dutiful anxiety aims at, though not through it. . . All that we do,—whatever we are doing,—whether we have time for more or time for less,—yet our work, finished or unfinished, will be acceptable, if done for Him. There is no inconsistency, then, in watching yet working, for we may work without setting our hearts on our work. Our sin will be if we idolize the work of our hands; if we love it so well as not to bear to part with it. The test of our faith lies in our being able to fail without disappointment.

P.S., vi, 268-9.

306

The while that we are still on earth, and our duties are in this world, let us never forget that, while our love must be silent, our faith must be vigorous and lively. Let us never forget that in proportion as our love is "rooted and grounded" in the next world, our faith must branch forth like a fruitful tree into this. The calmer our hearts, the more active be our lives; the more tranquil we are, the more busy; the more resigned, the more zealous; the more unruffled, the more fervent. This is one of the many paradoxes in the world's judgment of him, which the Christian realizes in himself.

P.S., ii, 341.

II. OUTGROWING THE WORLD

10

I am speaking of the conduct of the world at large, called Christian; but what has been said applies, and necessarily, to the case of a number of well-disposed or even religious men. I mean, that before men come to know the realities of human life, it is not wonderful that their view of religion should be unreal. Young people who have never known sorrow or anxiety, or the sacrifices which conscientiousness involves, want commonly that depth and seriousness of character which sorrow only and anxiety and self-sacrifice can give. I do not notice this as a fault, but as a plain fact, which may often be seen, and which it is well to bear in mind. This is the legitimate use of this world, to make us seek for another. It does its part when it repels us and disgusts us and drives us elsewhere. Experience of it gives experience of that which is its antidote, in the case of religious minds; and we become real in our view of what is spiritual by the contact of things temporal and earthly.

P.S., v, 40-1.

11

The great rule of our conduct is to take things as they come. He who goes out of his way as shrinking from the varieties of human life which meet him, has weak faith, or a strangely perverted conscience,—he wants elevation of mind. The true Christian rejoices in those earthly things which give joy, but in such a way as not to care for them when they go. For no blessings does he care much, except those which are immortal, knowing that he shall receive all such again in the world to come. But the least and the most fleeting, he is too religious to contemn, considering them God's gift; and the least and most fleeting, thus received, yield a purer and deeper, though a less tumultuous joy.

Only look upon the world in this light : its sights of sorrows are to calm you, and its pleasant sights to try you. There is a bravery in thus going straightforward, shrinking from no duty little or great, passing from high to low, from pleasure to pain, and making your principles strong without their becoming formal. Learn to be as the Angel, who could descend among the miseries of Bethesda, without losing his heavenly purity or his perfect happiness. Gain healing from troubled waters. Make up your mind to the prospect of sustaining a certain measure of pain and trouble in your passage through life; by the blessing of God this will prepare you for it,—it will make you thoughtful and resigned without interfering with your cheerfulness.

P.S., i, 333-4.

12

It is His will that all we do should be done, not unto men, or to the world, or to self, but to His glory; and the more we are enabled to do this simply, the more favoured we are. Whenever we act with reference to an object of this world, even though it be ever so pure, we are exposed to the temptation—(not irresistible, God forbid!) still to the temptation—of setting our hearts upon obtaining it. And, therefore, we call all such objects *excitements,* as stimulating us incongruously, casting us out of the serenity and stability of heavenly faith, attracting us aside by their proximity from our harmonious round of duties, and making our thoughts converge to something short of that which is infinitely high and eternal. Such excitements are of perpetual occurrence, and the mere undergoing them, so far from involving guilt in the act itself or its results, is the great business of life and the discipline of our hearts. . . . it is a part of Christian caution to see that our engagements do not become pursuits. Engagements are our portion, but pursuits are for the most part of our own choosing. . . . It is at once our privilege and our duty—the Christian portion of having engagements of this world without pursuing objects.

P.S., ii, 349-50, 352-4.

13

Such is God's merciful consideration of us; He does not separate us from this world, though He calls us out of it; He does not reject our old nature when He gives us a new one; He does but redeem it from the curse, and purify it from the infection which came through Adam, and is none of His. He especially blesses the creation to our use, though we be regenerate.

He does not bid us renounce the creation, but associates us with the most beautiful portions of it. He likens us to the flowers with which He has ornamented the earth, and to the birds that live solitary under heaven, and makes them the type of a Christian. He denies us Solomon's regal magnificence, to unite us to the lilies of the field and the fowls of the air.

P.S., v, 274-5.

14

Let us not so plunge ourselves in the sense of our offences, as not withal to take delight in the contemplation of our privileges. Let us rejoice while we mourn. Let us look up to our Lord and Saviour the more we shrink from the sight of ourselves; let us have the more faith and love the more we exercise repentance. Let us, in our penitence, not substitute the Law *for* the Gospel, but add the Law *to* the Gospel. . . . in like manner, as we must not defraud ourselves of Christian privileges, neither need we give up God's temporal blessings. All the beauty of nature, the kind influences of the seasons, the gifts of sun and moon, and the fruits of the earth, the advantages of civilized life, and the presence of friends and intimates; all these good things are but one extended and wonderful type of God's benefits in the Gospel. Those who aim at perfection will not reject the gift, but add a corrective; they will add the bitter herbs to the fatted calf and the music and dancing; they will not refuse the flowers of earth, but they will toil in plucking up the weeds. Or if they refrain from one temporal blessing, it will be to reserve another; for this is one great mercy of God, that while He allows us a discretionary use of His temporal gifts, He allows a discretionary abstinence also; and He almost enjoins upon us the use of some, lest we should forget that this earth is His creation, and not of the evil one.

S.D., 123-4.

III. ABANDONMENT

15

The Bible begins with the history of the curse pronounced on the earth and man; it ends with the book of Revelation, a portion of Scripture fearful for its threats, and its prediction of judgments. . . . Human tales and poems are full of pleasant sights and prospects; they make things better than they are, and portray a sort of imaginary perfection ; but Scripture (I repeat) seems to abstain even from what might be said in praise of human life as it is. We read, indeed, of the feast made when Isaac was weaned, of Jacob's marriage, of the domestic and religious festivities of Job's family; but these are exceptions in the tenor of the Scripture history. "Vanity of vanities, all is vanity"; "man is born to trouble:" these are its customary lessons. In truth, this view is the ultimate *true* view of human life. But this is not all; it is a view which it concerns us much to know. It concerns us (I say) much to be told that this world is, after all, in spite of first appearances and partial exceptions, a dark world; else we shall be obliged to learn it (and, sooner or later, we must learn it) by sad *experience;* whereas, if we are forewarned, we shall unlearn false notions of its excellence, and be saved the disappointment which follows them. And, therefore,

310

it is that Scripture omits even what might be said in praise of this world's pleasures,—not denying their value, such as it is, or forbidding us to use them religiously, but knowing that we are sure to find them out for ourselves without being told of them, and that our danger is on the side, not of undervaluing, but of overvaluing them; whereas, by being told of the world's vanity, *at first*, we shall learn (what else we should only attain *at last*), not indeed to be gloomy and discontented, but to bear a sober and calm heart under a smiling cheerful countenance.

P.S., i, 326-9.

16

Ten thousand things come before us one after another in the course of life, and what are we to think of them? what colour are we to give them? Are we to look at all things in a gay and mirthful way? or in a melancholy way? in a desponding or a hopeful way? Are we to make light of life altogether, or to treat the whole subject seriously? Are we to make greatest things of little consequence, or least things of great consequence? Are we to keep in mind what is past and gone, or are we to look to the future, or are we to be absorbed in what is present? *How* are we to look at things? this is the question which all persons of observation ask themselves, and answer each in his own way. They wish to think by rule; by something within them, which may harmonise and adjust what is without them. Such is the need felt by reflective minds. Now, let me ask, what *is* the real key, what is the Christian interpretation of this world? What is given us by revelation to estimate and measure this world by? Crucifixion of the Son of God.

It is the death of the Eternal Word of God made flesh which is our great lesson how to think and how to speak of this world. His Cross has put its due value upon every thing which we see, upon all fortunes, all advantages, all ranks, all dignities, all pleasures; upon the lust of the flesh, and the lust of the eyes, and the pride of life. It has set a price upon the excitements, the rivalries, the hopes, the fears, the desires, the efforts, the triumphs of mortal man. It has given a meaning to the various, shifting course, the trials, the temptations, the sufferings, of his earthly state. It has brought together and made consistent all that seemed discordant and aimless. It has taught us how to live, how to use this world, what to expect, what to desire, what to hope. It is the tone into which all the strains of this world's music are ultimately to be resolved. . . .

The doctrine of the Cross does but teach, though infinitely more forcibly; still after all it does but teach the very same lesson which this world teaches to those who live long in it, who have much experience in it, who know it. . . . The doctrine of the Cross of Christ does but anticipate for us our experience of the world. It is true, it bids us grieve for our sins in the midst of all that smiles and glitters around us; but if we will not heed it, we shall at length be forced to grieve for them from undergoing their fearful punishment. If we will not acknowledge that this world has been made miserable by sin, from the sight of Him on whom our sins were laid, we shall experience it to be miserable by the recoil of those sins upon ourselves. . . . They alone are able truly to enjoy this world who begin with the world unseen. They alone enjoy it who have first abstained from it. . . . they alone inherit it who take it as a shadow of the world to come, and who for that world to come relinquish it.

P.S., *vi*, 84-5, 87-8, 93.

17

I call resignation a more blessed frame of mind than sanguine hope of present success, because it is the truer, and the more consistent with our fallen state of being, and the more improving to our hearts; and because it is that for which the most eminent servants of God have been conspicuous. To expect great effects from our exertions for religious objects is natural indeed, and innocent, but it arises from inexperience of the kind of work we have to do,—to change the heart and will of man. It is a far nobler frame of mind to labour, not with the hope of seeing the fruit of our labour, but for conscience' sake, as a matter of duty; and again, in faith, trusting good *will* be done, though we see it not. Look through the Bible, and you will find God's

312

servants, even though they began with success, end with disappointment; not that God's purposes or His instruments fail, but that the time for reaping what we have sown is hereafter, not here; that here there is no great visible fruit in any one man's lifetime. Moses, for instance, began with leading the Israelites out of Egypt in triumph; he ended at the age of a hundred and twenty years, before his journey was finished and Canaan gained, one among the offending multitudes who were overthrown in the wilderness. Samuel's reformations ended in the people's wilfully choosing a king like the nations around them. Elijah, after his successes, fled from Jezebel into the wilderness to mourn over his disappointments. Isaiah, after Hezekiah's religious reign, and the miraculous destruction of Sennacherib's army, fell upon the evil days of his son Manasseh. Even in the successes of the first Christian teachers, the Apostles, the same rule is observed. After all the great works God enabled them to accomplish, they confessed before their death that what they experienced, and what they saw before them, was reverse and calamity, and that the fruit of their labours would not be seen till Christ came to open the books and collect His saints from the four corners of the earth. "Evil men and seducers shall wax worse and worse, deceiving and being deceived," is the testimony of St. Peter, St. Paul, St. John, and St. Jude.

P.S., viii, 129-131.

18

The true Christian feels as he would feel, did he know for certain that Christ would be here to-morrow. For he knows for certain, that at least Christ will come to him when he dies; and faith anticipates his death, and makes it just as if that distant day, if it *be* distant, were past and over. One time or another Christ will come, for certain: and when He once *has* come, it matters not what length of time there was before He came;—however long that period may be, it has an end. When we lie on the bed of death, what will it avail us to have been rich, or great, or fortunate, or honoured, or influential? All things will then be vanity. Well, what this world is will be understood by all to be then such as it is felt to be by the Christian now. He looks at things as he then will look at them, with an uninterested and dispassionate eye, and is neither pained much, nor pleased much at the accidents of life because they are accidents . . .

The truth is, as soon and in proportion as a person believes that Christ is coming, and recognises his own position as a stranger on earth, who has but hired a lodging in it for a season, he will feel indifferent to the course of human affairs. He will be able to look on, instead of taking a part in them. They will be nothing to him. He will be able to criticise them, and pass judgment on them, without partiality. This is what is meant by "our moderation" being acknowledged by all men. Those who have strong interests one way or the other, cannot be dispassionate observers and candid judges. They are partisans; they defend one set of people, and attack another. They are prejudiced against those who differ from them, or who thwart them. They cannot make allowances or show sympathy for them. But the Christian has no keen expectations, no acute mortifications. He is fair, equitable, considerate towards all men, because he has no temptation to be otherwise. He has no violence, no animosity, no bigotry, no party feeling. He knows that his Lord and Saviour must triumph; he knows that He will one day come from heaven, no one can say how soon. Knowing then the end to which all things tend, he cares less for the road which is to lead to it. So is it with the Christian. He knows Christ's battle will last till the end; that Christ's cause will triumph in the end; that His Church will last till He comes. He knows what is truth and what is error, where is safety and where is danger; and all this clear knowledge enables him to make concessions, to own difficulties, to do justice to the erring, to acknowledge their good points, to be content with such countenance, greater or less, as he himself receives from others. He does not fear; fear it is that makes men bigots, tyrants, and zealots; but for the Christian, it is his privilege, as he is beyond hopes and fears, suspense and jealousy, so also to be patient, cool, discriminating, and impartial;—so much so, that this very fairness marks his character in the eyes of the world, is "known unto all men."

P.S., v, 62-5.

19

The foundations of the ocean, the vast realms of water which girdle the earth, are as tranquil and as silent in the storm as in a calm. So is it with the souls of holy men. They have a well of peace springing up within them unfathomable; and though the accidents of the hour may make them seem agitated, yet in their hearts they are not so. Even Angels joy over sinners repentant, and, as we may therefore suppose, grieve over sinners impenitent,—yet who shall say that they have not perfect peace? Even Almighty God Himself deigns to speak of His being grieved, and angry, and rejoicing,—yet is He not the unchangeable? And in like manner. . . the Christian has a deep, silent, hidden peace, which the world sees not,—like some well in a retired and shady place, difficult of access. He is the greater part of his time by himself, and when he is in solitude, that is his real state. What he is when left to himself and to his God, that is his true life. He can bear himself; he can (as it were) joy in himself, for it is the grace of God within him, it is the presence of the Eternal Comforter, in which he joys. He can bear, he finds it pleasant, to be with himself at all times,—"never less alone than when alone." He can lay his head on his pillow at night, and own in God's sight, with overflowing heart, that he wants nothing,—that he "is full and abounds,"—that God has been all things to him, and that nothing is not his which God could give him. More thankfulness, more holiness, more of heaven he needs indeed, but the thought that he can have more is not a thought of trouble, but of joy. It does not interfere with his peace to know that he may grow nearer God. Such is the Christian's peace, when, with a single heart and the Cross in his eye, he addresses and commends himself to Him with whom the night is as clear as the day.

P.S., v, 69-76.

20

Ignorance is the root of all littleness; he who can realize the law of moral conflicts, and the incoherence of falsehood, and the issue of perplexities, and the end of all things, and the Presence of the Judge, becomes, from the very necessity of the case, philosophical, long-suffering, and magnanimous.

Prepos., 391.

XVIII:
BETWEEN THIS WORLD AND THE NEXT

ANALYTICAL SUMMARY

Thus is the Christian one who lives "between this world and the next"; to the world he is a contradiction, indeed a stumbling block, a scandal, so that his virtues seem vices, his wisdom folly, his meekness cunning, until the opposition between them ends in hatred and persecution even to death.

(Nos. 1-6.)

The Christian's true life is hidden from the world; even as the world neither knew nor understood Christ when He came into it, to the natural eye Christians are indistinguishable from ordinary men.

(Nos. 7-9.)

But to the Christian this deceitful world is in process of dissolution, until like a cloud or veil it can hardly conceal any longer the growing light of the heavenly sunrise.

(Nos. 10-19.)

He walks as a pilgrim and stranger the streets and lanes of this world, but he is not therefore homeless; he finds his home in holy Church, the blessed forecourt of his everlasting home, and in the mystery which invests her altars he breathes the air of heaven.

(Nos. 20-26.)

I. CONTRADICTING THE WORLD

I

There is an inward world, which none see but those who belong to it; and though the outside robe be many-coloured, like Joseph's coat, inside it is lined with camel's hair, or sackcloth, fitting those who desire to be one with Him who fared hardly in the wilderness, in the mountain, and on the sea. There is an inward world into which they enter who come near to Christ, though to men in general they seem the same as before. They hold the same place as before in the world's society; their employments are the same, their ways, their comings in and goings out. If they were high in rank, they are still high; if they were in active life, they are still active; if they were wealthy, they still have wealth. They have still great friends, powerful connexions, ample resources, fair name in the world's eye; but, if they have drunk of Christ's cup, and tasted the bread of His Table in sincerity, it is not with them as in time past. A change has come over them, unknown indeed to themselves, except in its effects, but they have a portion in destinies to which other men are strangers, and, as having destinies, they have conflicts also. They drank what looked like a draught of this world, but it associated them in hopes and fears, trials and purposes, above this world. They came as for a blessing, and they have found a work. They are soldiers in Christ's army; they fight against "things that are seen," and they have "all these things against them." To their surprise, as time goes on, they find that their lot is changed. They find that in one shape or other adversity happens to them. If they refuse to afflict themselves, God afflicts them. One blow falls, they are startled; it passes over, it is well; they expect nothing more. Another comes; they wonder; "Why is this?" they ask; they think that the first should be

319

their security against the second; they bear it, however; and it passes too. Then a third comes; they almost murmur; they have not yet mastered the great doctrine that endurance is their portion. O simple soul, is it not the law of thy being to endure since thou camest to Christ? Why camest thou but to endure? Why didst thou taste His heavenly feast, but that it might work in thee? Why didst thou kneel beneath His hand, but that He might leave on thee the print of His wounds? Why wonder then that one sorrow does not buy off the next? Does one drop of rain absorb the second? Does the storm cease because it has begun?

P.S., v, 295-6.

2

True Christians are little understood by the world because they are not of the world; and hence it sometimes happens that even the better sort of men are often disconcerted and vexed by them. . . . The immortality of truth, its oneness, the impossibility of falsehood coalescing with it, what truth is, what it should lead one to do in particular cases, how it lies in the details of life,— all these points are mere matters of debate in the world, and men go through long processes of argument, and pride themselves on their subtleness in defending or attacking, in making probable or improbable, ideas which are assumed without a word by those who have lived in heaven, as the very ground to start from. In consequence, such men are called bad disputants, inconsecutive reasoners, strange, eccentric, or perverse thinkers, merely because they do not take for granted, nor go to prove, what others do,—because they do not go about to define and determine the sights (as it were), the mountains and rivers and plains, and sun, moon, and stars, of the next world. And hence in turn they are commonly unable to enter into the ways of thought or feelings of other men, having been engrossed with God's thoughts and God's ways. Hence, perhaps, they seem abrupt in what they say and do; nay, even make others feel constrained and uneasy in their presence. Perhaps they appear reserved too, because they take so much for granted which might be drawn out, and because they cannot bring themselves to tell all their thoughts from their sacredness, and because they are drawn off from free conversation to the thought of heaven, on which their minds rest. Nay, perchance, they appear severe, because their motives are not understood, nor their sensitive jealousy for the honour of God and their charitable concern for the good of their fellow-Christians duly appreciated. In short, to the world they seem like *foreigners*. . . . Such is the effect of divine meditations: admitting us into the next world, and withdrawing us from this; making us children of God, but withal "strangers unto our brethren, even aliens unto our mother's children." Yea, though the true servants of God increase in meekness and love day by day, and to those who know them will seem what they really are; and though their good works are evident to all men, and cannot be denied, yet such is the eternal law which goes between the Church and the world—we cannot be friends of both; and they who take their portion with the Church, will seem, except in some remarkable cases, unamiable to the world, for the "world knoweth them not," and does not like them though it can hardly tell why; yet (as St. John proceeds) they have this blessing, that "when He shall appear, they shall be like Him, for they shall see Him as He is."

P.S., iv, 234-37.

3

1. Innocence, simplicity, implicit obedience to God, tranquility of mind, contentment, these and the like virtues are themselves a sort of wisdom;—I mean, they produce the same results as wisdom, because God works for those who do not work for themselves; and thus Christians especially incur the charge of craft at the hands of the world, because they pretend to so little, yet effect so much. . . . It appears to be craft, and is wisdom, in many ways. . . .

Accordingly, as persons have deep feelings, so they will find the necessity of self-control, lest they should say what they ought not. All this stands to reason, without enlarging upon it. And to this must be added, that those who would be holy and blameless, the sons of God, find so much in the world to unsettle and defile them, that they are necessarily forced upon a strict self-restraint, lest they should receive injury from such intercourse with it as is unavoidable; and this self-restraint is the first thing which makes holy persons seem wanting in openness and manliness.

2. The world. . . cannot believe that men will deliberately sacrifice this life to the next; and when they profess to do so, it thinks that of necessity there must be something behind which they do not divulge. And, again, all the reasons which religious men allege, seem to the world unreal, and all the feelings fantastical and strained; and this strengthens it in its idea that it has not fathomed them, and that there is some secret to be found out. And indeed it has not fathomed them, and there is a secret; but it is the power of Divine grace, their state of heart, which is the secret; not their motives or their ends, which the world is told to the full. Here is a second reason why the dove seems but a serpent. Christians give up worldly advantages; they sacrifice rank or wealth; they prefer obscurity to station; they do penance rather than live delicately; and the world says, "Here are effects without causes sufficient for them; here is craft."

3. . . . . There are a multitude of cases, and very various, where it is our duty to obey those who nevertheless have no power over our belief or conviction. When, however, religious men outwardly conform, on the score of duty, to "the powers that be," the world is easily led into the mistake that they have renounced their opinions as well as submitted their actions; and it feels or affects surprise to learn that their opinions remain ; and this it considers or calls an inconsistency, or a duplicity. It argues that they are breaking promise, cherishing what they disown, or resuming what they professed to abandon. And thus the very fact that they are so harmless, so inoffensive, that they do so much in the way of compliance, becomes a ground of complaint against them. . . . that they do not do more—that they do not do more than they have a right to do. They yield outwardly; to assent inwardly would be to betray the faith; yet they are called deceitful and double-dealing because they do as much as they can and not more than they may.

4. Again: the cheerfulness, contentment, and readiness with which religious men resign their cause into God's hands, and are well-pleased that the world should seem to triumph over them, have still further an appearance of craft and deceit. For why should they be so satisfied to give up their wishes, unless they knew something which others did not know, or were really gaining while they seemed to lose? . . .

5. And still stronger is this delusion on the part of the world, when the event justifies the confidence of religious men. The truest wisdom is to stand still and trust in God, . . . God fights for those who do not fight for themselves; such is the great truth . . . . Do nothing, and you have done everything. The less you do, the more God will do for you. The more you submit to the violence of the world, the more powerfully will He rise against the world, who is irresistible. The less you ward off the world's blows from you, the more heavy will be His blows upon the world, if not in your cause, at least in His own. When, then, the world at length becomes sensible that it is faring ill, and receiving more harm than it inflicts, yet is unwilling to humble itself under the mighty hand of God, what is left but to attribute its failure to the power of those who seem to be weak? that is, to their craft, who pretend to be weak when really they are strong. . . .

6. And of course all this happens to the surprise of Christians as well as of the world; they can but marvel and praise God, but cannot account for it more than the world. "When the Lord turned again the captivity of Sion," says the Psalmist, "then were we like unto them that dream." Or as the Prophet says of the Church, "Thine heart shall fear and be enlarged; because the abundance of the sea shall be converted unto thee, the forces of the Gentiles shall come unto thee," and here again the Christian's true wisdom looks like craft. It is true wisdom to leave the event to God; but when they are prospered, it looks like deceit to show surprise and to disclaim the work themselves. Moreover, meekness, gentleness, patience, and love, have in themselves a strong power to melt the heart of those who witness them. Cheerful suffering, too, leads spectators to sym-

323

pathy, till, perhaps, a reaction takes place in the minds of men, and they are converted by the sight, and glorify their Father which is in heaven. But it is easy to insinuate when men are malevolent, that those who triumph through meekness, have affected the meekness to secure the triumph.

S.D., 299-305.

4

Though . . . . in their principles, and in their future prospects, the Church is one thing, and the world is another, yet in present matter of fact, the Church is of the world, not separate from it; for the grace of God has but partial possession even of religious men, and the best that can be said of us is, that we have two sides, a light side and a dark, and that the dark happens to be the outermost. Thus we form part of the world to each other, though we be not of the world. . . .

It is only the actions of others which we see for the most part, and since there are numberless ways of doing wrong, and but one of doing right, and numberless ways too of regarding and judging the conduct of others, no wonder that even the better sort of men, much more the generality, are, and seem to be, so sinful. God only sees the circumstances under which a man acts, and why he acts in this way and not in that. God only sees perfectly the train of thought which preceded his action, the motive, and the reasons. And God alone (if aught is ill done, or sinfully) sees the deep contrition afterwards,—the habitual lowliness, then bursting forth into special self-reproach,—and the meek faith casting itself wholly upon God's mercy. Think for a moment, how many hours in the day every man is left wholly to himself and his God, or rather how few minutes he is in intercourse with others—consider this, and you will perceive how it is that the life of the Church is hid with God, and how it is that the outward conduct of the Church must necessarily look like the world, even far more than it really is like it, and how vain, in consequence, the attempt is (which some make) of separating

324

the world distinctly from the Church. Consider, moreover, how much there is, while we are in the body, to stand in the way of one mind communicating with another. We are imprisoned in the body, and our intercourse is by means of words, which feebly represent our real feelings. Hence the best motives and truest opinions are misunderstood, and the most sound rules of conduct misapplied by others. And Christians are necessarily more or less strange to each other; nay, and as far as the appearance of things is concerned, almost mislead each other, and are, as I have said, the world one to another. It is long, indeed, before we become at all acquainted with each other, and we appear the one to the other cold, or harsh, or capricious, or self-willed, when we are not so. So that it unhappily comes to pass, that even good men retire from each other into themselves, and to their God, as if retreating from the rude world.

P.S., *vii*, 36-8.

5

Human Society is an ordinance of God, to which He gives His sanction and His authority; but from the first an enemy has been busy in its depravation. Hence it is, that while in its substance it is divine, in its circumstances, tendencies, and results it has much of evil. Never do men come together in considerable numbers, but the passion, self-will, pride, and unbelief, which may be more or less dormant in them one by one, bursts into a flame, and becomes a constituent of their union. Even when faith exists in the whole people, even when religious men combine for religious purposes, still, when they form into a body, they evidence in no long time the innate debility of human nature, and in their spirit and conduct, in their avowals and proceedings, they are in grave contrast to Christian simplicity and straightforwardness. This is what the sacred writers mean by "the world," and why they warn us against it; and their description of it applies in its degree to all collections and parties of men, high and low, national and professional, lay and ecclesiastical.

It would be hard, then, if men of great talent and of special

325

opportunities were bound to devote themselves to an ambitious life, whether they would or not, at the hazard of being accused of loving their own ease, when their reluctance to do so may possibly arise from a refinement and unworldliness of moral character. Surely they may prefer more direct ways of serving God and man; they may aim at doing good of a nature more distinctly religious; at works, safely and surely and beyond all mistake meritorious; at offices of kindness, benevolence, and considerateness, personal and particular; at labours of love and self-denying exertions, in which their left hand knows nothing that is done by their right.

O.S., 271-2.

6

[The true Christian] is ever dying while he lives; he is on his bier, and the prayers for the sick are saying over him. He has no work but that of making his peace with God, and preparing for the judgment. He has no aim but that of being found worthy to escape the things that shall come to pass and to stand before the Son of man. And therefore day by day he unlearns the love of this world, and the desire of its praise; he can bear to belong to the nameless family of God, and to seem to the world strange in it and out of place, for so he is.

And when Christ comes at last, blessed indeed will be his lot. He has joined himself from the first to the conquering side; he has risked the present against the future, preferring the chance of eternity to the certainty of time; and then his reward will be but beginning, when that of the children of this world is come to an end.

P.S., *iv*, 238.

II. HIDDEN FROM THE WORLD

7

Holy souls take a separate course; they have risen with Christ, and they are like persons who have climbed a mountain and are reposing at the top. All is noise and tumult, mist and darkness at its foot; but on the mountain's top it is so very still, so very calm and serene, so pure, so clear, so bright, so heavenly, that to their sensations it is as if the din of earth did not sound below, and shadows and gloom were no where to be found. . . . I do not mean, of course, that a man can be religious who neglects his duties of this world; but that there is an inner and truer life in religious men, beyond the life and conversation which others see, or, in the words of the text, their "life is hid with Christ in God." Christ, indeed, Himself worketh hitherto, as His Father worketh, and He bids us also "work while it is day;" yet, for all this, it is true that the Father and the Son are invisible, that they have an ineffable union with each other, and are not in any dependence upon the mortal concerns of this world; and so we, in our finite measure, must live after their Divine pattern, holding communion with them, as if we were at the top of the Mount while we perform our duties towards that sinful and irreligious world which lies at the foot of it. . . .

It is then the duty and the privilege of all disciples of our glorified Saviour, to be exalted and transfigured with Him; to live in heaven in their thoughts, motives, aims, desires, likings, prayers, praises, intercessions, even while they are in the flesh; to look like other men, to be busy like other men, to be passed over in the crowd of men, or even to be scorned or oppressed, as other men may be, but the while to have a secret channel of communication with the Most High, a gift the world knows not of; to have their life *hid* with Christ in God.

P.S., *vi*, 209-11, 214.

8

Religious men, in the words of Scripture, "live by the faith of the Son of God, who loved them and gave Himself for them": but they do not tell this to all men; they leave others to find it out as they may. Our Lord's own command to His disciples was, that when they fast, they should "anoint their head and wash their face." Thus they are bound not to make a display, but ever to be content to look outwardly different from what they are really inwardly. They are to carry a cheerful countenance with them, and to control and regulate their feelings, that those feelings, by not being expended on the surface, may retire deep into their hearts and there live. And thus "Jesus Christ and He crucified" is, as the Apostle tells us, "a hidden wisdom;"—hidden in the world, which seems at first sight to speak a far other doctrine,—and hidden in the faithful soul, which to persons at a distance, or to chance beholders, seems to be living but an ordinary life, while really it is in secret holding communion with Him who was "manifested in the flesh," "crucified through weakness," "justified in the Spirit, seen of Angels, and received up into glory."

P.S., vi, 88-9.

9

We have these startling appearances:—Persons brought up without Baptism may show themselves just the same in character, temper, opinions, and conduct, with those who have been baptized; or when these differ from those, this difference may be sufficiently or exactly accounted for by their education.

An unbaptized person may be brought up with baptized persons, and acquire their tone of thought, their mode of viewing things, and their principles and opinions, just as if he were baptized. He may suppose that he has been baptized, and others may think so; and on inquiry it may be found out that he has not been baptized.

On the other hand, a baptized person may acquire the ways of going on, and the sentiments and modes of talking of those who despise Baptism, and seem neither better nor worse than they, but just the same.

An unbaptized person may in after-life be baptized; and if quiet and religious before, may remain so afterwards, with no change of any kind in his own consciousness about himself, or in the impression of others about him.

Or, he may have had a formed character before Baptism, and not a pleasing one; he may have been rude and irreverent, or worldly-minded. He may have improved; he may have had faith sufficiently to bring him to Baptism, and, as far as we can

328

judge, may have received it worthily; yet he may remain, improved indeed just so much as is implied in his having had faith to come to Baptism, but apparently in no greater measure.

Or, he may come to Baptism and improve after it, but only in such way as to all appearance he might have improved without having received it when he did; viz. from the intercourse of friends, from reading religious books, from study and thought, or from the trials of life.

Again, he may come to Baptism as a mere form, or from worldly motives, and yet in appearance be no worse than he was before. If he had a mixture of good and evil in him before, the same apparently remains.

And again, whether he has received Baptism or not, he is liable to the same changes of mind, to the same religious influences, nay, may run through the same spiritual course, may be gradually moulded on the same habits,—perhaps be affected in some remarkable way, so remarkable that it may be called a conversion, and what he himself may incorrectly call a regeneration,—which it cannot be, if we judge according to Scripture, and not appearance, since he either has been already regenerated in Baptism, or has not yet been regenerated, being unbaptized. Yet the same religious experience (as it sometimes is called) may befall him, whether he has been baptized or not.

It is indeed most obvious and striking how, in all systems, whether we take our own, or that which principally obtains abroad, or that of any dissenting bodies, we find the same sort of moral character attaching to this or that class of persons; how rank, wealth or power forms men every where alike; how all systems have their freethinkers; how all have the same parties. Men are formed every where by the influence of visible things on the same types, and correspond one to another, as if proving against the Word of God, that baptism and grace are not the really influential principles among men, but the world that is seen.

S.D., 68-70.

10

The principle under consideration is this: that, whereas God is one, and His will one, and His purpose one, and His work one; whereas all He is and does is absolutely perfect and complete, independent of time and place and sovereign over creation whether inanimate or living, yet that in His actual dealings with this world that is, in all in which we see His Providence (in that man is imperfect, and has a will of his own, and lives in time, and is moved by circumstances), He seems to work by a process by means and ends, by steps, by victories hardly gained, and failures repaired, and sacrifices ventured. Thus it is only when we view His dispensations at a distance, as the Angels do, that we see their harmony and their unity.

P.S., ii, 34.

11

How, it may be asked, can this world have upon it tokens of His presence, or bring us near to Him? Yet certainly so it is, that in spite of the world's evil, after all, He is in it and speaks through it, though not loudly. When He came in the flesh "He was in the world, and the world was made by Him, and the world knew Him not." Nor did He strive nor cry, nor lift up His voice in the streets. So it is now. He still is here; He still whispers to us, He still makes signs to us. But His voice is so low, and the world's din is so loud, and His signs are so covert, and the world is so restless, that it is difficult to determine when He addresses us, and what He says. Religious men cannot but feel, in various ways, that His providence is guiding them and blessing them personally, on the whole; yet when they attempt to put their finger upon the times and places, the traces of His presence disappear. Who is there, for instance, but has been favoured with answers to prayer, such that, at the time, he has felt he never could again be unbelieving? Who has not had strange coincidences in his course of life which brought before him, in an overpowering way, the hand of God? Who has not had thoughts come upon him with a sort of mysterious force, for his warning or his direction? And

330

some persons, perhaps, experience stranger things still. Wonderful providences have before now been brought about by means of dreams; or in other still more unusual ways Almighty God has at times interposed. And then, again, things which come before our eyes, in such wise take the form of types and omens of things moral or future, that the spirit within us cannot but reach forward and presage what it is not told from what it sees. And sometimes these presages are remarkably fulfilled in the event. And then, again, the fortunes of men are so singularly various, as if a law of success and prosperity embraced a certain number, and a contrary law others. All this being so, and the vastness and mystery of the world being borne in upon us, we may well begin to think that there is nothing here below, but, for what we know, has a connexion with every thing else; the most distant events may yet be united, the meanest and highest may be parts of one; and God may be teaching us and offering us knowledge of His ways, if we will but open our eyes, in all the ordinary matters of the day. This is what thoughtful persons come to believe, and they begin to have a sort of faith in the Divine meaning of the accidents (as they are called) of life, and of readiness to take impressions from them, which may easily become excessive, and which, whether excessive or not, is sure to be ridiculed by the world at large as superstition. Yet, considering Scripture tells us that the very hairs of our head are all numbered by God, that all things are ours, and that all things work together for our good, it does certainly encourage us in thus looking out for His presence in every thing that happens however trivial, and in holding that to religious ears even the bad world prophesies of Him.

Yet, I say, this religious waiting upon God through the day, which is so like that spirit of watching which is under consideration, is just as open to objection and scoffing from the world. God does not so speak to us through the occurrences of life, that you can persuade others that He speaks. He does not act upon such explicit laws, that you can speak of them with certainty. He gives us sufficient tokens of Himself to raise our minds in awe towards Him; but He seems so frequently to undo what He

Has done, and to suffer counterfeits of His tokens, that a conviction of His wonder-working presence can but exist in the individual himself. It is not a truth that can be taught and recognized in the face of men; it is not of a nature to be urged upon the world at large, nay, even on religious persons, as a principle. God gives us enough to make us inquire and hope; not enough to make us insist and argue.

P.S., ii, 248-50.

12

This is the law of Providence here below; it works beneath a veil, and what is visible in its course does but shadow out at most, and sometimes obscures and disguises what is invisible. The world in which we are placed has its own system of laws and principles, which, as far as our knowledge of it goes, is, when once set in motion, sufficient to account for itself,—as complete and as independent as if there was nothing beyond it. Ordinarily speaking, nothing happens, nothing goes on in the world, but may be satisfactorily traced to some other event or fact in it, or has a sufficient result in other events or facts in it, without the necessity of our following it into a higher system of things in order to explain its existence, or to give it a meaning. We will not stop to dwell on exceptions to this general statement, or on the narrowness of our knowledge of things: but what is every day said and acted on proves that this is at least the impression made upon most minds by the course of things in which we find ourselves. The sun rises and sets on a law; the tides ebb and flow upon a law ; the earth is covered with verdure or buried in the ocean, it grows old and it grows young again, by the operation of fixed laws. Life, whether vegetable or animal, is subjected to a similar external and general rule. Men grow to maturity, then decay and die. Moreover they form into society, and society has its principles. Nations move forward by laws which act as a kind of destiny over them, and which are as vigorous now as a thousand years ago. And these laws of the social and political world run into the physical, making all that is seen one and one only system; a horse stumbles, and an

oppressed people is rid of their tyrant; a volcano changes popu-
lous cities into a dull lake; a gorge has of old times opened, and
the river rolls on, bearing on its bosom the destined site of some
great mart, which else had never been. We cannot set limits
either to the extent or the minuteness of this wonderful web
of causes and effects, in which all we see is involved. It reaches
to the skies; it penetrates into our very thoughts, habits, and will.

Such is confessedly the world in which our Almighty Creator
has placed us. If then He is still actively present with His own
work, present with nations and with individuals, He must be
acting by means of its ordinary system, or by quickening or, as it
were, stimulating its powers, or by superseding or interrupting it;
in other words, by means of what is called nature or by miracle;
and whereas strictly miraculous interference must be, from the
nature of the case, rare, it stands to reason that, unless He has
simply retired and has left the world ordinarily to itself,—content with having originally imposed upon it certain general
laws, which will for the most part work out the ends which He
contemplates,—He is acting through, with, and beneath those
physical, social and moral laws, of which our experience informs
us . . . . [Accordingly] it is not too much to say that this is the
one great rule on which the Divine Dispensations with mankind have been and are conducted, that the visible world is the
instrument, yet the veil, of the world invisible,—the veil, yet
still partally the symbol and index: so that all that exists or
happens visibly conceals and yet suggests, and above all sub-
serves, a system of persons, facts, and events beyond itself. . . .

All that is seen,—the world, the Bible, the Church, the civil
polity, and man himself,—are types, and in their degree and
place representatives and organs of an unseen world, truer and
higher than themselves.

Ess., ii, 190-3.

13

When Providence would make a Revelation, He does not
begin anew, but uses the existing system; He does not visibly
send an Angel, but He commissions or inspires one of our own

333

fellows. When He would bless us, He makes a man His priest. When He would consecrate or quicken us, He takes the elements of this world as the means of real but unseen spiritual influences. When He would set up a divine polity, He takes a polity which already is, or one in course of forming. Nor does He interfere with its natural growth, development, or dependence on things visible. He does not shut it up in a desert, and there supply it with institutions unlike those which might naturally come to it from the contact and intercourse of the external world. He does but modify, quicken, or direct the powers of nature or the laws of society. Or if He works miracles, still it is without superseding the ordinary course of things. He multiplies the flocks or the descendants of Jacob, or in due season He may work signal or public miracles for their deliverance from Egypt; but still the operation of ordinary causes, the influence of political arrangements, and what is called the march of events, are seen in such providences as truly, and can be pointed out as convincingly, as if an Angel and a pillar of cloud were not with them.

Thus the great characteristic of Revelation is addition, not substitution. Things look the same as before, though an invisible power has taken hold of them. This power does not unclothe the creature, but clothes it. Men dream everywhere: it gives visions. Men journey everywhere: it sends "the Angels of God to meet them." Men may elsewhere be hospitable; now they entertain Angels. Men carry on a work; but it is a blessing from some ancestor that is breathing on and through it unseen. A nation migrates and seizes on a country: but all along its proceedings are hallowed by prophecy, and promise, and providence beforehand, and used for religious ends afterwards. Israel was as much a political power as man is an animal. The rites and ceremonies enjoined upon the people might be found elsewhere, but were not less divine notwithstanding. Circumcision was also practised in Egypt, frequent ablutions may be the custom of the East, the veil of Moyses may have been the symbol of other rulers (if so be) before him,—though the fact has to be proved; a Holy of Holies, an altar, a sacrifice, a

334

sacerdotal caste, *in* these points the Mosaic law resembled, yet *as to* these it differed from, the nations round about. The Israelitish polity had a beginning, a middle, and an end, like other things of time and place; its captivities were the natural consequences, its monarchy was the natural expedient, of a state of political weakness. Its territory was a battle-ground, and its power was the alternate ally, of the rival empires of Egypt and Assyria. Heathen travellers may have surveyed the Holy Land, and have thought it but a narrow slip of Syria. . .

What is true of Judaism is true of Christianity. The Kingdom of Christ, though not of this world, yet is in the world, and has a visible, material, social shape. It consists of men, and it has developed according to the laws under which combinations of men develop. It has an external aspect similar to all other kingdoms. We may generalize and include it as one among the various kinds of polity, as one among the empires, which have been upon the earth. It is called the fifth kingdom; and as being numbered with the previous four which were earthly, it is thereby, in fact, compared with them. We may write its history, and make it look as like those which were before or contemporary with it, as a man is like a monkey.

Ess., ii, 144-5.

14

Men, who are plunged in the pursuits of active life, are no judges of its course and tendency on the whole. They confuse great events with little, and measure the importance of objects, as in perspective, by the mere standard of nearness or remoteness. It is only at a distance that one can take in the outlines and features of a whole country. It is but holy Daniel, solitary among princes, or Elijah the recluse of Mount Carmel, who can withstand Baal, or forecast the time of God's providences among the nations. To the multitude all things continue to the end, as they were from the beginning of the creation. The business of state affairs, the movements of society, the course of nature, proceed as ever, till the moment of Christ's coming. "The sun was risen upon the earth," bright as usual, on that very day of

335

wrath in which Sodom was destroyed. Men cannot believe their own time is an especially wicked time; for, with Scripture unstudied and hearts untrained in holiness, they have no standard to compare it with. They take warning from no troubles or perplexities, which rather carry them away to search out the earthly causes of them, and the possible remedies. They consider them as conditions of this world, necessary results of this or that state of society. When the power of Assyria became great (we might suppose), the Jews had a plain call to repentance. Far from it; they were led to set power against power: they took refuge against Assyria in Egypt, their old enemy. Probably they reasoned themselves into what they considered a temperate, enlightened, cheerful view of national affairs; perhaps they might consider the growth of Assyria as an advantage rather than otherwise, as balancing the power of Egypt, and so tending to their own security. Certain it is, we find them connecting themselves first with one kingdom, and then with the other, as men who could read (as they thought) "the signs of the times," and made some pretences to political wisdom. Thus the world proceeds till wrath comes upon it and there is no escape. "To-morrow," they say, "shall be as this day, and much more abundant."

And in the midst of this their revel, whether of sensual pleasure, or of ambition, or of covetousness, or of pride and self-esteem, the decree goes forth to destroy. The decree goes forth in secret; Angels hear it, and the favoured few on earth; but no public event takes place to give the world warning. The earth was doomed to the flood one hundred and twenty years before the "decree brought forth," or men heard of it. The waters of Babylon had been turned, and the conqueror was marching into the city, when Belshazzar made his great feast. Pride infatuates man, and self-indulgence and luxury work their way unseen,— like some smouldering fire, which for a while leaves the outward form of things unaltered. At length the decayed mass cannot hold together, and breaks by its own weight or on some slight and accidental external violence.

P.S., ii, 112-14.

336

15

Satan cannot discern the Hand of God in what goes on; and though he would fain meet it and encounter it, in his mad and blasphemous rebellion against heaven,—he cannot find it. Crafty and penetrating as he is, yet his thousand eyes and his many instruments avail him nothing against the majestic serene silence, the holy imperturbable calm which reigns through the providences of God. Crafty and experienced as he is, he appears like a child or a fool, like one made sport of, whose daily bread is but failure and mockery, before the deep and secret wisdom of the Divine Counsels. He makes a guess here, or does a bold act there, but all in the dark. He knew not of Gabriel's coming, and the miraculous conception of the Virgin, or what was meant by that Holy Thing which was to be born, being called the Son of God. He tried to kill Him, and he made martyrs of the innocent children; he tempted the Lord of all with hunger and with ambitious prospects; he sifted the Apostles, and got none but one who already bore his own name, and had been already given over as a devil. He rose against his God in his full strength, in the hour and power of darkness, and then he seemed to conquer; but with his utmost effort, and as his greatest achievement, he did no more than "whatsoever Thy hand and Thy counsel determined before to be done." He brought into the world the very salvation which he feared and hated. He accomplished the Atonement of that world, whose misery he was plotting. Wonderfully silent, yet resistless course of God's providence! "Verily, Thou art a God that hidest Thyself, O God of Israel, the Saviour;" and if even devils, sagacious as they are, spirits by nature and experienced in evil, cannot detect His hand, while He works, how can we hope to see it except by that way which the devils cannot take, by a loving faith? how can we see it except afterwards as a reward to our faith, beholding the cloud of glory in the distance, which when present was too rare and impalpable for mortal sense?

P.S., *iv*, 259-60.

16

We are in a world of mystery, with one bright Light before us, sufficient for our proceeding forward through all difficulties. Take away this Light and we are utterly wretched,—we know not where we are, how we are sustained, what will become of us, and of all that is dear to us, what we are to believe, and why we are in being. But with it we have all and abound. Not to mention the duty and wisdom of implicit faith in the love of Him who made and redeemed us, what is nobler, what is more elevating and transporting, than the generosity of heart which risks everything on God's word, dares the powers of evil to their worst efforts, and repels the illusions of sense and the artifices of reason, by confidence in the Truth of Him who has ascended to the right hand of the Majesty on high? What infinite mercy it is in Him, that He allows sinners such as we are, the privilege of acting the part of heroes rather than of penitents? Who are we "that we should be able" and have opportunity "to offer so willingly after this sort?"—"Blessed," surely thrice blessed, "are they who have not seen, and yet have believed!" We will not wish for sight; we will enjoy our privilege; we will triumph in the leave given us to go forward, "not knowing whither we go," knowing that "this is the victory that overcometh the world, even our faith."

P.S., *ii*, 215-16.

17

But the true Christian . . . knows how to "use this world as not abusing it." He *depends* on nothing in this world. He trusts not *its* sights against the revealed Word. "Thou wilt keep him in perfect peace whose mind is stayed on Thee, because he trusteth in Thee." Such is the promise made to him. And if he looks out into the world to seek, it is not to seek what he does not know, but what he does. He does not seek a Lord and Saviour. He has "found the Messias" long since; and he is looking out for *Him*. His Lord Himself has *bid* him look for Him in the signs of the world, and therefore he looks out. His Lord Himself has shown him, in the Old Testament, how He, the Lord of Glory, condescends to humble Himself to the things of heaven and earth. He knows that God's Angels are about the earth. He knows that once they were even used to come in human shape. He knows that the Son of God, ere now, has come on earth. He knows that He promised to His Church the presence of a miraculous agency, and has never recalled His promise. Again, he reads, in the Book of the Revelation, quite enough, not to show him what is coming, but to show him that now, as heretofore, a secret supernatural system is going on *under* this visible scene. And therefore he looks out for Christ, for His present providences, and for His coming; and, though often deceived in his expectation, and fancying wonderful things are coming on the earth, when they still delay, he uses, and comforts him with the Prophet's words, "I will stand upon my watch, and set me upon the tower, and will watch to see what He will say unto me, and what I shall answer when I am reproved. And the Lord answered me.... The vision is yet for an appointed time, but at the end it shall speak and not lie; though it tarry, wait for it, because it will surely come, it will not tarry. Behold, his soul, which is lifted up, is not upright in him; but the just shall live by his faith."

P.S., vi, 253-54.

18

As the gestures, speech, and expressive countenances of our friends around us enable us to hold intercourse with them, so in the motions of universal Nature, in the interchange of day and night, summer and winter, wind and storm, fulfilling His word, we are reminded of the blessed and dutiful Angels. . . . Thus, whenever we look abroad, we are reminded of those most gracious and holy Beings, the servants of the Holiest, who deign to minister to the heirs of salvation. Every breath of air and ray of light and heat, every beautiful prospect, is, as it were, the skirts of their garments, the waving of the robes of those whose faces see God in heaven.

P.S., ii, 361-2.

19

Who can live any time in the world, pleasant as it may seem on first entering it, without discovering that it is a weariness, and that if this life is worth anything, it is because it is the passage to another? It needs no great religion to feel this; it is a self-evident truth to those who have much experience of the world. The only reason why all do not feel it is, that they have not lived long enough to feel it; and those who feel it more than others have but been thrown into circumstances to feel it more. But while the times wax old, and the colours of earth fade, and the voice of song is brought low, and all kindreds of the earth can but wail and lament, the sons of God lift up their heads, for their salvation draweth nigh. Nature fails, the sun shines not, and the moon is dim, the stars fall from heaven, and the foundations of the round world shake; but the Altar's light burns ever brighter; there are sights there which the many cannot see, and all above the tumults of earth the command is heard to show forth the Lord's death, and the promise that the Lord is coming.

P.S., *vii*, 158.

IV. THE FORECOURT OF HEAVEN

20

The mind finds nothing to satisfy it in the employments and amusements of life, in its excitements, struggles, anxieties, efforts, aims, and victories. Supposing a man to make money, to get on in life, to rise in society, to gain power, whether in a higher or lower sphere, this does not suffice; he wants a home, he wants a centre on which to place his thoughts and affections, a secret dwelling-place which may soothe him after the troubles of the world, and which may be his hidden stay and support wherever he goes, and dwell in his heart, though it be not named upon his tongue. The world may seduce, may terrify, may mislead, may enslave, but it cannot really inspire confidence and love. There is no rest for us, except in quietness, confidence, and affection; and hence all men, without taking religion into account, seek to make themselves a home, as the only need of their nature, or are unhappy if they be without one. Thus they witness against the world, even though they be children of the world; witness against it equally with the holiest and most self-denying, who have by faith overcome it.

Here then Christ finds us, weary of that world in which we are obliged to live and act, whether as willing or unwilling slaves to it. He finds us needing and seeking a home, and making one, as we best may, by means of the creature, since it is all we can do. The world, in which our duties lie, is as waste as the wilderness, as restless and turbulent as the ocean, as inconstant as the wind and weather. It has no substance in it, but is like a shade or phantom; when you pursue it, when you try to grasp it, it escapes from you, or it is malicious and does you a mischief. We need something which the world cannot give: this is what we need, and this it is which the Gospel has supplied.

I say, that our Lord Jesus Christ, after dying for our sins on the Cross, and ascending on high, left not the world as He found it, but left a blessing behind Him. He left in the world what before was not in it—a secret home for faith and love to enjoy wherever they are found, in spite of the world around us. . . . . This is the Church of God, which is our true Home of God's providing, His own heavenly court, where He dwells with Saints and Angels, into which He introduces us by a new birth, and in which we forget the outward world and its many troubles.

P.S., iv, 189-90.

21

The world is no helpmeet for man, and a helpmeet he needs. No one, man nor woman, can stand alone; we are so constituted by nature; and the world, instead of helping us, is an open adversary. It but increases our solitariness. Elijah cried, "I, I only am left, and they seek my life to take it away." How did Almighty God answer him? by graciously telling him that He had reserved to Himself a remnant of seven thousand true believers. Such is the blessed truth which He brings home to us also. We may be full of sorrows; there may be fightings without and fears within; we may be exposed to the frowns, censure, or contempt of men; we may be shunned by them; or, to take the lightest case, we may be (as we certainly shall be) wearied out by the unprofitableness of this world, by its coldness, unfriendliness, distance, and dreariness; we shall need something nearer to us. What is our resource? It is not in arm of man, in flesh and blood, in voice of friend, or in pleasant countenance; it is that holy home which God has given us in His Church; it is that everlasting City in which He has fixed His abode. It is that Mount invisible whence Angels are looking at us with their piercing eyes, and the voices of the dead call us.

P.S., *iv*, 195-6.

22

Ever since Christianity came into the world, it has been, in one sense, going out of it. It is so uncongenial to the human mind, it is so spiritual, and man is so earthly, it is apparently so defenceless, and has so many strong enemies, so many false friends, that every age, as it comes, may be called "the last time." It has made great conquests, and done great works; but still it has done all, as the Apostle says of himself, "in weakness, and in fear, and in much trembling." *How* it is that it is always failing, yet always continuing, God only knows who wills it,—but so it is; and it is no paradox to say, on the one hand, that it has lasted eighteen hundred years, that it may last many years more, and yet that it draws to an end, nay, is likely to end any day. And God would have us give our minds and hearts to the latter side of the alternative, to open them to impressions *from* this side, viz. that the end is coming,—it being a wholesome thing to live as if *that* will come in our day, which may come any day.

P.S., *vi*, 239-40.

23

The earth that we see does not satisfy us; it is but a beginning; it is but a promise of something beyond it; even when it is gayest, with all its blossoms on, and shows most touchingly what lies hid in it, yet it is not enough. We know much more lies hid in it than we see. A world of Saints and Angels, a glorious

342

world, the palace of God, the mountain of the Lord of Hosts, the heavenly Jerusalem, the throne of God and Christ, all these wonders, everlasting, all-precious, mysterious, and incomprehensible, lie hid in what we see. What we see is the outward shell of an eternal kingdom; and on that kingdom we fix the eyes of our faith. Shine forth, O Lord, as when on Thy Nativity Thine Angels visited the shepherds; let Thy glory blossom forth as bloom and foliage on the trees; change with Thy mighty power this visible world into that diviner world, which as yet we see not; destroy what we see, that it may pass and be transformed into what we believe. Bright as is the sun, and the sky, and the clouds; green as are the leaves and the fields; sweet as is the singing of the birds; we know that they are not all, and we will not take up with a part for the whole. They proceed from a centre of love and goodness, which is God himself; but they are not His fulness; they speak of heaven, but they are not heaven; they are but as stray beams and dim reflections of His Image; they are but crumbs from the table. We are looking for the coming of the day of God, when all this outward world, fair though it be, shall perish; when the heavens shall be burnt, and the earth melt away. We can bear the loss, for we know it will be but the removing of a veil. We know that to remove the world which is seen, will be the manifestation of the world which is not seen. We know that what we see is as a screen hiding from us God and Christ, and His Saints and Angels. And we earnestly desire and pray for the dissolution of all that we see, from our longing after that which we do not see.

P.S., iv, 210-11.

24

What a day will that be when I am thoroughly cleansed from all impurity and sin, and am fit to draw near to my Incarnate God in His palace of light above! what a morning, when having done with all penal suffering, I see Thee for the first time with these very eyes of mine, I see thy countenance, gaze upon Thy eyes and gracious lips without quailing, and then kneel down with joy to kiss Thy feet, and am welcomed into Thy arms. O my only true lover, the only Lover of my soul, Thee will I love now, that I may love Thee then. What a day, a long day without ending, the day of eternity, when I shall be so unlike what I am *now*, when I feel in myself a body of death, and am perplexed and distracted with ten thousand thoughts, any one of which would keep me from heaven. O my Lord, what a day when I shall have done once for all with all sins, venial as well as mortal, and shall stand perfect and acceptable in Thy sight, able to bear Thy presence, nothing shrinking from Thy eye, not shrinking from the pure scrutiny of Angels and Archangels, when I stand in the midst and they around me.

M.D., 482-3.

25

If ever, through Thy grace, I attain to see Thee in heaven, I shall see nothing else but Thee, because I shall see all whom I see in Thee, and seeing them I shall see Thee. As I cannot see things here below without light, and to see them is to see the rays which come from them, so in that eternal City Claritas Dei illuminavit eam, et lucerna ejus est Agnus.

M.D., 587-8.

26

My God it was Thy supreme blessedness in the eternity past, as it is Thy blessedness in all eternities, to know Thyself, as Thou alone canst know Thee. It was by seeing Thyself in Thy co-equal Son and Thy co-eternal Spirit, and in Their seeing Thee, that Father, Son, and Holy Ghost, Three Persons, One God, was infinitely blessed. O my God, what am I that Thou shouldst make my blessedness to consist in that which is Thy own! That Thou shouldst grant me to have not only the sight of Thee, but to share in Thy very own joy! O prepare me for it, teach me to thirst for it.

M.D., 590.

XIX: IN GOD

ANALYTICAL SUMMARY

It was man's glory before the fall that he was raised above all created nature by an indescribable "participation of the Divine Nature."

Therefore the man restored in Christ and growing to the maturity of his complete restoration is one who lives his most personal life from God, for God and in God, and as he ascends, penetrates ever more deeply into God, so that God is His life, and, so to speak, his life's breath;

(Nos. 1-4.)

so that because "God is love," his life from and in God has become a life of love, into which all his other virtues flow, living Love, Love as Life;

(Nos. 5-6.)

so the "freedom of the children of God" is now the air which he breathes and "Abba Father" the substance of his unceasing prayer;

(Nos. 7-8.)

and finally an awe-inspiring consciousness of the Divine Majesty pregnant with sublimity thoroughly penetrates and invests him for the regale-sacerdotium *the royal priesthood of his spiritual life.*

(Nos. 9-11.)

345

1. PERFECT AS THE FATHER

1

A CHRISTIAN's life is not only moral as opposed to vice and crime, not only religious as opposed to unbelief and profaneness, not only renewed as opposed to the old Adam, but is spiritual, loving, pleasing, acceptable, available, just, justifying; not of course the origin or well-spring of our acceptableness (God forbid!) but we believe this,—that He who eighteen hundred years since purchased for us sinners the gift of life eternal, with His own blood, and who at our baptism spoke over each of us the Word of acceptance, and admitted us at once to His presence, by the same Word forthwith proceeded to realize His gracious purpose; that "His word ran very swiftly," as being "living and powerful, and sharper than any two-edged sword;" that it reached even to our hearts, conveying its virtue into our nature, making us what the Almighty Father can delight in, and so returning to Him not "void," but laden with the triumphs of His grace, the fruits of righteousness in us as "an odour of a sweet smell," as "spiritual sacrifices acceptable to God, by Jesus Christ." He works out His justification towards us, in us, with us, through us, and from us, till He receives back in produce what He gave in seed.

Jfc., 93-4.

2

To be Christians, surely it is not enough to be that which we are enjoined to be, and must be, even without Christ; not enough to be no better than good heathens; not enough to be, in some slight measure, just, honest, temperate, and religious. We must indeed be just, honest, temperate, and religious, before we can rise to Christian graces, and to *be* practised in justice and the like

347

virtues is the way, the ordinary way, in which we receive the fulness of the kingdom of God. . . . It is much more than honesty, justice, and temperance; and this [more] is to be a Christian. . . . We must have a deep sense of our guilt, and of the difficulty of securing heaven; we must live as in His presence, daily pleading His cross and passion, thinking of His holy commandments, imitating His sinless pattern, and depending on the gracious aids of His Spirit; that we may really and truly be servants of Father, Son, and Holy Ghost, in whose name we were baptized. Further, we must, for His sake, aim at a noble and unusual strictness of life, perfecting holiness in His fear, destroying our sins, mastering our whole soul, and bringing it into captivity to His law, denying ourselves lawful things, in order to do Him service, exercising a profound humility, and an unbounded, never-failing love, giving away much of our substance in religious and charitable works, and discountenancing and shunning irreligious men. This is to be a Christian; a gift easily described, and in a few words, but attainable only with fear and much trembling.

P.S., *i*, 78-80.

3

[The Saint] differs from an ordinary religious man, I say, in this,—that he sets before him as the one object of life, to please and obey God; that he ever aims to submit his will to God's will; that he earnestly follows after holiness; and that he is habitually striving to have a closer resemblance to Christ in all things. He exercises himself, not only in social duties, but in Christian graces; he is not only kind, but meek; not only generous, but humble; not only persevering, but patient; not only upright, but forgiving; not only bountiful, but self-denying; not only contented, but meditative and devotional. An ordinary man thinks it enough to do as he is done by; he will think it fair to resent insults, to repay injuries, to show a becoming pride, to insist on his rights, to be jealous of his honour, when in the wrong to refuse to confess it, to seek to be rich, to desire to be well with the world, to fear what his neighbours will say. He seldom thinks of the Day of Judgment, seldom thinks of sins past, says few prayers, cares little for the Church, has no zeal for God's truth, spends his money on himself. Such is an ordinary Christian, and such is not one of God's elect. For the latter is more than just, temperate, and kind; he has a devoted love of God, high faith, holy hope, overflowing charity, a noble self-command, a strict conscientiousness, humility never absent, gentleness in speech, simplicity, modesty and unaffectedness, an unconsciousness of what his endowments are, and what they make him in God's sight. This is what Christianity has done in the world; such is the result of Christian teaching; viz., to elicit, foster, mature the seeds of heaven which lie hid in the earth, to multiply (if it may be said) images of Christ.

P.S., iv, 158-9.

4

Childhood, virginity, martyrdom, are made in scripture at once the Types and Standards of religious Perfection. . . . Love is the essence of the Chriatian character—its chief characteristics [are] resignation and composure of mind, neither anxious for the morrow, nor hoping from this world—and its duties, almsgiving, self-denial prayer and praise.

P.S., ii, 201, 204.

II. LOVE

5

Love in one sense *is* all virtues at once . . . . it is the root of all holy dispositions, and grows and blossoms into them: they are its parts; and when it is described, they of necessity are mentioned. Love is the material (so to speak) out of which all graces are made, the quality of mind which is the fruit of regeneration, and in which the Spirit dwells. . . . We love because it is our nature to love, and it is our nature because God the Holy Ghost has made it our nature. Love is the immediate fruit and the evidence of regeneration. . . .

Love, then, is the seed of holiness, and grows into all excellences, not indeed destroying their peculiarities, but making them what they are. . . . the soul which is quickened with the spirit of love has faith and hope, and a number of faculties and habits, some of which it might have without love, and some not; but anyhow, in that soul one and all exist *in* love, though distinct from it; as stalk, leaves, and flowers are as distinct and entire in one plant as in another, yet vary in their quality, according to the plant's nature. . . .

Love then is the motion within us of the new spirit, the holy and renewed heart which God the Holy Ghost gives us; and, as being such, we see how it may exist in infants, who obey the inward law without knowing it, by a sort of natural service, as plants and trees fulfil the functions of their own nature; a service which is most acceptable to God, as being moral and spiritual, though not intellectual. . . . Love, then, is the life of those who know not an external world, but who worship God as manifested within them.

P.S., iv, 309-11, 313.

6

The text*. . . tells us that faith at most only makes a hero, but that love makes a saint; that faith can but put us above the world, but that love brings us under God's throne; that faith can but make us sober, but love makes us happy. It warns us that it is possible for a man to have the clearest, calmest, exactest view of the realities of heaven; that he may most firmly realize and act upon the truths of the Gospel; that he may understand that all about him is but a veil, not a substance; that he may have that full confidence in God's word as to be able to do miracles; that he may have such simple absolute faith as to give up his property, give up all his goods to feed the poor; that he may so scorn the world, that he may with so royal a heart trample on it, as even to give his body to be burned by a glorious martyrdom; and yet—I do not say, be without love; God forbid! I do not suppose the Apostle means there ever *was* actually such a case, but that it is abstractedly possible; that no one of the proper acts of faith,

* "Though I have all Faith, so that I could remove mountains, and have no Charity, I am nothing."

in itself, and necessarily, implies love; that it is distinct from love. He says this,—that, though a person *be* all that has been said, yet unless he be also something besides, unless he have love, it profiteth him nothing. O fearful lesson, to all those who are tempted to pride themselves in their labours, or sufferings, or sacrifices, or works! We are Christ's, not by faith merely, nor by works merely, but by love; not by hating the world, nor by hating sin, nor by venturing for the world to come, nor by calmness, nor by magnanimity,—though we must do and be all this; and if we *have* love in perfection we *shall*,—but it is love makes faith, not faith love. We are saved, not by any of these things, but by that heavenly flame within us, which, while it consumes what is seen, aspires to what is unseen. Love is the gentle, tranquil, satisfied acquiescence and adherence of the soul in the contemplation of God; not only a preference of God before all things, but a delight in Him because He is God, and because His commandments are good; not any violent emotion or transport, but as St. Paul describes it, long-suffering, kind, modest, unassuming, innocent, simple, orderly, disinterested, meek, pure-hearted, sweet-tempered, patient, enduring. Faith without Charity is dry, harsh, and sapless; it has nothing sweet, engaging, winning, soothing; but it was Charity which brought Christ down. Charity is but another name for the Comforter. It is eternal Charity which is the bond of all things in heaven and earth; it is Charity wherein the Father and the Son are one in the unity of the Spirit; by which the Angels in heaven are one, by which all Saints are one with God, by which the Church is one upon earth.

P.S., iv, 317-8.

III. SONSHIP

7

We know that God's service is perfect freedom, not a servitude; but this it is in the case of those who have long served Him; at first it *is* a kind of servitude, it is a task till our likings and tastes come to be in unison with those which God has sanctioned. It is the happiness of Saints and Angels in heaven to take pleasure in their duty, and nothing but their duty; for their mind goes that one way, and pours itself out in obedience to God, spontaneously and without thought or deliberation, just as man *sins* naturally. This is the state to which we are tending if we give ourselves up to religion; but in its commencement, religion is necessarily almost a task and a formal service. . . . We are *ever* but beginning; the most perfect Christian is to himself but a beginner, a penitent prodigal, who has squandered God's gifts, and comes to Him to be tried over again, not as a son, but as a hired servant. . . .

The servant is not in his lord's confidence, does not understand what he is aiming at, or why he commands this and forbids that. He executes the commands given him, he goes hither and thither, punctually, but by the mere letter of the command. Such is the state of those who *begin* religious obedience. They do not see anything come of their devotional or penitential services, nor do they take pleasure in them; they are obliged to defer to God's word simply because it is His word.

We *must begin* religion with what looks like a form. Our fault will be, not in beginning it as a form, but in continuing it as a form. For it is our duty to be ever striving and praying to *enter* into the real spirit of our services, and in proportion as we understand them and love them, they will cease to be a form and a task, and will be the real expressions of our minds. Thus shall we gradually be changed in heart from servants into sons of Almighty God.

P.S., *iii*, 91-4.

8

We begin it by using our privilege of calling on Almighty God in express words as "Our Father." We proceed, according to this beginning, in that waiting, trusting, adoring, resigned temper, which children ought to feel; looking towards Him, rather than thinking of ourselves; zealous for His honour rather than fearful about our safety; resting in His present help, not with eyes timorously glancing towards the future. His name, His kingdom, His will, are the great objects for the Christian to contemplate

352

and make his portion, being stable and serene, and "complete n Him," as beseems one who has the gracious presence of His Spirit within him. And, when he goes on to think of himself, he prays, that he may be enabled to have towards others what God has shown towards himself, a spirit of forgiveness and loving-kindness. Thus he pours himself out on all sides, first looking up to catch the heavenly gift, but, when he gains it, not keeping it to himself, but diffusing "rivers of living water" to the whole race of man, thinking of self as little as may be, and desiring ill and destruction to nothing but that principle of temptation and evil, which is rebellion against God;—lastly, ending, as he began, with the contemplation of His kingdom, power and glory ever-lasting. This is the true "Abba, Father," which the Spirit of adoption utters within the Christian's heart, the infallible voice of Him who "maketh intercession for the Saints in God's way." And if he has at times, for instance, amid trial or affliction, special visitations and comfortings from the Spirit, "plaints unutterable" within him, yearnings after the life to come, or bright and passing gleams of God's eternal election, and deep stirrings of wonder and thankfulness thence following, he thinks too reverently of "the secret of the Lord," to betray (as it were) His confidence, and, by vaunting it to the world, to exaggerate it perchance into more than it was meant to convey: but he is silent, and ponders it as choice encouragement to his soul, meaning something, but he knows not how much.

P.S., *ii*, 225-6.

IV. NOBILITY

9

The temper of the Christian Church is high and heavenly, noble, majestic, calm and untroubled. For it is the state of heart imparted by the Divine Paraclete, who stands by us to strengthen us and raise our stature, and, as it were, to straighten our limbs, and to provide us with the wings of Angels, wherewith to mount heavenward;—by Him who takes possession of us, and dwells in us, and makes us His agents and instruments, nay, in a measure,

353

His confidants and counsellors, till we "comprehend the breadth and length and depth and height, and know the love of Christ, which passeth knowledge, that we may be filled with all the fulness of God." Religious men, knowing what great things have been done for them, cannot but grow greater in mind in consequence. We know how power and responsibility change men in matters of this world. They become more serious, more vigilant, more circumspect, more practical, more decisive; they fear to commit mistakes, yet they dare more, because they have a consciousness of liberty and of power, and an opportunity for great successes. And thus the Christian, even in the way of nature, without speaking of the influence of heavenly grace upon him, cannot but change from the state of children to that of men, when he understands his own privileges. The more he knows and fears the gift committed to him, so much the more reverent is he towards himself, as being put in charge with it. . . .

"Whosoever shall confess that Jesus is the Son of God, God dwelleth in him, and he in God." Is it not plain, that such a doctrine as is here declared will exceedingly raise the Christian above himself, and, without impairing—nay, even while increasing his humility, will make him feel all things of earth as little, and of small interest or account, and will preserve him from the agitations of mind which they naturally occasion?

S.D., 142-4.

10

Christians are called upon to think little of the ordinary objects which men pursue—wealth, luxury, distinction, popularity, and power. It was this negligence about the world which brought upon them in primitive times the reproach of being indolent. Their heathen enemies spoke truly; indolent and indifferent they were about temporal matters. If the goods of this world came in their way, they were not bound to decline them; nor would they forbid others in the religious use of them; but they thought them vanities, the toys of children, which serious men let drop. Nay, St. Paul betrays the same feeling as regards our temporal callings and states generally. After discoursing about

354

them, suddenly he breaks off as if impatient of the multitude of words: "But this I say, brethren," he exclaims, "the time is short."

Hence, too, the troubles of life gradually affect the Christian less and less, as his view of his own real blessedness, under the Dispensation of the Spirit, grows upon him; and even though persecuted, to take an extreme case, he knows well that, through God's inward presence, he is greater than those who for the time have power over him, as Martyrs and Confessors have often shown.

And, in like manner, he will be calm and collected under all circumstances; he will make light of injuries, and forget them from mere contempt of them. He will be undaunted, as fearing God more than man; he will be firm in faith and consistent, as "seeing Him that is invisible"; not impatient, as one who has no self-will; not soon disappointed, who has no hopes; not anxious who has no fears; nor dazzled, who has no ambition. . . . And now further let it be observed . . . . that all this greatness of mind . . . . which in other religious systems degenerates into pride, is in the Gospel compatible . . . . with the deepest humility.

The self-respect of the Christian is no personal and selfish feeling, but rather a principle of loyal devotion and reverence towards that Divine Master who condescends to visit him. He acts, not hastily, but under restraint and fearfully, as understanding that God's eye is over him, and God's hand upon him, and God's voice within him. He acts with the recollection that his Omniscient Guide is also his future Judge; and that while He moves him, He is also noting down in His book how he answers to His godly motions. He acts with a memory laden with past infirmity and sin, and a consciousness that he has much more to mourn over and repent of, in the years gone by, than to rejoice in. Yes, surely, he has many a secret wound to be healed; many a bruise to be tended; many a sore, like Lazarus; many a chronic infirmity; many a bad omen of perils to come. It is one thing not to trust in the world; it is another thing to trust in one's self.

S.D., 145-8.

355

11

Contemplate then thyself, not in thyself, but as thou art in the Eternal God. Fall down in astonishment at the glories which are around thee and in thee, poured to and fro in such a wonderful way that thou art (as it were) dissolved into the kingdom of God, as though thou hadst nought to do but to contemplate and feed upon that great vision. This surely is the state of mind the Apostle speaks of in the text when he reminds us who are justified and at peace with God, that we have the access to His royal courts, and stand in His grace, and rejoice in hope of His glory. All the trouble which the world inflicts upon us, and which flesh cannot but feel, sorrow, pain, care, bereavement—these avail not to disturb the tranquillity and the intensity with which faith gazes upon the Divine Majesty. All the necessary exactness of our obedience, the anxiety about failing, the pain of self-denial, the watchfulness, the zeal, the self-chastisements which are required of us, as little interfere with this vision of faith as if they were practised by another, not by ourselves. We are two or three selves at once, in the wonderful structure of our minds, and can weep while we smile, and labour while we meditate.

P.S., *iv*, 146-7.

XX : THE ENTIRE MAN

ANALYTICAL SUMMARY

Man's prerogative before the fall was the beauty of an "entire man," in whom the limitations, contrasts and contradictions of the creature—a creature compounded of flesh and spirit—were reduced to unity. Therefore the man restored in Christ and growing to the maturity of his complete restoration is one in whom the limitations disappear so that the scattered fragments of his being coalesce in an inner integrity and universality which testifies to the presence within him of Him who is the One and Unity;

(Nos. 1-3.)

so that the reality of his Christian life is shown by the fact that it displays a mutual tension of contrasts, "of opposite virtues" fear and love, prayer and work, providential guidance and personal responsibility, solitude and society, strictness and gentleness, penance and joy—in which as their common substance all the paths of the Christian life meet.

(Nos. 4-8.)

I. INTEGRITY

I

In every age of Christianity, since it was first preached, there has been what may be called a *religion of the world,* which so far imitates the one true religion, as to deceive the unstable and unwary. The world does not oppose religion *as such.* I may say, it never has opposed it. In particular, it has, in all ages, acknowledged in one sense or other the Gospel of Christ, fastened on one or other of its characteristics, and professed to embody this in its practice; while by neglecting the other parts of the holy doctrine, it has, in fact, distorted and corrupted even that portion of it which it has exclusively put forward, and so has contrived to explain away the whole;—for he who cultivates only one precept of the Gospel to the exclusion of the rest, in reality attends to no part at all. Our duties *balance* each other; and though we are too sinful to perform them all perfectly, yet we may in some measure be performing them all, and preserving the balance on the whole; whereas, to give ourselves only to this or that commandment, is to incline our minds in a wrong direction, and at length to pull them down to the earth, which is the aim of our adversary, the Devil.

P.S., i, 309-10.

2

Did a man act merely a bold and firm part, he would have cause to say to himself, "Perhaps all this is mere pride and obstinacy." Were he merely yielding and forgiving,—he might be indulging a natural indolence of mind. Were he merely industrious,—this might consist with ill-temper, or selfishness. Did he merely fulfil the duties of his temporal calling,—he would have no proof that he had given his heart to God at all. Were he

359

merely regular at Church and Holy Commmunion,—many a man is such who has a lax conscience, who is not scrupulously fair-dealing, or is censorious, or niggardly. Is he what is called a domestic character, amiable, affectionate, fond of his family?— let him beware lest he put wife and children in the place of God who gave them. Is he only temperate, sober, chaste, correct in his language?—it may arise from mere dullness and insensibility, or may consist with spiritual pride. Is he cheerful and obliging?— it may arise from youthful spirits and ignorance of the world. Does he choose his friends by a strictly orthodox rule?—he may be harsh and uncharitable; or, is he zealous and serviceable in defending the Truth?—still he may be unable to condescend to men of low estate, to rejoice with those who rejoice, and to weep with those who weep. No one is without some good quality or other: Balaam had a scruple about misrepresenting God's message, Saul was brave, Joab was loyal, the Bethel Prophet reverenced God's servants, the witch of Endor was hospitable; and therefore, of course, no one good deed or disposition is the criterion of a spiritual mind. Still, on the other hand, there is no one of its characteristics which has not its appropriate outward evidence; and in proportion as these external acts are multiplied and varied, so does the evidence of it become stronger and more consoling. General conscientiousness is the only assurance we can have of possessing it; and at this we must aim, determining to obey God consistently with a jealous carefulness about all things, little and great. . . . If it be objected that an evidence from works is but a cold comfort, as being at best but faint and partial, I reply, that, after all, it is more than sinners have a right to ask,—that if it be little at first, it grows with our growth in grace,—and moreover, that such an evidence, more than any other, throws us in faith upon the loving-kindness and meritorious sufferings of our Saviour. Surely, even our best doings have that taint of sinfulness pervading them, which will remind us ever, while we regard them, where our True Hope is lodged. Men are satisfied with themselves, not when they attempt, but when they neglect the details of duty. Disobedience blinds the conscience; obedience makes it keen-sighted and sensitive. The more we *do*, the more shall we trust in Christ; and that surely is no morose doctrine, which, after giving us whatever evidence of our safety can be given, leads us to soothe our selfish restlessness, and forget our fears, in the vision of the Incarnate Son of God.

P.S., *ii*, 158-60.

3

Any spirit which is content with what is short of this, which does not lead us to utter self-surrender and devotion; which reserves something for ourselves; which indulges our self-will; which flatters this or that natural inclination or affection; which does not tend to consistency of religious character;—is not from God. The heavenly influence which He has given us is as intimately present, and as penetrating—as catholic—in an individual heart as it is in the world at large. It is everywhere, in every faculty, every affection, every design, every work. And the surest test that we are members of the Catholic Church is the evidence of this Catholic influence, or religious consistency. . . .

Thus the heart of every Christian ought to represent in miniature the Catholic Church, since one Spirit makes both the whole Church and every member of it to be His Temple. As He makes the Church one, which, left to itself, would separate into many parts; so He makes the soul one, in spite of its various affections and faculties, and its contradictory aims. As He gives peace to the multitude of nations, who are naturally in discord one with another, so does He give an orderly government to the soul, and set reason and conscience as sovereigns over the inferior parts of our nature. As He leavens each rank and pursuit of the community with the principles of the doctrine of Christ, so does that same Divine Leaven spread through every thought of the mind, every member of the body, till the whole is sanctified.

S.D., 131-2.

II.   A UNITY OF OPPOSITES

4

The very problem which Christian duty requires us to accomplish is the reconciling in our conduct opposite virtues. It is not difficult (comparatively speaking) to cultivate single virtues. A man takes some one partial view of his duty, whether severe or kindly, whether of action or of meditation: he enters into it with all his might, he opens his heart to its influence, and allows himself to be sent forward on its current. This is not difficult: there is no anxious vigilance or self-denial in it. On the contrary, there is a pleasure often in thus sweeping along in one way.

P.S., ii, 282.

5

Religion has (as it were) its very life in what are paradoxes and contradictions in the eye of reason. It is a seeming inconsistency how we can pray for Christ's coming, yet wish time to "work out our salvation," and "make our calling and election sure." It was a seeming contradiction how good men were to desire His first coming, yet be unable to abide it; how the Apostles feared, yet - rejoiced after His resurrection. And so it is a paradox how the Christian should in all things be sorrowful yet always rejoicing, and dying yet living, and having nothing yet possessing all things. Such seeming contradictions arise from the want of depth in our minds to master the whole truth. We have not eyes keen enough to follow out the lines of God's providence and will, which meet at length though at first sight they seem parallel.

P.S., v, 48.

6

It is by means of strong contrasts that Scripture brings out to us what is the real meaning of its separate portions. . . I do not say that this makes it at all easier to combine the separate duties to which they relate; that is a further and higher work; but thus much we gain at once, a better knowledge of these separate duties themselves. . . Let a man try both to fear and to rejoice, as Christ and His Apostles tell him, and in time he will learn how; but when he has learned, he will be as little able to explain how it is he does both, as he was before. He will seem inconsistent, and may easily be proved to be so, to the satisfaction of irreligious men, as Scripture is called inconsistent. He becomes the paradox which

362

Scripture enjoins. This is variously fulfilled in the case of men of advanced holiness. They are accused of the most opposite faults; of being proud, and of being mean; of being over-simple, and being crafty; of having too strict, and, at the same time, too lax a conscience; of being unsocial, and yet being worldly. . . . Men of the world, or men of inferior religiousness, cannot understand them, and are fond of criticising those who, in seeming to be inconsistent, are but like Scripture teaching. . . .

How deep and refined is the true Christian Spirit!—how difficult to enter into, how vast to embrace, how impossible to exhaust!

P.S., v, 10, 65-7.

7

Christianity, considered as a moral system, is made up of two elements, beauty and severity; whenever either is indulged to the loss or disparagement of the other, evil ensues. In heathen times, Greek and Barbarian in some sense divided these two between them; the latter were the slaves of dreary and cruel superstitions, and the former abandoned themselves to a joyous polytheism. And so, again, in these latter times, the two chief forms of heresy into which opposition to primitive truth has developed were remarkable, at least in their origin three hundred years ago, and at times since, the one for an unrefined and self-indulgent religiousness, the other for a stern, dark, cruel spirit, very unamiable, yet still inspiring more respect than the other.

. . . .

Religion has two sides, a severe side, and a beautiful; and we shall be sure to swerve from the narrow way which leads to life, if we indulge ourselves in what is beautiful while we put aside what is severe.

S.D., 120, 391.

8

And let us view such men as these, whom we rightly call Saints, in the combination of graces which form their character, and we shall gain a fresh insight into the nature of that sublime morality which the Spirit enforces. St. Paul exhibits the union of zeal and gentleness; St. John, of overflowing love with uncompromising strictness of principle. Firmness and meekness are another combination of virtues, which is exemplified in Moses, even under the first Covenant. To these we may add such as self-respect and humility, the love and fear of God, and the use of the world without the abuse of it. This necessity of being "sanctified wholly," in the Apostle's language, is often forgotten. It is indeed comparatively easy to profess one side only of moral excellence, as if faith were to be all in all, or zeal, or amiableness; whereas in truth, religious obedience is a very intricate problem, and the more so the further we proceed in it. The moral growth within us must be symmetrical, in order to be beautiful or lasting; hence mature sanctity is seldom recognized by others, where it really exists, never by the world at large. Ordinary spectators carry off one or other impression of a good man, according to the accidental circumstances under which they see him. Much more are the attributes and manifestations of the Divine Mind beyond our understanding, and, appearing inconsistent, are rightly called mysterious.

U.S., 47-8.

XXI : THE CHILD

ANALYTICAL SUMMARY

But the beauty of the "entire" man before the fall was not the painfully acquired and maintained "Unity" of the man matured by long years of introspection and self-mastery, but the "simplicity" of the child.

Therefore Christ's word: "Except ye become as little children," is the ultimate and most profound expression of genuine Christianity: of perfect Christianity because the perfect restoration of that state of original innocence.

And the perfect Christian is one in whom all the flawless beauty of genuine individuality shines forth—whose distinctive virtue is nothing but this individuality purified in Christ;

(Nos. 1-4.)

one in whom all the indispensable compulsion of his years of noviceship has yielded to freedom, freedom to be holy;

(Nos. 3-4.)

one therefore who has almost completely emerged from the long and complicated windings of laborious reflexion and observation of self, who has, so to speak, outgrown the effects of the fruit from the tree of knowledge of good and evil, whose life now wholly consists in an ingenuous simplicity and innocence which, like the angels, has no thought for this world and no thought for self—but for one thing alone, the ever-repeated Holy, Holy, Holy;

(Nos. 5-13.)

finally, therefore, one in whom that of which our actual childhood was presentiment and promise has at last become reality and shall be fulfilled even more perfectly to his delight—in whom Paradise blooms once more from out the debris and ruins of the millenia of fallen humanity—A Child in God, A Child for eternity.

(Nos. 14-17.)

I. INDIVIDUALITY

1

ALL good men have in their measure all graces; for He, by whom they have any, does not give one apart from the whole: He gives the root, and the root puts forth branches. But since time, and circumstances, and their own use of the gift, and their own disposition and character, have much influence on the mode of its manifestation, so it happens that each good man has his own distinguishing grace, apart from the rest, his own particular hue and fragrance and fashion, as a flower may have. As, then, there are numberless flowers on the earth, all of them flowers, and so far like each other; and all springing from the same earth, and nourished by the same air and dew, and none without beauty; and yet some are more beautiful than others: and of those which are beautiful, some excel in colour, and others in sweetness, and others in form; and then, again, those which are sweet have such perfect sweetness, yet so distinct, that we do not know how to compare them together, or to say which is the sweeter: so is it with souls filled and nurtured by God's secret grace.

P.S., v, 76-7.

2

It has been the plan of Divine Providence to ground what is good and true in religion and morals, on the basis of our good natural feelings. . . What is Christian-high-mindedness, generous self-denial, contempt of wealth, endurance of suffering, and earnest striving after perfection, but an improvement and transformation, under the influence of the Holy Spirit, of that natural character of mind which we call romantic? On the other hand, what is the instinctive hatred and abomination of sin (which confirmed Christians possess), their dissatisfaction with

367

themselves, their general refinement, discrimination, and caution, but an improvement, under the same Spirit, of their natural sensitiveness and delicacy, fear of pain, and sense of shame? They have been chastised into self-government by a fitting discipline, and now associate an acute sense of discomfort and annoyance with the notion of sinning. And so of the love of our fellow Christians and of the world at large, it is the love of kindred and friends in fresh shape; which has this use, if it had no other, that it is the natural branch on which a spiritual fruit is grafted.

P.S., ii, 53-4.

II. NATURALNESS

3

A religious man, in proportion as obedience becomes more and more easy to him, will doubtless do his duty unconsciously. It will be *natural* to him to obey, and therefore he will *do* it *naturally*, i.e., without effort or deliberation. It is difficult things which we are obliged to think about before doing them. When we have mastered our hearts in any matter (it is true) we no more think of the duty while we obey than we think how to walk when we walk, or by what rules to exercise any art which we have thoroughly acquired. *Separate acts* of faith aid us only while we are *unstable*. As we get strength, but one extended act of faith (so to call it) influences us all through the day, and our whole day is but one act of obedience also. Then there is no minute distribution of our faith among our particular deeds. Our will runs parallel to God's will. This is the very privilege of confirmed Christians; and it is comparatively but a sordid way of serving God, to be thinking when we do a deed, "if I do not do this, I shall risk my salvation; or, if I do it, I have a chance of being saved;"—*comparatively* a grovelling way, for it is the best, the only, way for sinners such as we are to *begin* to serve God in. Still as we grow in grace we throw away childish things; then we are able to stand upright like grown men, without the props and aids which our infancy required. This is the noble manner of serving God, to do good without thinking about it, without any calculation or reasoning, from love of the good, and hatred of the evil;— though cautiously and with prayer and watching, yet so generously, that if we were suddenly asked why we so act, we could only reply "because it is our way," or "because Christ so acted;" so spontaneously as not to know so much that we *are* doing right as that we are *not* doing wrong; I mean, with more of instinctive fear of sinning than of minute and careful appreciation of the *degrees* of our obedience. Hence it is that the best men are ever the most humble; as for other reasons, so especially because they *are accustomed* to be religious. They surprise *others*, but not themselves; they surprise others at their very calmness and freedom from thought about themselves. This is to have a great mind, to have within us that "princely heart of innocence" of which David speaks. Common men see God at a distance; in their attempts to be religious they feebly guide themselves as by a distant light, and are obliged to calculate and search about for the path. But the long practised Christian, who, through God's mercy, has brought God's presence near to him, the elect of God, in whom the Blessed Spirit dwells, he does not look out of doors for the traces of God; he is moved by God dwelling in him, and needs not but act on instinct. I do not say there is any man altogether such, for this is an angelic life; but it is the state of mind to which vigorous prayer and watching tend.

P.S., vi, 73-75.

4

Suppose a religious man, for instance, in the society of strangers; he takes things as they come, discourses naturally, gives his opinion soberly, and does good according to each opportunity of good. His heart is in his work, and his thoughts rest without effort on his God and Saviour. This is the way of a Christian; he leaves it to the ill-instructed to endeavour after a (so-called) spiritual frame of mind amid the bustle of life, which has no existence except in attempt and profession. True spiritual-mindedness is unseen by man, like the soul itself, of which it is a quality; and as the soul is known by its operations, so it is known by its fruits.

P.S., ii, 161.

III. SIMPLICITY

5

It is, I say, God's incommunicable attribute, as He did not create, so not to experience sin—and as He permits it, so also to know it; to permit it without creating it, to know it without experiencing it—a wonderful and incomprehensible attribute truly, yet involved, perhaps, in the very circumstance that He permits it. For He is everywhere and in all, and nothing exists except in and through Him. Mysterious as it is, the very prison beneath the earth, its chains and fires and impenitent inmates, the very author of evil himself, is sustained in existence by God, and without God would fall into nothing. God is in hell as well as in heaven, a thought which almost distracts the mind to think of. . . . Where life, is, there is He; and though it be but the life of death—the living death of eternal torment—He is the principle of it. And being thus intimately present with the very springs of thought, and the first elements of all being, being the sustaining cause of all spirits, whether they be good or evil, He is intimately present *with* evil, being pure from it—and knows what it is, as being with and in the wretched atoms which originate it. . . .

This is His wonderful incommunicable attribute; and man sought to share in what God was, but he could not without ceasing to be what God was also, holy and perfect. It is the incommunicable attribute of God to know evil without experiencing it. But man, when he would be as God, could only attain the shadow of a likeness which as yet he had not, by losing the substance which he had already. He shared in God's knowledge by losing His image. God knows evil and is pure from it—man plunged into evil and so knew it. . . . Such was the fruit of the forbidden tree as it remains in us to this day.

P.S., viii, 257-258, 256-57, 259.

6

We do not know in what the duty and happiness of other beings consist; but at least this seems to have been man's happiness in Paradise, not to think about himself or to be conscious of himself. Such, too, to recur to the parallel especially suggested on this day, seems to be the state of children. They do not reflect upon themselves. Such, too, seems to be the state of those orders of Angels whose life is said to consist in contemplation—for what is contemplation but a resting in the thought of God to the forgetfulness of self? Hence the Saints are described as "Virgins who *follow the Lamb whithersoever He goeth.*" But Adam, discontented with what he was, pined after a knowledge which he could not obtain from without—which he could only have from miserable experience within—from moral disorders within him, and from having his mind drawn to the contemplation of himself in consequence of those disorders. He obtained the wished-for knowledge; and his first recorded act afterwards was one of reflection upon self, and he hid himself among the trees of the garden. He was no longer fitted for contemplating glories without him; his attention was arrested to the shame that was upon him.

P.S., viii, 259.

7

Our righteousness is Christ, our propitiation "within us"; on it we rely, not on ourselves. It is our boast thus to look back from the ultimate manifestations of life, in which is our sanctification, upon that Glory within us, which is its fount, and our true justification. It is our blessedness to have our own glory swallowed up in Christ's glory, and to consider our works and our holiness, to avail merely as securities for the continuance of that glory; not as things to be dwelt upon and made much of for their own sake, but as a sort of sacramental rite addressed to Him, for the sake of which He may be pleased still to illuminate us, and as tokens that His grace is not in vain. And after all, what we are, whatever it is, could not avail, were it tried in the balance, for more than this, to prove our earnestness and diligence. Even what is acceptable in us is still so imperfect that the blood of Christ is necessary to complete what His Spirit has begun; and, as His regenerating grace has infused sweetness into what was bitter, so must His mercifulness overlook the remaining bitterness in what He has made sweet.

Jfc., 200.

8

We know two things of the Angels—that they cry Holy, Holy, Holy, and that they do God's bidding. Worship and service make up their blessedness; and such is our blessedness in proportion as we approach them. But all exercises of mind which lead us to reflect upon and ascertain our state; to know what worship is, and why we worship; what service is, and why we serve; what our feelings imply, and what our words mean, tend to divert our minds from the one thing needful, unless we are practised and expert in using them. All proofs of religion, evidences, proofs of particular doctrines, scripture proofs, and the like,—these certainly furnish scope for the exercise of great and admirable powers of mind, and it would be fanatical to disparage or disown them; but it requires a mind rooted and grounded in love not to be dissipated by them. As for truly religious minds, they, when so engaged, instead of mere disputing, are sure to turn inquiry into meditation, exhortation into worship, and argument into teaching.

P.S., *viii*, 265.

9

True faith is what may be called colourless, like air or water; it is but the medium through which the soul sees Christ; and the soul as little really rests upon it and contemplates it as the eye can see the air. . . . Bystanders see our minds, but our minds, if healthy, see but the objects which possess them. As God's grace elicits our faith, so His holiness stirs our fear, and His glory kindles our love. Others may say of us "here is faith," and "there is conscientiousness," and "there is love;" but we can only say "this is God's grace," and "that is His holiness," and "that is His glory."

And this being the difference between true faith and self-contemplation, no wonder that where the thought of self obscures the thought of God, prayer and praise languish, and only preaching flourishes. Divine worship is simply contemplating our Maker, Redeemer, Sanctifier, and Judge; but discoursing, conversing, making speeches, arguing, reading, and writing about religion, tend to make us forget Him in ourselves. The Ancients worshipped; they went out of their own minds into the Infinite Temple which was around them. They saw Christ in the Gospels, in the Creed, in the Sacraments and other Rites; in the visible structure and ornaments of His House, in the Altar, and in the Cross; and, not content with giving the service of their eyes, they gave Him their voices, their bodies, and their time, gave up their rest by night and their leisure by day, all that could evidence the offering of their hearts to Him. . . Unwavering, unflagging, not urged by fits and starts, not heralding forth their feelings, but resolutely, simply, perseveringly, day after day, Sunday and week-day, fast-day and festival, week by week, season by season, year by year, in youth and in age, through a life, thirty years, forty years, fifty years, in prelude of the everlasting chant before the Throne,—so they went on "continuing instant in prayer," after the pattern of Psalmists and Apostles, in the day with David, in the night with Paul and Silas, winter and summer, in heat and in cold, in peace and in danger, in a prison or in a cathedral, in the dark, in the day-break, at sun-rising, in the forenoon, at noon, in the afternoon, at eventide, and on going to rest, still they had Christ before them; His thought in their mind, His emblems in their eye, His name in their mouth, His service in their posture, magnifying Him, and calling on all that lives to magnify Him, joining with Angels in heaven and Saints in Paradise to bless and praise Him for ever and ever. . . . Such is the difference between those whom Christ praises and those whom He condemns or warns. The Pharisee recounted the signs of God's mercy upon and in Him; the Publican simply looked to God. The young Ruler boasted of his correct life, but

373

the penitent woman anointed Jesus' feet and kissed them. Nay, holy Martha herself spoke of her "much service;" while Mary waited on Him for the "one thing needful." The one thought of themselves; the others thought of Christ.

Jfc., 336-9.

10

But let us, finding ourselves in the state in which we are, take those means which alone are really left us, which alone become us. Adam, when he had sinned, and felt himself fallen, instead of honestly abandoning what he had become, would fain have hid himself. He went a step further. He did not give up what he now was, partly from dread of God, partly from dislike of what he had been. He had learnt to love sin and to fear God's justice. But Christ has purchased for us what we lost in Adam, our garment of innocence. He has bid us and enabled us to become as little children; He has purchased for us the grace of *simplicity*. . . that simple-mindedness which springs from the heart's being *whole* with God, entire, undivided. And those who think they have an idea of it, commonly rise no higher than to mistake for it a mere weakness and softness of mind, which is but its counterfeit. To be simple is to be like the Apostles and first Christians. Our Saviour says, "Be ye harmless," or simple, "as doves." And St. Paul, "I would have you wise unto that which is good, and *simple concerning evil.*" Again, "That ye may be *blameless and harmless*, the sons of God without rebuke, in the midst of a crooked and perverse nation." And he speaks of the "testimony of" his own "conscience, that in *simplicity* and godly sincerity, not with fleshly wisdom, but by the grace of God," he had his conversation in the world and towards his disciples. Let us pray God to give us this great and precious gift. . . . so that we may have the boldness and frankness of those who are as if they had no sin, from having been cleansed from it; the uncontaminated hearts, open countenances, and untroubled eyes of those who neither suspect, nor conceal, nor shun, nor are jealous; in a word, so that we may have confidence in Him, that we may stay on Him, and rest in the thoughts of Him, instead of plunging amid the thickets of this

374

world; that we may bear His eye and His voice, and know no knowledge but the knowledge of Him and Jesus Christ crucified, and desire no objects but what He has blessed and bid us pursue.

P.S., viii, 267-8.

11

Though religious men have gifts, and though they may know it, yet they do not realise them. . . . Serious men may know indeed, if it so be, what their excellences are, whether religious, or moral, or any other, but they do not feel them in that vivid way which we call realizing. They do not open their hearts to the knowledge so that it becomes fruitful. Barren knowledge is a wretched thing when knowledge ought to bear fruit; but it is a good thing, when it would otherwise act merely as a temptation. When men realize a truth it becomes an influential principle within them, and leads to a number of consequences both in opinion and in conduct. The case is the same as regards realizing our own gifts. But men of superior minds know them without realizing. They may know that they have certain excellences, if they have them, they may know that they have good points of character, or abilities, or attainments; but it is in the way of an unproductive knowledge, which leaves the mind just as it found it. And this seems to be what gives such a remarkable simplicity to the character of holy men, and amazes others so much that they think it a paradox or inconsistency, or even a mark of insincerity, that the same persons should profess to know so much about themselves, and yet so little,—-that they can bear so much praise, so much popularity, so much deference, and yet without being puffed up, or arrogating aught, or despising others; that they can speak about themselves, yet in so unaffected a tone, with so much nature, with such childlike innocence, and such graceful frankness.

P.S., vi, 263-4.

12

Men who indulge their passions have a knowledge, different in kind from those who have abstained from such indulgence; and when they speak on subjects connected with it, realize them in a

375

way in which others cannot realize them. The very ideas which are full of temptation to the former, the words which are painful to them to utter, all that causes them shame and confusion of face, can be said and thought of by the innocent without any distress at all. Angels can look upon sin with simple abhorrence and wonder, without humiliation or secret emotion; and a like simplicity is the reward of the chaste and holy; and that to the great amazement of the unclean, who cannot understand the state of mind of such a one, or how he can utter or endure thoughts which to themselves are full of misery and guilt.

P.S., vi, 264-5.

13

The Christian's character is formed by a rule higher than that of calculation and reason, consisting in a Divine principle or life, which transcends the anticipations and criticisms of ordinary men. Judging by mere worldly reason, the Christian ought to be self-conceited, for he is gifted; he ought to understand evil, because he sees and speaks of it; he ought to feel resentment, because he is conscious of being injured; he ought to act from self-interest, because he knows that what is right is also expedient ; he ought to be conscious and fond of the exercises of private judgment, because he engages in them; he ought to be doubting and hesitating in his faith, because his evidence for it might be greater than it is; he ought to have no expectation of Christ's coming, because Christ has delayed so long ; but not so : his mind and heart are formed on a different mould. In these, and ten thousand other ways, he is open to the misapprehensions of the world, which neither has his feelings nor can enter into them. Nor can he explain and defend them on considerations which all men, good and bad, can understand. He goes by a law which others know not; not his own wisdom or judgment, but by Christ's wisdom and the judgment of the Spirit, which is imparted to him,—by that inward incommunicable perception of truth and duty, which is the rule of his reason, affections, wishes, tastes, and all that is in him, and which is the result of persevering obedience. This it is which gives so unearthly a character to his whole life and conversation, which is "hid with Christ in God"; he has ascended with Christ on high and there "in heart and mind continually dwells"; and he is obliged in consequence to put a veil upon his face, and is mysterious in the world's judgment, and "becomes as it were a monster unto many," though he be "wiser than the aged," and have "more understanding than his teachers, because he keeps God's commandments." Thus "he that is spiritual judgeth all things, yet he himself is judged of no man"; and with him "it is a very small thing to be judged of man's judgment," for "He that judgeth him is the Lord."

P.S., vi, 266-7.

IV. A CHILD IN GOD

14

Such are the feelings with which men often look back on their childhood, when any accident brings it vividly before them. Some relic or token of that early time, some spot, or some book, or a word, or a scent, or a sound, brings them back in memory to the first years of their discipleship, and they then see, what they could not know at the time, that God's presence went up with them and gave them rest. Nay, even now perhaps they are unable to discern fully what it was which made that time so bright and glorious. They are full of tender, affectionate thoughts towards those first years, but they do not know why. They think it is those very years which they yearn after, whereas it is the presence of God which, as they now see, was then over them, which attracts them. They think that they regret the past, when they are but longing after the future. It is not that they would be children again but that they would be Angels and would see God; they would be immortal beings, crowned with amaranth, robed in white, and with palms in their hands, before His throne.

P.S., iv, 262-3.

377

15

What we were when children is a blessed *intimation*, given for our comfort, of what God will make us if we surrender our hearts to the guidance of His Holy Sprit,—a prophecy of good to come, —a foretaste of what will be fulfilled in heaven. And thus it is that a child is a pledge of immortality; for he bears upon him in figure those high and eternal excellences in which the joy of heaven consists, and which would not be thus shadowed forth by the All-gracious Creator, were they not one day to be realized.

P.S., ii, 67.

16

Childhood is a type of the perfect Christian state; our Saviour so made it when He said that we must become as little children to enter His kingdom. Yet it, too, is a thing past and over. We are not, we cannot be children; grown men have faculties, passions, aims, principles, views, duties, which children have not; still, however, we must become *as* little children; in them we are bound to see Christian perfection, and to labour for it with them in our eye. Indeed there is a very much closer connexion between the state of Adam in Paradise and our state in childhood than may at first be thought; so that in surveying Eden, we are in a way looking back on our own childhood; and in aiming to be children again we are aiming to be as Adam on his creation. . . . . Adam's state in Eden seems to have been like the state of children now—in being simple, inartificial, inexperienced in evil, unreasoning, uncalculating, ignorant of the future, or (as men now speak) unintellectual. . . .

In [both] these states the "knowledge of good and evil" is away, whatever be the meaning of that phrase, and that instead of it the Lord is our Light, "and in His light shall we see light." . . . . Far different is our state since the fall:—at present our moral rectitude, such as it is, is acquired by trial, by discipline: but what does this really mean? by sinning, by suffering, by correcting ourselves, by improving. We advance to the truth by experience of error; we succeed through failures. We know not how to do right except by having done wrong. We call virtue a mean,—that is, as considering it to lie between things that are wrong. We know what is right, not positively, but negatively;— we do not see the truth at once and make towards it, but we fall upon and try error, and find it is *not* the truth. We grope about by touch, not by sight, and so by a miserable experience exhaust the possible modes of acting till nought is left, but truth, remaining. Such is the process by which we succeed; we walk to heaven backward; we drive our arrows at a mark, and think him most skilful whose shortcomings are the least. . . .

This gift which sanctified Adam and saves children becomes the ruling principle of Christians generally when they advance to perfection. According as habits of holiness are matured, principle, reason, and self-discipline are unnecessary; a moral instinct takes their place in the breast, or rather, to speak more reverently, the Spirit is sovereign there. There is no calculation, no struggle, no self-regard, no investigation of motives. We act from love. Hence the Apostles say, "Ye have an unction from the Holy One, and ye know all things"; "Ye are the temple of the living God; as God hath said, I will dwell in them, and walk in them."

P.S., *v*, 102-3, 107-9.

17

Almighty God does not bring back the past, His dispensations move forward in an equable uniform way, like circles expanding about one centre;—the greater good to come being, not indeed the same as the past good, but nevertheless resembling it, as a substance resembles its type. In the past we see the future as if in miniature and outline. Indeed how can it be otherwise? seeing that all goods are but types and shadows of God Himself the Giver, and are like each other because they are like Him.

P.S., *v*, 100.

379

A